CW00829100

SUZUKI PRODUCTION MOTORCYCLES

1952–1980

Other Titles in the Crowood MotoClassics Series

SUZUKI PRODUCTION MOTORCYCLES

1952–1980

MICK WALKER

THE CROWOOD PRESS

First published in 2006 by
The Crowood Press Ltd
Ramsbury, Marlborough
Wiltshire SN8 2HR

www.crowood.com

British Library Cataloguing-in-Publication Data
A catalogue record for this book is available from the
British Library.

ISBN-10 1 86126 900 5
ISBN-13 978 1 86126 900 3

Acknowledgements
The following good people helped with information or
illustrations in the preparation of this book: Colin Gibson,
Jay Leeson, Heidi Cockerton, Andy and Alan Baldwin,
Pip Higham, Andy Lee, Dave Evans, Vic Bates, Phil
Kersey, Robert Saunders, the late Barry Sheene, David
Essex, Brenda Scivyer, Bill Robertson, Mick Oliver, Tony
Collison, George Schofield, Ian Holmes, the Suzuki
Motor Co., and members of the Suzuki Owners Club.

Dedication
This book is dedicated to my late friend
and fellow Suzuki enthusiast, Don Leeson,
who was tragically killed whilst racing in the
2005 Classic Manx Grand Prix; ironically
on a Honda.

Typeface used: Bembo.

Typeset and designed by
D & N Publishing, Lambourn Woodlands,
Hungerford, Berkshire.

Printed and bound in Great Britain by The Cromwell
Press, Trowbridge.

Contents

Preface

When I owned my first Suzuki (a two-fifty in Aden, during 1963), little did I dream that over four decades later I would be writing a book detailing the early history of this great company and its bikes between 1952 and 1980.

That T10 always struck me as a well-made, quality motorcycle, the Japanese design contrasting sharply with the various Italian and British machines that I had previously owned and ridden. The Italian and British bikes were good basic motorcycles – the Ducati 250 Daytona and Triumph Tiger 100 also offered excellent performance – but the Suzuki brought a level of sophistication previously unheard of, with features such as electric start/12-volt electrics, flashing indicators, mirrors, fully enclosed final-drive chain, hydraulically operated rear brake, and much more; all within the standard purchase price. Despite all these advantages, however, the Japanese still lagged behind in areas such as suspension, tyres and welding.

All pre-T20 (Super Six) Suzukis have a special character, very much of the Orient and not of the West. Their styling appears somewhat curious to Western eyes, but all the same they are often not without interest. Like those produced by Honda at the same time, Suzuki models of the 1960s seemed to have far more character than some of the 1970s creations (for example,

the GT250 series). However, as with Honda, Suzuki did manage some classics during this time, notably the GT750, GS750 and X7. The RE5 Rotary, on the other hand, was a commercial disaster, although the relatively small number that were built are much loved and admired by their owners today.

For much of the 1970s, I was an official Suzuki dealer. During this period I also got to know the late Barry Sheene, a friend of my shop manager, John Blunt, and a contracted rider for the Japanese marque at the time. This close relationship with the Suzuki brand – both through the dealership and via my friendship with Barry – has been of great help in compiling and writing this book, as has riding most of the bikes described in the following pages.

Back in 1963, my T10 seemed a massive motorcycle, but today it appears surprisingly small. Somehow, this is a sad reflection of how modern motorcycle design has evolved. Many modern bikes are actually heavier and certainly thirstier than a small car and even Suzuki has fallen into the trap of producing ever-larger bikes.

Do we really need these massive machines? While you ponder that question, I hope you enjoy reading *Suzuki Production Motorcycles 1952–1980* as much as I enjoyed writing it.

Mick Walker

1   Origins

Early Days

Michio Suzuki was born on 10 February 1887 in Hamamatsu, then a small village some 130 miles (210km) south-west of the Japanese capital, Tokyo. Today, that village is a thriving city and still the base for the modern-day Suzuki Motor Company. In 1909, at the age of 22, the young Michio went into business via the newly formed Suzuki Loom Works, manufacturing what Jeff Clew was to describe in his 1980 book *Suzuki* as 'a product that had no particularly outstanding features'. However, Suzuki was nothing if not inventive, and after only just over a year in business he came up with the idea of allowing his two-shuttle loom to weave cloth with stripes in it. This important innovation allowed his fledgling organization to achieve a considerable advance over its more established rivals. It was soon followed by another invention – a device regulating the warp – and eventually by the introduction of the Suzuki power loom, which firmly established the Suzuki brand name on the map of Japanese textile machinery.

On 15 March 1920, the enterprise was reorganized as the Suzuki Loom Manufacturing Company, going public with a share capital of 500,000 yen and seventy-two shareholders. It was an inauspicious day for the new enterprise to choose: the very day when, as Jeff Clew recalled, 'the rice, cotton yarn and silk yarn markets collapsed with dramatic suddenness', due to problems experienced by the Japanese economy at the end of the First World War. However, Suzuki rode out the storm, even though many small manufacturers ended up going bankrupt.

Founder Michio Suzuki was born on 10 February 1887 and first went into business in 1909 at the age of just 22, initially as a loom manufacturer. After the Second World War his business empire expanded into both motorcycles and cars. He finally retired in 1957.

By 1921, the new corporation was in a strong enough position to begin planning a new production facility and equipping itself with the latest machine tools. The shareholders agreed to the new venture and land was acquired on the outskirts of Hamamatsu, with both the production facilities and head office being located there.

Another setback to the Japanese economy occurred in 1923 with the huge Kanto earthquake. Fortunately this did only very minor damage to the Suzuki plant, but several of its customers were badly affected. Even so, when the financial year ended, Suzuki's accounts showed not only a profit, but even a dividend to shareholders.

In 1930 another milestone was reached when Michio Suzuki perfected the sarong-weaving loom. Demand for Japanese-made sarongs had increased substantially during the First World War, when European imports dried up. Initially, Japanese producers had lacked the ability to produce the traditional sarong patterns, but Michio's invention solved this problem, not only greatly helping the home producers, but also boosting the Suzuki corporation's bank balance. This in turn led to exports to countries such as China and, later, Thailand.

The First Motor Vehicles

The forward-thinking Michio Suzuki could see the growing importance of the motor vehicle, both in four- and two-wheel forms. During the early and mid-1930s Japan relied heavily upon imported automobiles and motorcycles, but Suzuki, along with certain other visionaries from industries outside the motor trade, soon began to study what his country would need in the future. By the mid-1930s Michio had been joined by his son-in-law Shunzo; following Japanese custom, he had adopted this man, so that he could have a male heir. It was Shunzo who was placed in charge of the motor vehicle development programme.

Shunzo's view was that the Japanese domestic market needed the smaller displacement vehicle, whether with two or four wheels. His first task was to import a British Austin 7 car during early 1937, and this led to the evaluation and ultimate construction of what can best be described as a cross between the Austin and British Ford design. Like the Austin, the Suzuki was powered by a liquid-cooled four-cylinder engine. The engine produced a claimed 13bhp at 3,500rpm and employed a four-speed constant mesh gearbox; all major castings were of aluminium alloy in a bid to reduce weight.

The first engine had been completed in late 1937, and by the beginning of 1939 several complete cars had been built and tested by Suzuki's experimental department. Work was also being carried out on a small-capacity motorcycle engine – indeed, it was at an advanced stage – but then came the news that, because of military considerations, all non-essential work was to cease in favour of the war programme. (The Japanese had been involved in a largely unreported conflict in mainland China for several years, and by 1939 this had also begun to involve the Russian forces, in a dispute over the Mongolian border.) Despite the setbacks, however, by April 1939 the Suzuki share capital had increased to the sum of 2 million yen, and a period of unprecedented growth followed. On 7 December 1941, following the Japanese attack on the Americans at Pearl Harbor, the Pacific war broke out. By the end of that year Suzuki's share capital had doubled to 4 million yen.

Aided by Japanese military contracts for munitions, the company's expansion continued apace and, even though the Americans were quickly gaining ascendancy in the war itself, at the end of 1944 Suzuki's share capital had risen to 9 million yen.

At the end of 1944, the Suzuki corporation suffered its first real setback, when a severe earthquake in December caused the partial destruction of two buildings on the Hamamatsu site.

At the Takasuka facility there was worse news, with three buildings totally destroyed. Both works were to sustain further damage due to an air raid in April 1945, and further raids followed in May and July. The war was brought to an abrupt cessation on 14 August 1945, after the Americans had dropped atomic bombs on Hiroshima (6 August) and then Nagasaki (9 August).

Producing a Powered Two-Wheeler

After the end of the conflict, in what can only be described as near total economic collapse, Suzuki built anything it could to stay in business. The early post-war products included farm implements, window-raising springs, electrical heaters and much more, simply to keep its thousands of workers on the payroll. Suzuki also returned to its core business of loom manufacture.

Generally, things appeared to be on the up, but Japan itself was on the very edge of revolution and Suzuki to many represented, as one commentator described it, 'the bad old days and ways of the military era'. In fact, Michio Suzuki was really only interested in the civilian way of life – and commercial activity – but others, including some of his own workforce, failed to see things that way. There was an ill-tempered dispute, followed by a six-month strike, which crippled production. It was eventually only ended in May 1950 thanks to the mediation services of the Shizuoka District Labour Commission.

At this time, Michio Suzuki was 63 years old. A keen fisherman, he would often seek some peace and quiet from the troubles of corporate life by going fishing. To reach his favourite water hole, Michio used a pedal cycle, and he soon began to think about fitting a small engine to it, to make the trip easier. This began a chain of events that was to lead the Suzuki brand into the world of motorcycles. In common with many other companies, notably Ducati and Honda, this transfer to a different area of industry was to be via a small auxiliary engine that could be fitted into a conventional pedal cycle.

Michio Suzuki was not only an engineer, but also someone who believed in being the best in his chosen field. Upon inspection of his potential rivals in this new field, he soon discovered that most efforts being manufactured and sold by Japanese producers at the time placed the engine to the rear of the frame, often above or to the side of the rear wheel, whilst others mounted it above the front wheel. Michio, aided by his adopted son Shunzo, realized that the best placing of the engine was definitely in the centre of the machine; in this position, the bicycle's chain could be used to transfer power from the engine to the rear wheel.

Suzuki did not consider buying up old war surplus engines as Soichiro Honda had done, or have any intention of acquiring assemblies from other manufacturers; instead, they planned to produce everything for the new project in-house, and set about designing a 36cc two-stroke engine. Every single component was made within the Suzuki works: the crankshaft oil seal (hand-made from leather), the flywheel magneto and high-voltage coil, and even the carburettor.

Suzuki's capacity to produce all these components is proof that the company was, right from the beginning, in a better position to build powered two-wheelers than most of its rivals.

Work began on the original prototype in November 1951, and was completed just four weeks later!

However, this engine, produced in a remarkably short period, proved on test to be in need of further development. A series of problems came to light, largely centred upon the home-made oil seals and carburettor glitches. With typical Japanese thoroughness, these problems were soon overcome, and in addition a double sprocket gear system was developed. This gear system enabled the rider either to pedal and thus assist the engine, or to disconnect the pedals, using the engine alone to propel the machine. As C.D. Bohon commented in the October 1978 issue of the American *Motorcyclist* magazine: 'This was such a revolutionary invention in Japan that the country's patent agency granted Suzuki a money subsidy to continue research into motorcycle engineering development'.

The Power Free and Diamond Free

The production version, the Power Free, was first put on the market in 1952. This was a conventional piston-port induction two-stroke, with a single, vertical cylinder. Early models retained the 36cc of the prototype, and a single-speed transmission, but this was soon changed to 50cc and two-speed.

In July 1952, only a month after its launch, the Power Free was able to demonstrate its credentials, when a team of five riders successfully completed a two-day trip from Hamamatsu and Tokyo, run in conjunction with the factory's first advertising campaign.

By February 1953 the company's share capital stood at 120 million yen. In that same month, the finishing touches were being made to the next two-wheel development, to be known as the Diamond Free, which was launched the following month. Displacing 58cc (43 × 40mm), although still employing a bicycle frame with unsprung front forks, the Diamond Free represented a considerable advance on the original Power Free model. The entire machine had much cleaner lines, and for the first time Suzuki employed what could be best described as a degree of styling in the design of both the engine and the cycle.

Compared with the Power Free, the newcomer produced exactly double the power output, at 2bhp, although at the same 4,000rpm. Other details of the Diamond Free's specification included a compression ratio of 7:1, a drum rear brake (compared with a rim type on the

Suzuki's first effort in the powered two-wheel industry, the 1952 36cc Power Free auxiliary engine.

The 58cc (43 × 40mm) Diamond Free debuted in 1953. Although it still employed a conventional pedal cycle frame, it was an altogether more advanced design.

Power Free), 1.375 × 24 tyres and a dry weight of 104lb (47kg).

In July 1953 Suzuki had their first taste of competitive motorcycling. This was an ascent of Mount Fuji, an event sponsored by Mainichi Shimbun, which attracted considerable public and media attention. The Diamond Free won its class and, according to one commentator, 'performed exceptionally well'. Not long afterwards another Diamond Free made a successful ascent of Mount Norikura, whilst in October 1953 a three-man squad left Sapporo on a 1,860-mile (3,000km) journey to Kagoshima in the southern area of Japan. Not a single mechanical breakdown was experienced during the eighteen-day exercise.

With production of the Diamond Free having built up to well over 4,000 units per month, the first Suzuki exports had begun – to Taiwan. All these early engines and complete machines were however not marketed under the Suzuki brand name, but instead under the name SJK (Suzuki Jidosha Kogyo, or Suzuki Automotive Industries); this policy was to continue for several years.

The Suzuki Motor Co.

With its share capital now standing at 250 million yen, in June 1954 the Suzuki Motor Company Ltd was established. The move came in response to the launch of the first real Suzuki motorcycle, the Colleda CO (*colleda* being the Japanese for 'this is it').

The CO was not only Suzuki's first motorcycle, but also its first four-stroke, using a 90.5cc (48 × 50mm) ohv single-cylinder engine and three-speed gearbox in unit. Official company figures claimed 4bhp at 5,000rpm. Other features included drum brakes front and rear, telescopic front forks, plunger rear suspension, and a dry weight of 188lb (53kg). Although underpowered, it none the less made history by being the first Japanese two-wheeler to be equipped with a speedometer as standard equipment.

Another model that made its entrance in 1954 was the Mini Free. This is best described as a moped, but very much on the lines of the Power Free and Diamond Free, featuring a 49.9cc (38 × 44mm) single-cylinder two-stroke engine, with belt final drive, conventional pedal-cycle frame and a drum rear brake. Power output was a claimed 2bhp at 4,500rpm.

In an attempt to overcome the poor performance of the CO, for 1955 Suzuki produced the COX. Essentially, this was a bored-out version of the smaller-engined model, with a 56mm (instead of 48mm) piston; the stroke remained unchanged at 50mm. With a similar dry weight, the larger-engined ohv single did provide improved performance, but in truth the COX was a mere stop-gap. The first of a new breed of two-stroke motorcycles was waiting in the wings and was launched very shortly thereafter, effectively meaning that the CO and the new COX did not survive beyond 1955.

The ST

The new two-stroke, the ST, was not only a better-performing engine but also offered increased development potential, and was cheaper and easier to manufacture. In addition, it gave its owners fuel economy that was almost as good as that of the COX four-stroke. It had a CZ-like appearance and was the first really modern Suzuki, pointing the way forward for the company, which was to remain two-stroke-orientated for the next two decades. In the process, Suzuki was to rise to the very pinnacle in two-stroke-engine technology.

Like the CO/COX, the ST employed a channel steel frame, telescopic front forks and plunger rear suspension. The latter was soon axed in favour of a rigid frame after the increase in power caused some problems; Suzuki were clearly more interested in reliability than comfort.

Although the cycle parts might have been linked, the engine most certainly was not, its

123cc (52 × 58mm) piston-port induction single-cylinder being of particularly clean design. Inside it boasted no less than four main bearings and, for the first time on a Suzuki design, a caged roller big-end. The three-speed gearbox was, like that of the CO/COX, in unit with the engine, whilst the electrics set new standards for the Japanese industry, thanks to a Suzuki-developed six-pole flywheel magneto for the ignition and a 25-watt battery-operated headlamp. To complete the picture there was an alloy head, cast-iron cylinder barrel and vertically split aluminium crankcases. Before putting the ST on sale, Suzuki ran no fewer than five prototypes for 6,000 miles (almost 10,000km) each on a demanding endurance run. Fifteen test riders, working three shifts around the clock, demonstrated the newcomer's potential in terms of both performance and reliability.

The success of the ST125 signalled the end of the two four-strokes and in late 1955 the budget-priced Porter Free arrived. It retained the 52mm bore size of the ST, but the stroke was reduced to 48mm, giving a displacement of 101.9cc. It shared the same design characteristics as the ST125, but it had a rigid frame from the start, plus a less luxurious specification (for example, a painted tank, instead of the chrome version of the larger-engined model), and, whereas the ST produced 5.5bhp, the Porter Free managed only 4.2 – both at 5,000rpm.

The Export Market

Like Siochiro Honda (*see Honda Production Motorcycles 1946–1980*, Crowood Press), Shunzo Suzuki realized the importance of the export market, and this was to make a major contribution to the ultimate success of his company. Like his Honda counterpart, Shunzo visited both the United States of America (in August 1955) and Europe (in October 1956); by that time, he was Senior Managing Director, whilst his father Michio, although still company

President, was now operating in a less executive role.

Both father and son must be credited with getting the Suzuki motorcycle project up and running during the firm's two-wheel pioneering days of the 1950s. However, it was the younger man who realized the potential of the world stage for the company's products. He felt strongly that, in order to achieve this, Suzuki needed a 'top-of-the-range' prestige model and, as 1955 was coming to a close, the company's engineers were working flat out to achieve this goal.

The new model, a two-fifty twin-cylinder motorcycle, was officially launched for the 1956 season as the SJK Colleda TT (the TT suffix having no connection at that time with the Isle of Man races). It was Suzuki's first-ever twin and, in another first for Suzuki, it also included direction indicators. At its heart was a 247cc piston-port two-stroke with separate alloy heads and inclined cast-iron cylinders. With bore and stroke dimensions of 54 × 54mm, the Suzuki engineers were already employing the same square dimensions that were later adopted by the top two-stroke racing teams, including MZ and

Suzuki's first twin, the Colleda TT two-fifty of 1956. Its 247cc (54 × 54mm) engine was clearly based on the German Adler design.

The TT was followed by the TP in 1957. It now sported telescopic instead of Earles-type front forks, while the frame had been redesigned to include duplex front downtubes.

Suzuki themselves. However, in virtually every other respect, the TT was clearly intended to be a reliable, comfortable touring machine, rather than an out-and-out sportster.

Actually, the TT was a strange mixture, with a technical specification that was impressive for the period, up-to-the-minute suspension, and a massive headlamp that featured a fog lamp at its base; one commentator described it as 'a styling debacle'. Certainly, to Western eyes it was strange, but so too were many other Japanese motorcycles of the same era. It also had a massive pressed-steel backbone frame, whilst there was an Earles fork at the front and a swinging arm with twin shock absorbers at the rear (again a first for Suzuki). Like other 'first stage' Suzuki two-fifty twins up to and including the T10, the TT featured a four-speed transmission. Another feature was the standard fitment full rear chain enclosure; 3.25 × 16 tyres were specified front and rear.

Suzuki claimed 16bhp (at 6,000rpm) and an optimistic 81mph (130km/h) for the 1956 TT. In appearance, the TT power unit was a dead ringer for the German Adler MB250's bottom-end styling, with 54 × 54mm bore and stroke measurements and even the same inclined cylinders. Some observers have associated Yamaha with using Adler technology, but surely the Suzuki TT owes far more to the German design than Yamaha does!

A Fully Automated Line

As motorcycle output and sales continued to climb, production facilities had to be reviewed to cope with the increased demand. Mass production had arrived at Suzuki. A new plant was finished and opened during January 1957, providing Suzuki with a fully automated assembly line that was ultra-modern in design, and only the second such motorcycle operation in Japan. (Honda were the first to have used the techniques.)

In February 1957, on his seventieth birthday, Michio Suzuki retired from active participation in the company he had founded, and his adopted son Shunzo took over as President.

To benefit fully from the new mass production facilities, Shunzo Suzuki took the decision in early 1958 to streamline the range to three basic models: the ST125, the two-fifty twin (now known as the Colleda TP) and the SM, which was new for that year. The latter ('SM' for 'Suzu Moped') employed the now discontinued Mini Free engine unit mounted in a pressed-steel spine frame, with leading link forks (also formed from pressed steel, as was the swinging arm). The first year's production had belt final drive, but this gave way to a chain thereafter.

As for the revised two-fifty, its major change was the fitment of conventional telescopic front forks in place of the Earles type previously used. Several other changes were made, notably 3.00 × 18 tyres, a smaller headlamp (although still with a flat-bottom rim, which was to characterize all the two-fifty twins, up to and including the T10), revised bodywork, and an increase in power to 18bhp.

Later that year, in October 1958, the first use was made of the now-famous Suzuki 'S' logo. At the same time the initials SJK ceased to be used.

A brand-new, smaller-capacity twin, known as the 125 Seltwin, was launched on to the market in July 1959. The power unit is best described as a miniature version of the TT/TP unit, with its alloy heads and inclined cast-iron cylinders. Using bore and stroke dimensions of 42 × 45mm, the engine displaced 124cc, producing

10bhp at 8,000rpm, running on a compression ratio of 7:1. Like the two-fifty, the 125 used a four-speed gearbox; later, a 150cc version was also offered. Perhaps the most notable feature of the 125 Seltwin twin was its styling, which Suzuki described as 'Jet Age'. It is best described as angular, but not quite as squared-off as the Honda Benley (C92/95) or Dream (C72/77) models. The initial production version of the Seltwin twin was the SB, which ran until 1963, by which time the coding had reached SL.

ABOVE: *1959 SB125 Colleda Seltwin with 125cc (42 × 45mm) twin-cylinder engine.*

RIGHT: *Ian Holmes with his 1959 SB125 at the Classic Motor Cycle Show, Stafford, April 2006.*

Hydraulic Braking

At several points in its history, Suzuki attempted to exploit technically interesting engineering in its motorcycle production; one of its experiments was the unforgettable RE5 Rotary (*see* Chapter 11). A similar project – which also ultimately led to a dead end – was the use of hydraulically operated drum brakes. Interestingly, both projects had their origins in Germany, not in Japan.

The innovative use of hydraulically operated drum brakes began with the Colleda TA Twin Ace, a new twofifty twin that arrived for the 1960 model year, replacing the Colleda TP. Interestingly, the TA featured revised

bore and stroke dimensions of 52 × 58mm (which were continued on the TB and also, finally, the T10).

The first experiments with the hydraulic brake setup involved a TA equipped with the operation for its front drum only. Later, both front and rear drums were operated by hydraulics, and linked together. Sharing a common master cylinder, they were operated by the rear brake pedal, the pressure being distributed by a prearranged ratio of rear to front of 9:5. Jeff Clew explained the system:

> This ratio had been determined after extensive tests, to ensure the front brake did not lock and the forks did not depress excessively under fierce brake application. An over-ride arrangement ensured the front brake could be used independently, by means of a conventional control cable and handlebar lever, or be used to supplement the combined hydraulic braking effort, if desired…. It was, in fact, an ingenious model adaptation of the cable-operated linked braking system that had been used by Rudge Whitworth and others in the pre-war era. Sadly it proved to be impracticable in the end and was abandoned, like earlier attempts to perfect such a system. It was found almost impossible to establish a 'norm' for the optimum division of the braking effort under widely varying conditions.

Later, in the mid-1970s, the Italian Moto Guzzi factory began producing a linked system, but with disc brakes front and rear. As for Suzuki, the rear brake only continued to be hydraulically operated on both the TB and T10 before the whole programme was abandoned.

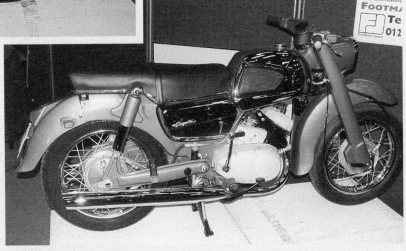

ABOVE: Close-up of the TA engine unit: virtually a new design from what had gone before, but still with four speeds and petroil mixture.

RIGHT: New for the 1960 model year, the 246cc (52 × 58mm) TA twin. One notable feature was its hydraulically operated drum brakes.

Other Early Twin-Cylinder Model Features

In basic terms, the TA-T10 series was characterized by having a pressed-steel backbone frame – which was common to the vast majority of Japanese motorcycles of the period – and the front downtubes of the original TT/TP machines. There was also telescopic fully shrouded front forks (with the TA giving the impression that it had the trailing link type), swinging-arm rear suspension via non-adjustable fully-shrouded shock absorbers, a fully enclosed final-drive chain, direction indicators, and full-width drum brakes on both wheels. All were powered by an outwardly similar 246cc piston-ported engine with petroil lubrication, integral four-speed gearbox (with an unusual 'rotary' gear-selection method) and twin stub-mounted 20mm Mikuni (licensed Amal) carburettors.

Many of the above features were also utilized on the 125/150 Seltwin twin series of machines.

For a full technical development of the final model in the TA-T10 series, *see* Chapter 3.

The Selped MA

In mid-1958 Honda put into production its C100 Super Cub. During its first year, this model sold an amazing 755,589 examples! Suzuki's response to such huge sales figures was the Selped MA, which was launched in January 1960. In many respects it was virtually a direct copy of the Honda design, except for two major differences: being a Suzuki, the Selped had a two-stroke engine, and it was not a true 'step-thru' like the Honda but instead featured a more conventional centrally mounted fuel tank above the power unit.

The 49.9cc (41 × 38) two-stroke single-cylinder engine had an alloy head and inclined cast-iron cylinder barrel; it produced a claimed 4bhp at 8,000rpm and in contrast to the Honda Super Cub, had four instead of three speeds. However, the balance of the new Suzuki ultra-

Crankcase assembly in the Suzuki factory, circa 1960.

In June 1960 Suzuki followed rival Honda's example of a year earlier by sending a team of three machines to compete in the Isle of Man Ultra Lightweight (125cc) TT. Entered under the Colleda name, all three finished. The highest placed, Toshio Matsumoto (seen here), came home fifteenth.

lightweight mirrored the successful Honda design, with its pressed steel frame, deeply valanced mudguard (the rear being an integral part of the frame structure), full-width brakes, leading link front forks, 17in wheels and swinging-arm rear suspension.

A Strive for Exports

In June 1960, Suzuki took part in the famous Isle of Man TT for the first time, entered under the Colleda name, with three specially constructed 125cc twin-cylinder machines. Again, they were following Honda, who had made their TT debut (in the same class) a year earlier. Honda and Suzuki were entering the races for the same reason: to publicize their products prior to a major sales drive into the lucrative European market.

Although neither Suzuki nor Honda enjoyed a victory on their first TT visit, the trip none the less proved the reliability of Suzuki's machinery, with Toshio Matsumoto gaining a bronze replica by coming home fifteenth at an average speed of 71.88mph (115.65km/h); Michio Ichino was one place further back, and Englishman Ray Fay came in eighteenth.

In spring 1961, Suzuki opened an office in London, although at that time there was no UK distributor; this was to come a couple of years later. However, by the end of 1961 there were a number of what Suzuki described as 'Authorized Distributors' outside Japan. The full listing was as follows:

Aden (now *South Yemen*): Noman Abdo Thabet, Crater;
Africa, East: Sohan Singh & Co, Gulzaar, Nairobi, Kenya;
Africa, West: Boulos Enterprises, 207–208 Akanni Street, Lagos, Nigeria;
Belgium: Suzuki Belgium, S71 Grote Steenweg, Berchem, Antwerp;
France: Pierre Bonnet, 78 Avenue du General Leclerc, Boulogne–Billancourt;
Kuwait: The Mutawa Alkazi Company, Sha'b-Gate, Kuwait;
Saudi Arabia: The Saied Bin Omar Barayan, Jeddah.

The two African distributors were not only responsible for the sales to their own country but also to the Republic of South Africa,

Rhodesia (now Zimbabwe), Ghana, Uganda, Angola, Mozambique, Malawi, Tanzania and Zambia. Total African Suzuki sales in 1961 numbered in the region of 10,000 units.

In addition, Suzuki themselves had already opened up the 'local' South East Asian market, and had begun exporting to Hong Kong, Indonesia, Laos and Pakistan.

The original Taiwanese exports deal (dating back to 1952) signed with the Taiwanese Trading Company had by 1960 progressed into a major operation – Suzuki Industrial Co Ltd – and by 1961 some 2,000 machines were being shipped annually to Taiwan, as well as a further 4,000 to Indonesia, where assembly took place in Jakarta.

The London office opened in May 1961 by the Suzuki Motor Company was housed in a small building with living accommodation, at 25 Montrose Court in the south-west of the city. It was run by Jimmy Matsumiya, who was employed on a full-time basis.

Testing the Twins

Below the London office were a couple of garages, which were used to house test machines. These included a pair of 250TB twins (registration numbers 274 DLW and 275 DLW). Although the model was not yet on sale in the UK, 274 DLW was tested by *Motorcycle Mechanics* in its June 1962 issue. Brian Smith reported as follows:

> Comfortable, safe and fast – these three points are outstanding in the Suzuki 250TB which I've been testing this month. In fact, I'd say that it is the most comfortable machine I've ever ridden, despite the fact that it is intended as a sports model. The riding position is very good but the suspension is soft. This gives the comfort all right, but means that roadholding at higher speeds is not as good as it might be otherwise. I don't want to give the impression that the machine frightened me or anything like that, because it is really delightful to

> throw round corners. But you can't have everything – and I would take the machine as it is every time, particularly for fast touring.

As for braking performance, *MCM* considered that the Suzuki had better brakes than all other machines tested around the same time: 'The front brake on its own was capable of locking the wheel and yet it does not require a terrific grip to do it.' As for the hydraulically operated rear brake, 'this makes the action very light, yet the mechanism has been designed so that it is difficult to lock the wheel. These two brakes together gave fantastic stopping power with complete safety.'

Smith also praised the handlebar layout: 'The excellent workmanship in the lever units puts British machines to shame. The levers and switches are incorporated in one alloy casting which is highly polished and looks even better than chrome.' Credit was also given to: the standard fitment electric starter; the penetrating note from the horn; the twin handlebar mirrors (again standard equipment); the 'unique' fuel-level gauge (a level strip on the nearside front of the tank); 'easily operated' prop and centre stands, the 'well-positioned and easy-to-use' fuel tap; the 'large' knee-grips; and the 'exceptionally neat' choke control.

According to Brian Smith, there were just a few faults: 'the chrome on the indicators, handlebars and silencers rusted and started to peel in places'; there was no valancing on the front mudguard; and the position on the pillion was 'rather cramped'.

MCM achieved 80mph (129km/h) and a fuel consumption figure of 72mpg (almost 4ltr/100km) overall during the test period, which covered 950 miles (almost 1,600km). *Motor Cycling* also tested 275 DLW and its review was published in the 13 June 1962 issue:

> In general terms, the 246cc Suzuki 250TB is a quick twin-cylinder two-stroke with above-average acceleration and the lavish specification that

we are coming to expect of the Japanese models. In particular, its conventionally ported engine is silky smooth, very quiet and has a quite unusual spread of power in top gear from 20mph (32km/h) up to a best one-way speed of 75mph (121km/h)… And gearing makes best use of the 18bhp available from the engine, particularly in terms of acceleration.

The *Motor Cycling* tester went on to describe the Nippon Denso electric starter-cum-dynamo:

Starting was achieved by closing the butterfly chokes of both carburettors (opened by a single, easy-to-reach lever), flooding both float chambers (operated by separate 'ticklers') and pressing the starter button on the right-hand handlebar. From cold it was necessary to use the starter for two or three seconds, but hot starting was genuinely instantaneous.

Although gearbox action was described as 'practically faultless', the selection process was more difficult:

The gearbox selector cam being of the rotary type [as on all the Suzuki twins at that time], neutral

could be engaged directly from either top or bottom gear – a situation fraught with problems to the novice… changing up (assuming neutral as the 'bottom' position) was made by pressing the rocking pedal with the toe; and changing down with the heel…. One disadvantage of the rotary cam is that the rider can only too easily become 'lost in the gears'. A count must be kept but it does have the advantage of allowing the rider to slip into neutral from top gear when pulling up.

A definite plus was: 'a beautifully light clutch – with a comfortably shaped and lengthy lever', which 'aided easy gear changing. It also withstood the punishment of many full-bore sprint starts and engaged and disengaged smoothly and quietly.' The 'transmission smoothness – assisted by a large rubber vane-type shock absorber in the rear sprocket – was delightful'.

Like Brian Smith, writing for *Motorcycle Mechanics*, the *Motor Cycling* tester was not entirely satisfied with the 250TB's handling:

The suspension springs were rather too soft for fast cornering. Thrusting the machine into a bumpy corner resulted in slight pitching at the front – but the Suzuki always maintained its line, even though

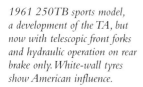

1961 250TB sports model, a development of the TA, but now with telescopic front forks and hydraulic operation on rear brake only. White-wall tyres show American influence.

Engine	Air-cooled parallel twin, two-stroke, with piston-port induction, alloy heads, cast-iron barrels and horizontally split aluminium crankcases	Front suspension	Telescopic forks; fully enclosed
		Rear suspension	Pressed-steel swinging-arm, with twin fully enclosed shock absorbers
Bore	52mm	Front brake	165mm full-width drum, SLS
Stroke	58mm	Rear brake	165mm full-width drum, SLS (hydraulically operated)
Displacement	246cc	Tyres	3.00 × 17 front and rear
Compression ratio	7:1		
Lubrication	Petroil; ratio 20:1	*General specifications*	
Ignition	Battery/coil, Nippon Denso 12v 100w dynamo; electric start	Wheelbase	53.2in (1,351mm)
		Ground clearance	5.3in (134mm)
Carburettor	2 × Amal, made under licence by Mikuni, Type 392, 22mm	Seat height	30in (76mm)
		Fuel tank capacity	2.2gal (10ltr)
Primary drive	Gears	Dry weight	310lb (147kg)
Final drive	Chain	Maximum power	18bhp @ 7,000rpm
Gearbox	Four-speed, foot-change	Top speed	76mph (122km/h)
Frame	Spine type of pressed steel; rear section (bolted up) forms rear half of mudguard		

★ Note also 250TC touring model with valanced painted front mudguard, touring handlebars, chrome tank panels, etc.

the prop stand was grounding…. Rear springing was also soft and sometimes caused a slight rhythmic pitching. However, both front and rear forks were well damped on compression and rebound and bottoming never occurred.

Motor Cycling also agreed with *MCM* about the seat, which 'otherwise very comfortable' was 'not long enough for a pillion'.

Accessibility was deemed to be 'particularly good': 'the dynamo/electric starter, the contact breaker points and the clutch withdrawal mechanism are exposed by removing three Phillips screws around a single alloy cover', whilst the 'battery (enclosed in by transparent plastic, fuse, flasher unit and voltage regulator) is contained within the offside cover'. The reporter also praised the finish – 'practically everything about the Suzuki is of a very high quality' – describing the tool kit as 'comprehensive' and the tools themselves 'well made'. However, like the *Mechanics* tester, he was inclined to criticize the chrome plating.

Motor Cycling's test came to a favourable conclusion: 'Without doubt the Suzuki 250 TB is an excellent example of Japanese know-how and engineering – and there's nothing quite like it in Britain.'

Prior to the two machines being tested by the press, both had been used for course-learning exercises for the Isle of Man TT by the Suzuki factory riders.

Geoff Duke's Japanese visit

In spring 1960, six-times World Champion Geoff Duke spent around three weeks in Japan at the invitation of Fumito Sakai, President of

OPPOSITE PAGE:
TOP: 1961 Suzuki brochure showing the Model TA Colleda Twin 250cc motorcycle and Suzulight Model TL 360cc car.

BOTTOM: 1961 Suzuki range specifications, plus 50cc, 125cc and 150cc machines; Model MA Selpet, Model SB Seltwin and Model SB-S Seltwin Sports respectively.

"SUZULIGHT"
Model TL (360 c.c.)

Simply beautiful-mighty powered-wonderfully handy is the SUZULIGHT Light-van with 4 seat.
Front wheel-drive for lightness and stability.
All mechanical parts under the bonnet.
When rear seat is folded down, 300 kgs luggage is loaded.

Exciting, Dynamic "COLLEDA TWIN-ACE"
Model TA (250 c.c.)

World most advanced motorcycle.
A new high in motorcycle performance
Co-action front and rear oil brake
Twin cylinder, twin carburettor
Dynamo starter
More top speed   Nice riding comfort

SUZUKI MOTOR CYCLES

SUZUKI MOTOR CO., LTD.

HEAD OFFICE & FACTORY 300, Takatsuka near Hamamatsu, Shizuoka Pref. Japan

TOKYO BRANCH No. 1 5-chome, Siba-shinbashi, Minatoku. TOKYO

267 35-3

The smart "COLLEDA SELTWIN"
Model SB (125 c.c.)

Safety handling, comfort riding fun
Top in beautifully jet lined
Top in performance-that's the new "COLLEDA SELTWIN"
With ; Dynamo starter
Twin cylinder   More horse power

The stylish "COLLEDA SELTWIN SPORTS"
Model SB-S (150 c.c.)

Tops for touring-comfortable, dependable.
Amazing performance
Unsurpassed road-holding
Technical superiority

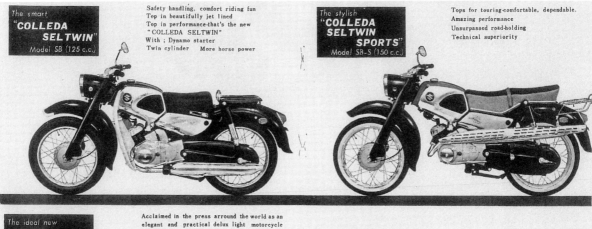

The ideal new "SUZUKI SELPET"
Model MA (50 c.c.)

Acclaimed in the press arround the world as an elegant and practical delux light motorcycle with :
Dynamo starter
Independent suspension
4 speed gearbox.

✱ SPECIFICATIONS

	SUZUKI SELPET	COLLEDA TWIN-ACE	COLLEDA SELTWIN	COLLEDA SELTWIN SPORTS	SUZULIGHT
Overall Length	1,760mm(69.4")	2,030mm(79.8")	1,985mm(77.8")	1,985mm(77.8")	2,990mm(117.7")
Overall Width	605mm(24.0")	690mm(27.1")	700mm(27.6")	645mm(25.0")	1,295mm(51.0")
Overall Height	890mm(35.0")	950mm(37.3")	930mm(36.6")	920mm(36.5")	1,380mm(54.3")
Wheel Base	1,150mm(45.0")	1,320mm(53.1")	1,280mm(51.1")	1,250mm(46.1")	2,050mm(78.21")
Ground Clearance	120mm(4.7")	130mm(4.8")	130mm(5.1")	130mm(5.1")	150mm(5.3")
Tires Front, Rear	2.25"-17"-4p	2.75"-16"-4p	2.75"-17"-4p	2.75"-17"-4p	4.50"-12"-4p
Engine	2 cycle ∫ cylinder, 50 c.c.	2 cycle 2 cylinder, 250 c.c.	2 cycle 2 cylinder 125 c.c.	2 cycle 2 cylinder 150 c.c.	2 cycle 2 cylinder, 360 c.c.
Bore × Stroke	41mm×38mm	52mm×58mm×2	42mm×45mm(×2)	46mm×45mm(×2)	59mm×66mm(×2)
Compression Ratio	8.5:1	6.5:1		7:1	7.2:1
Ignition	Battery Ignition	Battery Ignition	Battery Ignition	Battery Ignition	Battery Ignition
Starting System	Dynamo Starter	Dynamo Starter	Dynamo Starter	Dynamo Starter	Dynamo Starter
Battery	12V, 6AH	12V, 12 AH	12V, 11 AH	12V, 11 AH	12V, 24 AH
Maximum horse power	4.0 HP/8,000 r.p.m.	18 HP/7,000 r.p.m.	10 HP/7,000 r.p.m.	10 HP/7,000 r.p.m.	21 HP/5,500 r.p.m.
Climbing Ability	⅕	⅓	⅕	⅕	⅕
Brake Stopping Distance	5m(25 km/h)	8m(35 km/h)	8m(35km/h)	8m(35km/h)	6m(35 km/h)
Fuel Consumption	75km/l(25km/h)	70km/l(40km/h)	60km/l(40km/h)	60km/h/40km/h)	30 km/l
Fuel Tank Capacity	4 litre	9 litre	9.2 litre	9.2 litre	22 litre
Clutch	multiple wet disk clutch	multiple wet disk clutch	Multiple wet disk clutch	Multiple wet disk clutch	Multiple wet disk clutch
Transmission	4 speed foot operated	4 speed foot operated	4 speed foot operated	4 speed foot operated	3 speed from 1 back
Operating system	Rotary system by left foot	Rotary system by left foot	Rotary system by left foot	Rotary system by left foot	Remote Control System
Suspension system Front	Bottom Link System	Telescopic System	Telescopic System	Telescopic System	Transvers Leaf-spring
Rear	Pivot System	Pivot System	Pivot System	Pivot System	Independent Suspension

the Japan Motorcycle Federation and publisher of the Japanese magazine, *Motorcyclist*. During his visit, Duke not only witnessed sporting events but also visited the Honda, Yamaha and Suzuki factories. He later reported that 'during the whole of my stay at the Suzuki factory, I was showered with questions from every direction regarding the TT, and racing in general. And it was quite apparent that their approach to racing was both enthusiastic and serious, backed up with considerable technical knowledge' (*Geoff Duke In Pursuit of Perfection*, Osprey 1988).

He also wrote about his impressions in an article entitled 'My Japanese Journey', published in the 2 June 1960 issue of *Motor Cycling*:

> The Suzuki company was our next port of call, and this one of the two Japanese factories supporting this year's TT was approached on 19 April, with great interest. And it turned out to be a highly efficient organization, manufacturing motorcycles only since the war [1952 actually] and now producing machines at a rate of 8,500 per month!

During his 1960 visit, Geoff Duke was also able to test several machines, including the 50cc Selpet (on the lines of moped, but with footrests in place of pedals and equipped with electric start and flashing indicators); the latest SB125 and TA250 twins, plus a works 125cc twin-cylinder racer (of the type to be used in the 1960 TT).

His 1960 Japanese visit certainly gave Geoff Duke something on which to reflect upon his return to Great Britain:

> On the plane home, I had some time to think and made certain notes which I thought might serve to stir some of our manufacturers out of their complacency. But alas, this was not to be. Edward Turner of Triumph/BSA later visited Japan on a fact-finding tour, but appeared to be unmoved. Perhaps the 'facts' were too shattering! (*Geoff Duke In Pursuit of Perfection*, Osprey 1988)

Further Developments

During 1961 several changes were made to the Suzuki corporate structure, to cope with existing and expected future growth. In the most important move, the textile machinery division was separated from the automotive manufacturing operation. During the same year, the firm's own foundry was opened, so that castings no longer had to be purchased from outside suppliers. Shortly thereafter, Suzuki was in a position to manufacture its own forgings too. These developments not only gave Suzuki a firmer grip on its quality control, but also improved profit margins and at the same time made the company less dependent upon outside sources.

During August 1961, the share capital had reached 300 million yen. In November of the same year, the 125 twin was modernized into the SK, and later the SL.

Another important aspect of Suzuki's emergence as a major force, not only in the Japanese home market but also the wider world, was its policy of market research. This had revealed that there was a need to offer a more comprehensive range of up to 100cc class machines. As one commentator put it, 'potential customers sought a machine that would have the performance capabilities of a typical 125cc model of that era but a retail price more in keeping with that of the average 50cc model'. Also having a bearing on Suzuki's future direction in this ultra-light-weight field was the Japanese home market, where legislation at the same time meant that prices could be more competitive with engines not exceeding 90cc. This explains why, from that time, Suzuki was to offer a range of models with engine sizes not exceeding 89.9cc! As the 1960s unfolded, the M series was joined by the K, A, F and U ranges; for the full story of the development of all these small singles, *see* Chapter 2.

Through the 1950s, Suzuki made the transition from Japan's to the world's number 2. The Japanese invasion of the European and, ultimately, the American markets had begun.

2 Small Singles

Like several other major companies in both Japan and Europe, Suzuki began its two-wheel activities during the immediate post-war era by producing small single cylinder motorcycles, mopeds and scooters; other producers of similar two-wheelers included Honda and Yamaha, as well as Ducati, Agusta (MV), Piaggio (Vespa) and Innocenti (Lambretta). Whilst the very early Suzuki models – 'bread-and-butter' machines – rarely hit the headlines, they none the less represent a vital segment in any history of the Japanese marque.

The K and M Series

During the early 1960s Suzuki offered an entire range of inexpensive commuter-type models, including MA, MC, ME, M12, M15, M30, K10 and K11. These humble bikes were vitally important to the success of the company – no fewer than 520,000 examples of the K10 and K11 models alone being manufactured during their five-year production run. The significance of these small machines in Suzuki's initial drive for export sales cannot be underestimated. The various twins may have generated more publicity, but the cheap-to-buy, economical and ultra-reliable small, single-cylinder creations were the bedrock upon which Suzuki built its world-wide sales armada.

AMC

In June 1963 the news leaked out that AMC (Associated Motor Cycles), the manufacturers of AJS, Matchless, Norton, Francis-Barnett and

James, were to handle the import of Suzuki motorcycles into the UK, via a completely new organization – Suzuki (Great Britain) Ltd – to

Heidi Cockerton with her 1963 M15 from the first batch imported by AMC (Associated Motor Cycles).

be based in Birmingham. Full-scale distribution was planned to begin later the same year. Negotiations between Suzuki and AMC had begun several months earlier, but were only finalized during the visit to the UK by Shunzo Suzuki himself. Shunzo had been in the Isle of Man in early June to witness his works entries score a magnificent 1-2-3 victory over great rivals Honda, in the Ultra Lightweight (125cc) TT.

Between October 1963 and October 1964, with Alan Kimber in charge, and working from the back door of the James factory in Golden Hillock Road, Green, Birmingham, some 18,000 machines were imported. Suzuki GB's earliest imports were a trio of fifties, the M12, M15 and M15D, the 80 and K10, plus the T10 two-fifty twin (*see* Chapter 3). However, the vast majority of Suzukis to find British owners in that first twelve-month period were the K and M singles. The K11 arrived a few months later in spring 1964, following a visit to Japan by Kimber.

Early Models for the British Market
Electric Start
The only 50cc motorcycle on the British market in 1964 with an electric start was the Suzuki M15D Sovereign, which *Motor Cycling* described as having 'a standard specification which is lavish, even by Japanese standards'. For an outlay of £114 9s, the buyer got not only 12-volt electrics but also leg shields, direction indicators, chrome-plated carrier, leading link pressed-steel front forks and speedometer. A kickstart-only version with 6-volt electrics, the M15 Sportsman, sold for the lower price of £95 11s. The third member of the 50cc trio was the M12 Super Sport. This was equipped with a hi-level exhaust, narrow front mudguard and exposed stanchion oil-damped telescopic forks.

All versions shared a pressed-steel fabricated stressed backbone-type frame, fully enclosed final-drive chain, and 2.25 × 17 tyres at both front and rear.

The 50cc M12 Super Sport was probably the most popular of all early Suzuki imports into Great Britain.

1963 M12 Specification

Engine	Air-cooled single with piston-port induction, slightly inclined cylinder, alloy head, cast-iron barrel, caged needle roller small- and big-ends, vertically split aluminium crankcases	Front suspension	Telescopic forks with exposed springs
		Rear suspension	Swinging-arm, with twin shock absorbers
		Front brake	100mm full-width drum, SLS
		Rear brake	100mm full-width drum, SLS
Bore	41mm	Tyres	2.25 × 17 front and rear
Stroke	38mm		
Displacement	49cc	*General specifications*	
Compression ratio	6.7:1		
Lubrication	Petroil, 20:1 ratio	Wheelbase	45in (1,143mm)
Ignition	Flywheel magneto, 6-volt	Ground clearance	4.7in (119mm)
Carburettor	15mm	Seat height	28in (711mm)
Primary drive	Gears, 15/66	Fuel tank capacity	1.3gal (6ltr)
Final drive	Chain, 13/32	Dry weight	145lb (66kg)
Gearbox	Four-speed, foot-change	Maximum power	4.2bhp @ 8,000rpm
Frame	Pressed-steel construction, no front downtube or cradle	Top speed	50mph (80km/h)

Built from 1963 through to 1967, the M12 Super Sport could reach 50mph (80km/h).

Displacing precisely 49cc, the M12/15 series piston-port induction engine had bore and stroke dimensions of 41 × 38mm – slightly over-square. The power output of all three versions was the same – 4.2bhp at 8,000rpm – as was the compression ratio of 6.7:1. Like all the first Suzukis imported into the UK during 1963/64, the 50cc engine was petroil lubricated and featured an alloy head and cast-iron barrel, a four-speed gearbox built-in unit, wet, multi-plate clutch, gear primary drive and roller bearing big- and small-ends. All the singles featured vertically split crankcases. Maximum speed of the M-series Suzuki 50 was 50mph (80km/h).

The 80 Range

The 80 K10 Standard was part of the first Suzuki GB shipment, which arrived in October 1963. A second model, the K11 Sports, reached the UK a few months later (*see* page 24). Like the fifties, both 80s shared the same 79.5cc (45 × 50mm), four-speed piston-port engine with petroil lubrication. However, although still of the pressed-steel backbone type, the frame of the larger-engined machines had a tubular steel front downtube, wider-section 2.50 tyres, slightly higher gear ratios and no electric start option.

Motor Cycle News' Sean Wood considered the K11 Sport model to be 'as light as a fifty and as powerful as a 125', whilst the 'suspension was just right' and the controls 'as light as a feather'.

LEFT: *K10 engine with alloy head, cast-iron barrel, four speeds and petroil lubrication.*

BELOW: *A 1963 79.5cc (45 × 50mm) K10, with single seat, built-in carrier and leg shields.*

1967 K11P 80 Sport; now with pump ('P') lubrication, but otherwise much as before.

1963 K11 Specification

Engine	Air-cooled single with piston-port induction, slightly inclined cylinder, alloy head, cast-iron barrel, caged needle-roller small- and big-ends, vertically split aluminium crankcases
Bore	45mm
Stroke	50mm
Displacement	79.5cc
Compression ratio	6.7:1
Lubrication	Petroil
Ignition	Flywheel magneto, 6-volt
Carburettor	17mm
Primary drive	Gears, 19/73
Final drive	Chain, 14/30
Gearbox	Four-speed, foot-change
Frame	Pressed-steel construction, with front downtube brace
Front suspension	Telescopic fork with exposed springs
Rear suspension	Swinging-arm, with twin shock absorbers
Front brake	110mm full-width drum, SLS
Rear brake	110mm full-width drum, SLS
Tyres	2.50 × 17 front and rear

General specifications

Wheelbase	45.7in (1,160mm)
Ground clearance	5.3in (134mm)
Seat height	28in (711mm)
Fuel tank capacity	1.5gal (7ltr)
Dry weight	155lb (70kg)
Maximum power	8bhp @ 7,500rpm
Top speed	60mph (97km/h)

In June 1964 the K10 Standard retailed at £122 17s and the K11 Sport cost £128 10s.

The K11 had also proved its worth in competition, being campaigned in several British and International events with considerable success. On-the-road maximum speed for both eighties was 56mph (90km/h), but the real advantage over the smaller-engined machines was much-improved engine torque – which made the eighty so successful off-road.

A Step-Thru

June 1964 saw the debut of a 50cc step-thru model on the British market, to compete with Honda's ultra-successful C100 Super Cub. Coded M30, this had been available in other markets (as had the M12/15 machines) prior to imports arriving in Great Britain. Priced at £93 9s, the M30 was marketed in the UK as the Suzi. It featured an automatic three-speed gearbox, dual seat, leg shields, mirrors and indicators – all included in the asking price. Available in grey, red, blue or green (with off-white leg shields), the M30 could clock 43mph (69km/h)

NOW YOU TOO CAN ENJOY THE THRILL OF A SUZUKI

50 CC MOTOR CYCLES FOR THE YOUNG AND YOUNG AT HEART

On Grand Prix tracks all over the world, Suzuki 50 cc machines have been adding a new dimension to motor cycling ... piling success on success in a relentless stream. These compact dynamos of power – designed along youthful, racy lines with a performance to match – give you everything you could wish for in one ultra-modern machine ... superior engineering, comfort, manoeuvrability, speed, fuel economy! The ultimate in practical, safe, all round transportation! And now – for the first time – Suzuki models are available in this country backed by the comprehensive service facilities of the world's largest manufacturer of 2-stroke motor cycles.

M15 Sportsman 91 gns.—or £19.0.0. deposit and 14/- per week for 3 years.
M15D Sovereign (with press button self-starter) 109 gns—or £23.10.0 deposit and 17/- per week for 3 years.
NO 'EXTRAS' NEEDED — standard equipment includes 4-speed gearbox · neutral gear warning light · indicator winkers · mirrors · parking lights · dual seat · carrier · stop lights · passenger foot rests. Both these models give you maximum speeds in the fifties and a fuel consumption of 185 m.p.g.

SUZUKI
FLYWEIGHT CHAMPIONS OF THE WORLD   M15 Sportsman

Suzuki GB advertisement, dated February 1964: '50cc Motorcycles for the Young – and Young at Heart.'

and up to 180mpg (1.5ltr/100km). Dry weight was 123lb (56kg). The full-width drum brakes, 2.25 × 17 tyres and leading link forks were shared with the M15/M15D models.

With a slightly reduced compression ratio of 6.3:1, power output was 4bhp at the lower 6,800rpm. Lubrication was again by petroil.

Like all the 1964 Suzuki range, the accent was very much on comfort, ease of handling and reliability, plus, in the 50/80 single-cylinder models, a budget purchase price and excellent fuel economy figures. Another star point for

such small engine sizes was a surprising amount of flexibility. (Of course, this was pre-Super Six days, when Suzuki was to jump – successfully – on the performance bandwagon as a priority.)

Rider Comfort and Protection

With their leg shields, decent mudguarding, fully enclosed drive chain and comfortable seat, the touring versions of the fifty and eighty models had obviously been designed to provide the rider with as much protection and comfort as possible without having to resort to a scooter. Likewise the rocking gear pedal. As one commentator of the day described it: 'You don't have to put your foot under it, so you don't damage your best shoes. It's simply four down [he was testing an 80 K10] on the front to change up, and four down on the back of the pedal for down.'

The full-width drum brakes were adjudged 'exceptional'. Not only this but they worked precisely the same in both the wet and dry, which was something that could not be said of certain Suzuki models of the 1970s with disc front stoppers!

The K125

At the end of 1964 Suzuki produced their first disc-valve induction series production model, the K125. Examples of this machine arrived in the UK (for the ISDT) in September 1965, but the K125 was never offered for sale in Britain, even though it was a notable success in Japan and developing countries well into the 1980s.

The centre of the machine was a 124cc (54 × 54mm) single-cylinder engine with twin exhaust header pipes. The cast-iron cylinder barrel was split into two, to feed a silencer on each side of the machine; many observers wrongly thought it was a twin! The cylinder head was of aluminium and featured a centrally positioned spark plug.

Motor Cycle News reported the bikes' arrival in its 15 September 1965 issue: 'Hastily modified at the Birmingham factory, the machines arrived

The K125 arrived at the end of 1964 and was Suzuki's first production disc-valve roadster. It also featured a twin-port exhaust, which made it look like a twin. Production was to continue until well into the 1980s.

from Japan last week, after being delayed in America. Three will be ridden by Don Barratt, Mick Miller and John Stone. Two more will be used by members of the Irish Vase team. Two other 125s were damaged in transit.'

However, the K125's baptism in what was the fortieth running of the ISDT, is best described as a disaster, as *MCN* recounted: 'The new 125s with rotary-valve induction were the worst hit. Don Barratt blew his cylinder head off; Mick Miller holed his piston and John Stone just survived a complete seizure.' And this was all on the first day!

The ISDT bikes had 2.75 × 19 front and 3.50 × 16 rear tyres (16in on both wheels on the standard roadster). The exhausts had been cut and raised to clear the QD (quickly detachable)

rear-wheel spindle, and the stock close-fitting metal front mudguard had been replaced by an off-road-type fibreglass component, suitable for the larger-diameter wheel. The carburettor was mounted under a cover on the offside (right) of the crankcase, whilst the opposite side extension housed an electric start, making for a rather wide power unit.

As for the cycle parts, there was a pressed-steel beam frame that was conventional for the period. The front brake was reported as being 'a smaller edition of the twin-leading shoe stoppers fitted to the six-speed ISDT Suzuki twins'. These latter machines – ridden by John Harris, Peter Fletcher and Eddie Crooks – were in fact specially prepared versions of the T20 Super Six (*see* Chapter 3).

Pump Lubrication

From the mid-1960s, Suzuki introduced a distinctive feature, represented by a 'P' at the end of the model code, which helped both in terms of reputation and reliability. This was a simple but exceedingly effective mechanically operated pump, which metered the flow of oil from a separate tank to the vital component parts of the engine unit. The same fitment was made on many other Suzukis in later years. This replaced the previous petroil (petrol/oil) mixture, which Suzuki engineers realized was a messy nuisance for commuter-orientated customers.

To ensure that the system was responsive to engine requirements, the pump was linked to the throttle so that the delivery rate was increased as the throttle was opened, and it would not have to rely solely on the speeding up of the pump drive as the engine responded. This more refined system significantly diminished the possibility of an engine being starved of vital lubrication in the event of coasting down a lengthy incline, which could occur with the petroil system. In the latter case, if the throttle remained shut, no oil would reach the engine's working components until it was opened again.

The pump system was not an entirely new innovation, the British marque Velocette having employed the same basic principle during the inter-war period, with its GTP model. However, the Suzuki CCI (controlled crankshaft injection) system was more refined, pumping oil direct to the vital engine internals via a series of external plastic pipes fitted with one-way valves. There was no question of having to rely upon a jet set into the side of the inlet passage, or in the carburettor itself, immediately behind the slide. The latter technique was not much different from the petroil system, even though it eliminated the need for messy and time-consuming petrol and oil mixing.

By ensuring a direct, positive feed of undiluted oil, the Suzuki approach to two stroke lubrication was a significant step forward, which had not, hitherto, been applied to a series production motorcycle that was really mass-produced. Besides brand-new models with the Posi-Force system (for example the T20 Super Six), Suzuki also adopted various existing engines, such as the K10 and K11, adding the 'P' after the original letters (for example, K10P) to denote pump lubrication.

The B100/120 Series

Besides the K125, another Suzuki single-cylinder machine was to have an exceptionally long production life – the B100/120 series, which became known as the 'Bloop', and was likened by many observers to the equally long-running British BSA Bantam (1948–71). The two models were both launched during 1964, but, whereas the K125 was to remain virtually unchanged throughout its life, the 'Bloop', or to be more precise its engine assembly, was to appear in several different guises.

The 1964 B100 displaced 118cc with bore and stroke dimensions of 52 × 56mm respectively, with a particularly clean design for the unit construction piston-port engine/gearbox assembly. Suzuki claimed a power output of 10bhp at 7,000rpm.

Initially, the B100 was not imported into the UK. As Don Leeson recalled, 'Suzuki had

only just become established in [Britain] with a range of 50cc and 80cc singles, and the 250cc T10 twin. For whatever reason – uncertainty about their overall reception, thinking they had enough utility models already, or perhaps more likely because of the comparatively high price of the new model – the B100 was not offered for sale in the UK.' In fact, British buyers were in for a relatively long wait, as the first examples of the model did not reach their market until May 1966. This motorcycle was identical to the original B100 in practically all respects, except for the addition of an oil pump. B100P (the 'P' suffix representing the oil pump) was soon accorded the nickname 'Bloop' by the British press and owners alike.

On the B100 engine the addition of Suzuki's Posi-Force pump lubrication system (*see* above) was achieved by an extension outboard of the offside (right) crankshaft and front helical drive primary gear. This extension drove the oil pump. A pair of gears and a ball bearing formed a special gearbox within a modified offside engine side-cover, to dispense with the 20:1 pre-mix employed by the original B100, to the state-of-the-art B100P, at what Don Leeson described as 'minimal cost'. A single tube from the pump supplied oil between the two nearside (left) crankshaft bearings. The only mechanical modifications were an oil guide plate between the nearside crankwheel and revised inner main bearing. Main jet size on the B100P was 95 whereas the petroil B100 had a larger 110 jet to ensure sufficient lubrication/fuel. Both used a Mikuni VM20 instrument.

The Clutch
The clutch was mounted on the offside of the engine unit, with five friction (bonded material) and six plain steel plates. Originally, Suzuki had employed plates from the K series 80cc models. However, this proved to be a mistake, and the diameter was increased from 111 to 118mm (from engine number B100-90165). The release mechanism consisted of a quick thread worm set-up located in the offside engine side-cover.

During its entire production life the B100P and later B120P models always used a four-speed gearbox. This had the useful feature of primary kickstart operation – in other words, the engine could be started whilst in gear, provided the clutch lever was pulled in.

Engine
The B100P's engine was essentially a simple, straightforward and most of all reliable unit. A two-ring aluminium piston ran in a cast-iron cylinder liner, with two oversizes of piston being available from Suzuki. As was traditional in the marque's two-strokes at the time there were caged-roller small- and big-end bearings. The crankshaft featured a pressed-in crankpin, and the assembly ran on a trio of main bearings, within vertically split aluminium crankcases.

The 6-volt flywheel magneto (for both ignition and lights) was mounted on the nearside (left) end of the crank by woodruff key/taper. This set-up was responsible for the continuation of a maintenance glitch on the early Suzuki singles – contact breaker points were mounted inboard of the flywheel rotor, making it necessary to use a flywheel extractor to remove the flywheel prior to either simply adjusting the points gap or fitting a new set of points. Either way, it was a right nuisance! On the other side the primary-drive gear was also keyed to the crankshaft.

Suzuki introduced the B100P (soon nicknamed the 'Bloop') in 1966. It was derived from the earlier B100, the only real difference being pump lubrication (hence the 'P').

ABOVE: B100P engine, 118cc (52 × 56mm), piston-port induction, four speeds and flywheel magneto ignition.

BELOW: B100P speedometer with single neutral (green) warning light. Basic, but functional.

The Cycle Parts

Like the power unit, the cycle parts were simple yet sturdy. Again, as with many other early Suzuki single-cylinder models, the frame was of the pressed-steel open type (in other words, with no front downtube). In fact, the engine assembly was only held in place by a trio of bolts that passed through the rear of the crankcase. A pleated-paper air filter element was hidden inside the frame, with the 6-volt, 4-amp hour battery beneath the nearside (left) plastic side-cover. The petroil-lubricated B100 came with a polythene oil bottle to go behind the matching offside (right) plastic side-cover, whereas the B100P featured a metal oil tank of similar profile instead.

The fuel tank had a capacity of 1.75gal (8ltr) and was fitted with replaceable chrome-plated side panels and rubber knee grips.

Of 17in, the wheels sported 6in (150mm) full-width brake hubs, with single-leading shoe operation. For a machine with a dry weight of only 189lb (86kg), these were quite effective. In truth, anything more powerful would probably have been a liability for many B100P owners, who were quite often new to motorcycling.

An oil-damped telescopic front fork carried trendy (and effective) rubber gaiters and a slim, close-fitting steel mudguard. Twin-shock rear suspension was taken care of by fully shrouded, chrome-plate units, offering three-way adjustable damping. A Suzuki brochure of the period claimed that these provided 'the easy riding of a baby buggy'.

As on the other roadster singles, the pressed-steel swinging arm incorporated a fully enclosed chainguard on the nearside (left), minimizing both maintenance and cleaning chores, to say nothing of prolonging chain life itself.

On the offside (right) of the machine, a typically efficient Suzuki silencer hid the rod-operated rear brake mechanism, and also incorporated a separate exhaust header pipe, which not only aided maintenance, but kept down costs when a replacement was needed.

At the rear, an extension of the frame formed the rear mudguard and mounting for the rear light, number plate assembly and rear indicators.

For its size and performance, the 25/25W headlamp was generally seen as good for its day, as was the horn (which was located under the front of the fuel tank). Perhaps unsurprisingly, the instrumentation was basic, comprising an oval speedometer mounted in the top of the headlamp shell, containing neutral and indicator warning lamps.

With a UK launch price of £169 17s 6d, the B100P's standard specification included handlebar-mounted choke lever, steering lock, side and centre stands and pillion footrests. It came in red, blue or black, with off-white (best described as cream) side panels, together with a silver front mudguard.

Testing the Newcomer
The B100P (and the T20 Super Six) were both launched in the UK on 25 May 1966. To coincide with this, *Motor Cycle News* carried a comprehensive test of both machines in its issue dated the same day.

Alan Kimber, the Suzuki UK boss, had originally planned a big journalistic reception, with full road tests for the two newcomers after a Brands Hatch unveiling. However, Air France managed to mislay the goods, according to *MCN*, 'somewhere between Los Angeles and Birmingham'. The machines eventually arrived seventeen days later than planned, as Peter Howdle of *MCN* reported: 'They landed last week with nothing on their pretty clocks, too late for fully run-in testing but in time for a 200-mile (322km) spin. And those vanguards of big shipments now on the high seas from Tokyo gave a very good account of themselves.'

Peter Howdle and colleague Ken Warburton took the two brand-new bikes to Wales, where Howdle was covering the Welsh Three Day Trial.

After singing the praises of the new Posi-Force lubrication system, *MCN* explained that

the B100P's gearbox was 'a foolproof four-speeder with neutral at the top. A green light in the speedo dial tells when the box is in neutral. The drill is to remember to change down for down and up for up.' Starting was 'always instantaneous', but Howdle did admit to 'a spot of rough, rather forceful running-in once the 118cc engine began to loosen up. Although below full throttle, my Suzy cruised happily between 55 and 60mph [89 and 97km/h]. Once or twice I saw 70. In third gear, with the engine buzzing smoothly and pulling well, hills could be crested at 50.'

In Peter Howdle's view,

> Suzuki should be assured of good sales with both models in standard road trim. The "120" Suzy is the obvious step-up for folk weaned on 50cc or 80cc lightweights. Although suspension was a trifle hard, handling was as good as any 80cc or 125cc flyweight I have ridden… my only regret is that these exciting new models are not British made.

For the 1967 model year the specification remained unchanged. The designation was changed to B120, but the 'Bloop' nickname stuck. From the mid-1970s the B120 was marketed as the 'Student', and excellent sales and a good record in service meant that it was still available as the 1980s dawned. By then the chrome tank panel and distinctive knee grips had long since given way to a plain, painted tank finish, but otherwise it remained much as it had been back in 1967.

The following extract from a 1980 factory brochure provides a glimpse of how the company viewed this long-running model:

> The B120 is a mature bike that provides you with comfortable everyday motorcycling, fitted with Suzuki's unique CCI lubrication system and a four-speed gearbox as standard. It is really matured – sturdy, trouble-free, easy in maintenance, safety orientated and money saving. There is one more reason why it is getting so much wide popularity.

1970 B120P Specification

Engine	Air-cooled single with piston-port induction, slightly inclined cylinder, alloy head and barrel, the latter with replaceable liner, caged needle roller small- and big-ends, vertically split aluminium crankcases
Bore	52mm
Stroke	56mm
Displacement	118cc
Compression ratio	6.8:1
Lubrication	Pump
Ignition	Flywheel magneto, 6-volt
Carburettor	Amal VM20SH, 20mm
Primary drive	Gears, 16/50
Final drive	Chain, 14/31
Gearbox	Four-speed, foot-change
Frame	Pressed-steel construction, no front downtube or cradle
Front suspension	Telescopic fork with rubber gaiters
Rear suspension	Swinging-arm, with three-way adjustable shock absorbers
Front brake	140mm full-width drum, SLS
Rear brake	140mm full-width drum, SLS
Tyres	Front 2.50 × 17, rear 2.75 × 17

General specifications

Wheelbase	48in (1,219mm)
Ground clearance	5.9in (149mm)
Seat height	26.2in (665mm)
Fuel tank capacity	1.76gal (8ltr)
Dry weight	189lb (86kg)
Maximum power	10bhp @ 7,000rpm
Top speed	60mph (97km/h)

Versatility, commuting to and from either office or school, shopping. Leisure or whatever you call it – the B120 performs.

The A Series

The A100

The year 1967 brought another significant Suzuki lightweight, the A100 – another model that was to run on virtually unchanged until well into the 1980s.

However, unlike the 'Bloop', the A100 not only had a near-horizontal cylinder but also disc-valve induction. Because of its layout, the cylinder head fins were positioned horizontally rather than vertically. Both the head and barrel were of light alloy, the latter with an iron liner, and engine dimensions were 'square' at 50 × 50mm, giving a capacity of 98cc. Compression ratio was 6.5:1 and the disc valve was mounted on the offside of the crankcase. With

The A50's bigger brother, the A100, was launched in 1967. It sported disc-valve induction and a near-horizontal cylinder, 98.2cc (50 × 50mm), 9.5bhp and four speeds.

a healthy 9.5bhp at 7,500rpm and a dry weight of 176lb (80kg), the A100 was capable of a similar performance to the B120.

Unlike the 'Bloop', the A100 saw several changes over the years, both to styling and specification, including wheel sizes (17 to 18in from 1970), various sizes of fuel tank and also more sporting versions (the AC100 and AS100), although these latter models were offered only in 1970 and 1971.

RIGHT: 1973 A100K, with revised styling.

BELOW: Exploded view of the A100 engine with near-horizontal cylinder and vertically split crankcases.

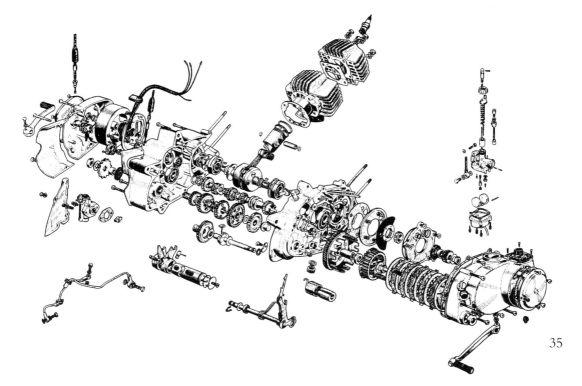

1968 A100 and AS100 Specifications*

Engine	Air-cooled single with disc-valve induction, near-horizontal cylinder, alloy head and barrel, the latter with replaceable liner, caged needle roller small- and big-ends, vertically split aluminium crankcases
Bore	50mm
Stroke	50mm
Displacement	98.2cc
Compression ratio	6.5:1
Lubrication	Pump
Ignition	Flywheel magneto, 6 volt
Carburettor	Amal 20mm
Primary drive	Gears, 16/50
Final drive	Chain, 15/32
Gearbox	Four-speed, foot-change
Frame	Pressed-steel construction, no front downtube or cradle
Front suspension	Telescopic fork with rubber gaiters
Rear suspension	Swinging-arm, with twin shock absorbers
Front brake	140mm full-width drum
Rear brake	140mm full-width drum

General specifications

Wheelbase	45.6in (1,158mm)
Ground clearance	5.3in (134mm)
Seat height	26.7in (678mm)
Fuel tank capacity	1.5gal (7ltr)
Dry weight	176lb (80kg)
Maximum power	9.5bhp @ 7,500rpm
Top speed	69mph (111km/h)

* A100 low-level exhaust; AS100 hi-level exhaust

1969 A50 and AS50 Specifications*

Engine	Air-cooled single with disc-valve induction cylinder, alloy head and barrel, the latter with replaceable liner, caged needle roller small- and big-ends, vertically split crankcases
Bore	41mm
Stroke	37.8mm
Displacement	49.9cc
Compression ratio	6.7:1
Lubrication	Pump
Ignition	Flywheel magneto, 6 volt
Carburettor	Amal 16mm
Primary drive	Gears 19/73
Final drive	Chain 12/32
Gearbox	Five-speed, foot-change
Frame	Pressed-steel construction, no front downtube or cradle
Front suspension	Telescopic fork with rubber gaiters
Rear suspension	Swinging-arm, with twin shock absorbers
Front brake	110mm full-width drum, SLS
Rear brake	110mm full-width drum, SLS
Tyres	2.25 × 19 front and rear

General specifications

Wheelbase	45.7in (1,160mm)
Ground clearance	5.9in (150mm)
Seat height	26.8in (681mm)
Fuel tank capacity	1.4gal (6.5ltr)
Dry weight	160lb (72.5kg)
Maximum power	4.9bhp @ 8,500rpm
Top speed	60mph (96.5km/h)

* A50 low-level exhaust; AS50 hi-level exhaust

A 50cc Version

There was also a smaller '50' version with the same disc-valve induction (49.9cc, 41 × 37.8mm), which, running on a compression ratio of 6.7:1, put out 4.9bhp at 8,500rpm. The A50 series also had the advantage of a five-speed instead of four-speed gearbox.

Over the years (starting with the sporty AS50 of 1968), various versions were built with the same basic engine, including the A50, the AC50 (like the AS50, with raised exhaust, abbreviated chainguard, and either exposed springs or gaitered forks), the A50P ('P' for pedals) and A50K (a restricted performance motorcycle).

There were even the A70 (as A50, but with four speeds), the A80 and A90 versions, plus in many cases sports variants, such as the AC90,

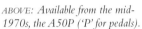

AC90G, AS90 and AS90G. Detailing each and every small single-cylinder Suzuki from the late 1960s to the late 1970s would take a book in itself, there were so many models, some for specific markets only, such as Japan, developing countries or the West.

ABOVE: Available from the mid-1970s, the A50P ('P' for pedals).

LEFT: 1971 A50, touring version of the AS50 sports model, with low-level exhaust, dual seat and fully enclosed final-drive chain.

1972 B120P, still essentially much as before – and still 118cc.

First offered in 1968, the AS50 was a brilliant little bike, its five-speed, 49.9cc (41 × 37.8mm) disc-valve engine developing 4.9bhp.

BELOW: Suzuki's UK model range and price list, April 1970, stretching from the U50 through to the T500 Mark II.

U for Utility

In 1966 Suzuki introduced the U50, which effectively replaced the M30, both machines being of the 'step-thru' type with their U-shape pressed-steel frame layout. However, even though the two looked very similar, technically they were quite different. The M30 had been piston-port induction and petroil lubrication, whereas the new U50 (also sold as the U50D with electric start and 12-volt electrics) not only featured disc-valve induction but pump lubrication. The D variant of the U50 also had coil, rather than flywheel magneto ignition, which was fitted to both the M30 and U50 standard models.

The U50 did retain the three-speed, automatic clutch (there being no conventional clutch lever on either machine for the rider to worry about), 2.25 × 17 tyres, leading-link front forks and the wide use of plastics for components such as leg shields. Also retained was the fully enclosed final-drive chain and heel and toe gear lever. There was also a larger-engined version, the U70 (69.8cc, 46 × 42mm).

At the start of 1969, the U50 and U70 were replaced by the new F50/70 models with essentially the same basics of three speeds, leading link forks, fully enclosed chain, leg shields, and rocking heel and toe gear pedal with automatic clutch; but brand-new styling (almost a copy of

Honda C100 Super Cub) and a change from disc to the more advanced reed-valve induction.

The new reed-valve engines were not only smoother, but also, more importantly, provided

SUZUKI FR70

Suzuki: built to take on the country.

ABOVE LEFT: After the M30 and U50, the next Suzuki 'step-thru' was the F50, which arrived in 1969. A distinctive feature was its advanced reed-valve induction. 70 and 90cc versions were also offered.

ABOVE RIGHT: The FR50 replaced the F50 from the 1974 model year, and once again 70 (shown) and 90 versions were offered, depending upon country.

a better spread of power throughout the rev range. The F50 produced 4.5bhp at 6,000rpm (against the U50's 4.1bhp at the same revolutions) whilst the F70 put out slightly less power: 6.1bhp at 6,500rpm compared with the U70's 6.5bhp at 7,000rpm.

For the 1974 model year (K) the two machines became the FR50 and FR70. New features included a fog lamp (mounted on the steering column shield and below the handlebars/headlamp), revised front indicators (now on the handlebars, rather than leg shields), revised mid-section of frame and new panelling, and a newly designed speedometer console, featuring fuel warning and neutral lights. There were also new headlight and tail-light assemblies.

The FZ50 and GP Series

Towards the end of the 1970s Suzuki had something of a rethink concerning its smaller-capacity models. This not only saw the introduction

of the ultra-modern FZ50 Suzy, but also a pair of excellent new ultra-lightweight motorcycles, the GP100 and GP125. The GP series effectively replaced the long-running A100/B120 machines in many markets.

The FZ50 was very much a design for the 1980s rather than the 1970s. Suzuki called it 'The Family Bike' and claimed, 'If you can ride a bicycle you can ride a Suzy.' With a two-speed transmission and no gear change, the rider simply had to steer, accelerate and brake. The FZ50 was ultra-safe, with a special 'Safety Start' engine that would not start *until* the rider applied the rear brake; a feature that proved very popular with lady owners. Maintenance-free electronic 6-volt ignition, 12in alloy wheels with 3.00 section tyres and a low seat height also helped sales. The comprehensive standard specification also included indicators, helmet lock, front and rear carriers, and protective leg shields. The 49cc air-cooled two-stroke engine (with horizontal alloy head and cast-iron cylinder barrel) provided up to 100mpg (2.8ltr/100km). Available in blue or orange, this brilliant little bike, which weighed just 130lb (59kg) dry, was a massive sales success for Suzuki. After years of trailing behind Honda with its M30/U/F/FR step-thrus, the company at last had a machine to take on its rival – and win in the showroom.

The GP duo used disc-valve engines of 98cc (50 × 50mm) and 123cc (56 × 50mm), five-speed, putting out 12bhp at 8,500rpm (GP100) and 15bhp at 8,000rpm (GP125). (Many 125s for the British market were sold in 12bhp guise after the new learner laws were introduced during 1981.) Depending upon the market and the exact model, buyers got either disc or drum front brakes and wire or cast-alloy wheels. All models had 6-volt contact-breaker electrics. The 100 could reach 68mph (110km/h), the 125 (in unrestricted guise), 75mph (121km/h). Other details included 18in wheels, oil-damped exposed stanchion telescopic front forks, twin mirrors, indicators and of course pump lubrication.

Later, by 1982, Suzuki made a switch to four-stroke lightweights – first, the GS125 (roadster) and then the DR125 (trail) – but it continued with several two-strokes for a time, particularly in markets in the developing world. The two-stroke engine was the one that had really put Suzuki on the map, and it was particularly important at the 'first-bike' stage of many budding motorcyclists' careers the world over.

ABOVE: During the late 1970s the FZ50 Suzy was one of the best-selling small machines on the market. Its automatic transmission meant no gear changing, as the Suzuki publicity material emphasized: 'Just steer, accelerate and brake.'

RIGHT: The GP125 (and GP100) also arrived at the end of the 1970s. Sharing many components, both offered excellent performance and economy for their respective engine sizes. The GP100 displaced 98cc (50 × 50mm). To achieve the larger 123cc engine size, the bore size of the GP125 was increased to 56mm; the stroke remained unchanged.

3 T20 and Other Early Twins

The first of Suzuki's two-fifty twin-cylinder models to take on the world seriously was the T10, which could trace its origins back to the 1960 TA (Twin Ace), itself a derivative of the company's first two-fifty twins, the initial 1956 TT and subsequent TP models. At that time the brand name Colleda was in use instead of the now-familiar Suzuki, which was introduced when exports to Western countries began in earnest during the period late 1961 to early 1962. Following the TA came the TB, the TBB (also known confusingly in some markets as the TC) and, finally, the T10.

Origins

Although the T10 was the first Suzuki twin to be offered for sale in the UK, it was not the first on British roads. Jimmy Matsumiya, Suzuki Japan's first British representative, was accorded this honour with a pair of TBs available in 1962; these were used for magazine road tests and by the works team for TT course learning.

The *Motorcycle Mechanics* road test of a 250 TB in June 1962 (*see* Chapter 1) was headlined 'A Superb Machine – That's the Suzuki'. Tester Brian Smith and other British riders were particularly impressed by one unusual feature – the rotary gear change – described by the late Don Leeson in the May 1986 issue of *Motorcycle Enthusiast* as 'a common feature of Japanese machines of the time'. *Motorcycle Mechanics* considered it to be 'a tremendous advance in design'. Don Leeson explained the system in more detail: 'The rotary change allowed two methods of selecting neutral from top gear –

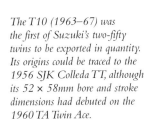

The T10 (1963–67) was the first of Suzuki's two-fifty twins to be exported in quantity. Its origins could be traced to the 1956 SJK Colleda TT, although its 52 × 58mm bore and stroke dimensions had debuted on the 1960 TA Twin Ace.

either back down the 'box through third, second and first in the normal manner, or by changing *up* once more!' It was a great asset for the Japanese commuter in the crowded stop–go conditions of central Tokyo, where one dab after a crash stop would get the rider back to neutral. However, it was to prove less beneficial in Europe and America, particularly when five- and six-speed 'boxes began to appear. According to Don Leeson, 'It was all too easy to lose count, think the resulting burst of revs was a result of a missed gear and hook the lever up one more time. Rotary change didn't seem such a good idea when you found yourself doing 80mph in first!' Suzuki soon got the message, and the feature was never offered on T10s for the UK market, which began to receive imported stock in October 1963.

The T10

Many believe wrongly that the T10 was the progenitor of the model that replaced it, the much better-known T20. Actually, the model designations are the closest point of commonality. In truth the T10 represented the end of one design family, while the T250 (up to the T250C) was the beginning of another. The T20 came somewhere in the middle and shared practically nothing in the way of components with either.

The TA-T10 was characterized by the open pressed-steel frame common to many Japanese manufacturers at the time, telescopic fully enclosed front forks, swinging-arm rear suspension via non-adjustable shocks, and a fully shrouded final-drive chaincase integral with the swinging arm. All were powered by an outwardly similar 246cc-engined piston-port induction two-stroke twin with unit construction of the four-speed gearbox and wet clutch assemblies. Lubrication was by petroil at a mixture of 20:1, fed by twin 20mm stub-mounted Mikunis (built under licence from the British Amal concern).

The carburettors were enclosed by cast-alloy shields, which added to the exceptionally clean lines of the power unit. A small black plastic lever protruded through the nearside (left) cover, and operated linked butterfly chokes. Mixture enrichment was achieved by brass ticklers at the top of each unit. The inside of the frame pressing functioned as an airbox, each carburettor being fed by an individual rubber hose and rectangular paper filter element.

A 1963 T10 of the type owned by the author in Aden (now South Yemen) that year, while serving in the Royal Air Force. The machine was very much a high-quality, de luxe touring bike, with electric start, 17in wheels, full-width drum brakes (the rear hydraulically operated), petroil lubrication and a four-speed gearbox.

The Engine

The engine of the T10 followed what was by then traditional Suzuki twin-cylinder design, with both cast-iron cylinder barrels being flange-mounted to the horizontally split aluminium crankcases, the alloy heads bolting down on to copper/asbestos gaskets. The four ball-race-bearing crankshaft assembly featured two bearings and an oil seal within a substantial cylindrical holder on the nearside (timing), and a single seal and bearing in the centre and on the offside (right). Caged roller big-ends and bronze bushed small-ends were fitted. Compared with the T20 and all subsequent Suzuki two-fifty twins, the T10 (and its forerunners, except the TT and TP) employed long-stroke 52 × 58mm bore and stroke dimensions, compared with square 54 × 54mm ones.

The helical gear primary drive operated a mainshaft-mounted clutch, this being fitted

T10 engine with alloy heads and cast-iron cylinder barrels.

with five steel and five fibre plates. A Siba-type starter/generator was keyed to the timing side of the crank. For those unfamiliar with Greeves Invarcars and certain British scooters of the late 1950s and early 1960s, this type of starter was an extremely bulky device. It was wound so that application of current from the 12-volt, 12-amp hour battery would drive the rotor, thereby starting the engine, at which point the unit then functioned as a generator. Activation was achieved via a push-button mounted on the offside (right) handlebar to a relay within the voltage control box. Cranking speed was slow because of the relatively low torque available, there being no reduction gear ratio with the rotor mounted directly to the crankshaft.

Running on a compression ratio of 6.3:1, the T10 put out a claimed 21bhp at 8,000rpm

British Imports

As the T10 was Suzuki's range leader at the time, it was the subject of considerable press and public interest alike, and first news of pending British imports appeared in various magazines at the end of June 1963. *Motor Cycling*'s report read: 'Holders of the 50cc World Road Race Championship and clear leaders in the current 125cc title contest, the Japanese Suzuki company is about to launch a massive onslaught on the British and Eire two-stroke markets through Associated Motor Cycles Ltd; one of Britain's two major manufacturing groups.' (The full story of this tie-up and its ultimate fate is recorded in other chapters; it was of significant interest to both parties – for entirely different reasons – for its initial period.)

First supplies of Suzuki machines arrived in the UK at the beginning of October 1963, *Motor Cycling* commenting: 'Six models of the 10-strong range have arrived and are headed by the T10 250 twin roadster.'

A sample of the T10 was supplied by the newly appointed concessionaires, who were based at the James factory in Greet, Birmingham. Out on the road it was found to provide 'ample power'. In what was described as a 'short run', a *Motor Cycling* journalist seemed pretty happy, even though the 'model was not fully run in':

> The engine was very smooth and the acceleration impressive, provided that the revs were kept up in the intermediate gears. The rocking pedal gave light and positive selection of the four ratios, although one had to become accustomed to the 'neutral-under-bottom-and-over-top' arrangement provided by a rotary cam-plate. The hydraulic rear brake was powerful without 'grabbing'. Both brakes together stopped the machine just within 10 yards from 30mph. The exhaust was notably quiet.

T10s were offered for sale in Great Britain in either black or white, the colour being applied to the frame, forks, chaincase/swinging arm, headlamp shell and fuel tank. The majority of the aluminium components were finished in a dull silver paint with the handlebar controls being polished and lacquered. Don Leeson made note of the 'copious use… of chromium plate, with the vertical surfaces of the side-covers sporting an attractive dull grain effect', and felt that the chrome seat-trim fitting was also worthy of mention. Normally, Suzuki fitted this *under* the seat grab-strap, and indeed a couple of early factory photographs showed this set-up. Clearly this was the designer's intention, but, as Leeson went on to explain, 'presumably the production line had a woman with the straps before the woman with the trims, since most photos (including factory ones) show the trim passing over the grab strap. This arrangement holds true for every T10 seat I have seen in original condition, and poses a fitting problem for the would-be restorer with nice rechromed trims. Not only do they look wrong over the top of the strap, they don't fit very well either!'

Detail Changes
The T10 was marketed in the UK from 1963 through to 1967 (by which time it was running

alongside the T20). During this period a number of detail changes were carried out:

1. The initial batch sported steel headlamp shells with half-moon speedometer and 'top-hat'-type indicators, those at the rear being combined with the rear lamp bracket.
2. T10s manufactured after 13 August 1963 (from engine number 11860) changed over to a plastic headlamp shell with a rectangular speedometer, and the 'lollipop'-style indicators as employed on the K and M single-cylinder ranges.
3. Front mudguards up to engine number 12036, which was recorded as going through the factory on 9 September 1963, were chrome, thereafter painted silver.
4. Introduction of a strengthened steering column (stem) and modified fork shrouds was introduced from engine number 13501, on 25 December 1963.
5. The final version of the T10 (not imported into the UK) utilized brakes and handlebar controls from the T20, and also came with polished engine cases.

The above information relates to British market models, except where stated. Other countries' models (including the T10) were apt to differ, in some cases quite considerably. Also most British-market T10s came with leg shields and twin mirrors.

Testing the T10
The very first time the British press corp got to ride the newly imported T10 was at a special test day organized by importers AMC. Sales boss Alan Kimber brought a number of bikes representative of the Suzuki range, from Birmingham in six Vauxhall-towed trailers, to Crystal Palace in south London, on Wednesday 23 October 1963. These, including a couple of T10s, were lined up for what was described as a 'try-it-yourself' demonstration for motorcycle journalists.

The test session was carried out along the Grandstand section of the race circuit, which, as one journalist complained, 'was too short to allow a full appreciation of the largest machine [the T10]'. Even so, *Motor Cycling*'s editor Bob Holliday felt that the model 'impressed enormously with its urgent acceleration, comfortable riding position and powerful yet smooth braking'.

Despite this test day, the British public had to wait for some time until the first real press road tests began to appear. One of the most interesting of these was published by *Motor Cycle News* in its 3 June 1964 issue, under an impressive headline: 'The Suzuki T10 is like a Rolls-Royce on two wheels.' Up to that time only Brough Superior and BMW had been referred to in such terms, so the Japanese newcomer had clearly made quite an impression with the three-man test team of Charlie Rous, Pat Braithwaite and Sean Wood.

Sean Wood penned the main test report, and was generous in his praise for the T10:

'Designed for pleasure riding.' These are the words chosen by Suzuki to describe their 250cc two-stroke twin, the T10; and it is no idle boast. A more luxurious machine it would be hard to find. Electric starter, direction indicators, leg shields, rear carrier, mirrors and a hydraulic rear brake are all

Carburettors are hidden under this enclosure on the T10 model.

included for the competitive price of £248 17s. The 'extras' are standard. There is even a provision for a wander inspection lamp light. The engine is turbine smooth, even smoother than the average twin two-stroke. Riding the Suzuki is like sitting in a well-ventilated 'Rolls'. If you want it to show a turn of speed, it will do so in no uncertain manner, but it is primarily intended as a touring machine.

The likes of pillion footrests and a prop stand were still cost options on British bikes, so it is understandable that the motoring journalists were impressed by the T10's specification. However, it should also be pointed out that an Ariel Arrow retailed at £192 – nearly one-third cheaper than the Suzuki!

MCN said the maximum speed was '78mph (125.5km/h) in neutral conditions, and with an eleven-stone rider'.

As well as the smoothness of the engine and its good performance, a number of other features of the T10 came in for praise – the brakes and the electrical system (notably the efficiency of the starter), the lights and the horn.

On the negative side, interestingly, the *MCN* test revealed an uncertainty concerning the T10's gearing: 'The Suzuki importers are experimenting with the overall gear ratios on the twin and they feel that it may be slightly over-geared.' During *MCN*'s test period the standard twelve-tooth gearbox sprocket was replaced by an eleven-tooth component. This reduced top gear from 6:1 to 6.65. As Sean Wood pointed out, this decreased fuel economy by some 5mpg, whilst acceleration with the lower gearing was 'not noticeably improved'. However, maximum speed 'showed a slight increase of approximately 5mph [8km/h]'. And because the speedometer was driven from the gearbox, it ultimately proved 'impossible to get any exact idea of the advantages to be gained by the modification'.

In addition, all three testers complained about the handling and roadholding when 'pressing on'. Although the T10 was deemed supremely comfortable for touring, Charlie Rous was less complimentary about 'the wallowy rear suspension. It was far too soft. On even the slightest of bends, it would screw itself into a mild corkscrew pitch.' According to Pat Braithwaite, 'The bike's handling suffers because of its jelly-like suspension.' The dual seat was also criticized for being 'so resilient that once or twice I could actually feel the metal pan underneath'.

I was a T10 owner back in the mid-1960s, when stationed in Aden, serving in the RAF, and I would agree with most of what *MCN* wrote. There is no doubt that the T10 was a luxury tourer, not a sports bike. It impressed me with its sophistication. It was heavy, for a two-fifty, but this weight – 330lb (150kg) dry – gave it a reassuringly solid and robust feel, hence the 'Rolls-Royce' tag.

Another relevant feature was the T10's low seat height of only 27in (686mm), which related to the use of 17in rims (3.00-section tyres both front and rear). Of course, Japanese motorcycles of this era were fitted with Japanese tyres, which at the time were depressingly poor in the wet. This did not much affect me in the Middle East, where I was based as a T10 owner and rider, as it hardly ever rained! However, owners in Britain often carried out a couple of modifications: fitting British tyres and after-market shock absorbers.

Sales and Reputation

The T10 was never a big seller in the UK, partly because of its relatively high price and partly because of its styling, which, although standard Japanese for the early 1960s, was decidedly strange to Western eyes. In March 1965, the price was reduced to £224 19s.

A T20 on display on the company's stand at the 1966 London Earls Court Show; it is hitched to a single-seat Flight sidecar.

As with the RE5 Rotary (*see* Chapter 11), another sophisticated, well-equipped and thus expensive machine released on to a largely unreceptive public, the T10 still engenders fierce loyalty amongst owners and former owners.

In the final analysis, the T10 was essentially a home-market model that just happened to be exported. Later designs from the Suzuki stable were aimed at a wider world. They also benefited from vital feedback to the factory, and much of this was provided via the T10. As such, the T10 has an important place in Suzuki's history. A study of it certainly allows an appreciation of the rapid progress made by the Japanese in the following decade and more.

T20 Super Six

If the T10 was the forerunner of the Suzuki two-fifty twin-cylinder family in world markets, the machine that followed it did much to establish the breed. The T20 (known in the American market as the X6 Hustler) had in fact three separate designations back home in Japan: T20, T21 and T250. The bike known in the West as the 'T250' has the oil pump mounted on top of the crankcase; on the T20/X6, the pump sits on the side of the engine behind the clutch. As Don Leeson once pointed out: 'Would-be restorers

please note – there is minimal interchangeability of parts between the two motors…'.

How It All Began

During 1964 Masanao Shimizu quit running Suzuki's Grand Prix team to design their new range leader. Alert as he was to motorcycle technical advances both on and off the race circuit, he realized that the company needed a 250cc sports/touring model that could take on the world. It was not a task that could be achieved by any future development of the existing T10 design.

Masanao Shimizu's idea was to capitalize fully on Suzuki's GP racing successes and resultant publicity. By taking on board a 'racing improves the breed' slogan, he did much to make the Suzuki brand as respected on the street as it had become on the track.

Two prototypes were to emerge at the Tokyo Show in November 1964. One was the T20, featuring the engine design that was to be used for the production machines, together with the familiar tank, seat and mudguards. Overall styling, however, looked much heavier than what was to appear for sale; using enclosed T10-type front forks and rear shock absorbers.

The other machine was the R250, with tank, seat and front mudguard following the T10 pattern, whilst the cylinder heads and barrels had the square-cut finning that was later to become a Yamaha trademark. However, the real technical interest centred on the induction system's rotary disc valves. The carburettors were in full view, rather than hiding under covers (as favoured by Bridgestone and Kawasaki). Each carb was equipped with a large funnel-shaped air filter assembly. Suzuki staff claimed an impressive 32bhp, whilst the sporting image was enhanced by exposure of both the front and rear springing, and alloy wheel rims.

As history shows, the disc-valve R250 was not given production status; instead, this interesting prototype-only merely bequeathed its exposed springing to the production T20.

Japan Tops Two Million Sales

At the very same time when the two prototype machines were being displayed in Tokyo, the Japanese motorcycle industry topped two million sales in a single year for the first time. This was an incredible figure given that, as recently as 1946 (the first year for which production figures were made available), the entire output of the country's industry was a mere 219 machines. In 1947 it had increased to 2,010, in 1948 it was 7,717, and in 1949 it had risen to 9,189. By 1953, with an output of 166,429 units, the industry had broken the 100,000 figure. By 1959, production had really begun to accelerate, with 880,659 machines coming out of Japan's factories, over a million in 1960 and up to 1,922,750 in 1963. In 1964, some 200,000 machines were produced every month. The vast majority were mopeds or ultralight motorcycles, but this output was still by far the largest of any country in the world.

Reasons for this extraordinary expansion were multi-faceted: a virgin home market, government aid to industry, and low wages. Probably most significant of all was the combination of sporting success and the simple fact that Japanese bikes were technically good and reliable.

Designations

Like the other Japanese producers during the early/mid-1960s, Suzuki used a combination of letters and numbers to designate different models. In Suzuki's case, M denoted 50cc machines; K, 80cc; B, 120cc; and S, 125/150cc twins. The T series of 250cc twins dated back to 1956 when the first TT arrived, followed by the TP, TA, TB, TC and T10, all of which bore a strong family likeness.

At the time of the T20's design, Japanese bike exports were increasing, ranges were expanding and annual model changes were becoming the norm. To ease the resultant recognition problems, all manufacturers adopted a similar system of model designation. The prefix letter(s) would show the type of machine, followed by figures to show the nominal capacity. A suffix would then show either the model's sequential update (Honda and Kawasaki) or, as in the case of Suzuki ultimately, the model year.

Unfortunately the arrival of the T20 coincided with the transfer from one identification system to the other. According to Don Leeson, this led to a 'bewildering number of designations applying to the same machine'. First, Suzuki had a number of design exercises under way at the same time, code-named X1 to X6. The X3 was to become the still-born R250, using the designation Rotary 250, while the X6 went into production as the T20, which led many to assume that it was a development of the T10. In fact, the two were totally different machines, both in design and purpose.

In Japan, the machine was known as the Super Sport, identified as the T20 in 1965, the T21 in 1966 and the T250 in 1967. In Great Britain, the importers called it the Super Six, no doubt influenced by the Royal Enfield Super Five (the first British production two-fifty with a five-speed gearbox), but coded T20 throughout. In the USA, it began as the X6, then became the X6-Hustler, a name that, confusingly, the American distributors continued to use on the subsequent definitive T250.

Soichiro Honda and Shunzo Suzuki, the bosses of the two biggest factories, both promised more growth to come. The Suzuki works was being enlarged, following the completion of a magnificent new test circuit. In late 1964 there were over seven million machines on Japanese roads, whilst exports continued to

The Posi-Force Lubrication System

The British firm Velocette had pioneered the use of pump lubrication for two-strokes – regulated by throttle control – from 1932. But after the war, with Velocette having axed its GTP model, the idea was allowed to lapse. Post-war, both Puch (on their split singles) and DKW (on its three-cylinder cars) had used pump lubrication for all or part of the engine.

Yamaha reintroduced the concept, with its YA6 125cc single in spring 1964, followed by the YDS3 two-fifty twin in June. Yamaha's Auto-Lube system injected oil into the carburettor inlets. Suzuki refined the principle with its Posi-Force, introduced on the T20. It forced oil, via non-return check valves, into the outer main bearings. From there, lubricant passed through the crankpin to provide lubrication for the big-end; the excess was flung off to benefit the pistons and the small-ends. A junction box under the fuel tank split the throttle cable into three, two controlling the 24mm Mikuni carburettors, the other regulating the throw of the oil pump stroke. The oil pump was mounted on the offside (right) at the rear of the clutch, and was constantly driven at a speed proportional to engine revolutions. Oil for the central main bearing was provided by splash from the gearbox.

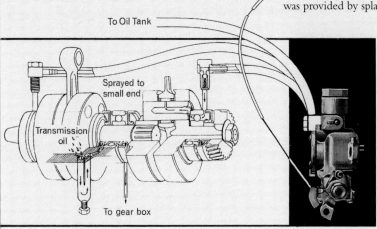

Suzuki's Posi-Force
lubrication system.

boom. Overseas sales were represented by 51 per cent USA, 20 per cent Asia, 15 per cent Europe; the remaining 14 per cent were destined for other markets, including Africa. At that time, anything above 100cc was of little use on the domestic market, as existing Japanese road conditions were best described as 'bad', and there was a universal speed limit of 60km/h (37mph). It was little wonder that virtually all bigger bikes went for export.

The Design

Although many names were applied to the T20 during its lifetime, nothing much changed in terms of mechanics or style from the initial production batch, which arrived in 1965.

At its heart was an all-alloy engine, with square 54 × 54mm bore and stroke dimensions (giving 247cc), the twin cylinder barrels being inclined slightly forward atop the horizontally split crankcases. Cast-iron liners were pierced by a bridged inlet, a pair of transfers and a single exhaust port. According to Don Leeson, it was 'all conventional stuff, but sufficient for the 54mm bore, twin-ring pistons to produce 29bhp when turning over at 7,500rpm'. The general engine specification was completed with a three-bearing crankshaft, the steel connecting rods featuring caged needle rollers at either end. Crankshaft oil seals, particularly on the timing side, were to prove something of a weakness, and needed to be watched by owners.

Six Ratios

It was the six-speed gearbox that generated much of the hype around the arrival of the T20.

An industry first on a series production motor-cycle, it was trumpeted by the Suzuki marketing department with the slogan, 'When the rest run out of stick, shift into sixth!' At the time, most manufacturers, including rivals Honda, were still using four-speed 'boxes. A few, notably Ducati and Royal Enfield, had reached five, but Suzuki were the first with six. It was quite a major innovation for the mid-1960s!

Neutral was between first and second gears, and to aid selection a positive stop was provided when going down through the box. As a result, two full throws of the lever were required to move from neutral to first. Changing up from first to second was as normal, with neutral obtained by a measured 'half-throw' of the pedal. (Suzuki had abandoned its notorious rotary change mechanism found on all its early twin-cylinder models.)

As for the ratios, they were as follows: 20.19, 13.23, 9.99, 8.173, 6.98 and 6.17:1. The unusual feature of the positive stop location when changing down from second gear was a consid-erable help in heavy urban traffic, but it did cause a somewhat noisy engagement of both first and second gears. With six cogs in the 'box, there was a ratio for every situation and this definitely gave the rider an advantage over other two-fifties in either racing or hilly terrain, making it much easier to keep the engine on the 'boil'.

Being a pioneer can lead to problems, and the fourth gear was weak on early models; dealers were provided with free update kits.

The clutch was of the wet, multi-plate type, and, like the gearbox, in unit with the engine.

Cycle Parts and Other Features

Cycle parts on the T20, whilst looking pretty straightforward today, were a major innovation at the time, particularly from Suzuki. The frame was a full double-cradle design, instead of the more usual pressed-steel backbone type with no downtube, as on the earlier Suzuki twins. It was also built for lightness and, although offering superb handling, it was not particularly strong. A frame brace had to be added into production between the two exhausts, as the front engine bolt was prone to breakage.

Even though it had a better-handling chassis, the T20 was a machine with no superfluous equipment and its priorities were completely changed from that of the T10. Its lighter dry weight of 298lb (135kg) was reflected in lean, low styling. An 8in (200mm) twin-leading shoe front brake, backed up by a similar, albeit SLS unit at the rear, were more than capable of pinning the T20 down from its maximum speed, which was nearly 100mph (160km/h).

It was acceleration rather than sheer speed that was the new Suzuki two-fifty's star attraction. To help it to fit more easily into its sportster role, it was provided with a nearside kickstarter only; the complication and additional weight of an electric starter was not considered to be worth the loss in performance that it would incur.

Once started, the rider could delight in playing tunes through the highly effective silencers,

The T20's duplex tubular steel frame was a major change in Suzuki design policy.

while monitoring the situation via the combined speedometer/tachometer mounted atop the traditional early Suzuki horseshoe-shaped plastic headlamp. Also in the headlamp were the ignition switch, neutral light and high-beam warning light.

As for paintwork, there was a metallic candy red (described by Don Leeson as 'glittering'), blue or black, set off by the highly polished aluminium of the engine outer cases and wheel hubs. Front and rear mudguards on British machines were silver-grey with a centre body stripe. In contrast, early Stateside imports of the T20 (X6) had stripeless mudguards, with oil tank and side-cover also in silver-grey. The final version in the USA featured chrome front 'guard and a race-styled tank and seat – in celebration of Ron Grant's 132mph (212km/h) record at the Bonneville Salt Flats on an American-prepared Suzuki racer.

Racing the T20

There is no doubt that the successes garnered by the T20 in sports and endurance-type racing did much to gain it a huge reputation, even though, at least in the UK, it was on sale for just three short years.

Its British racing debut, at least in a major event, came in 1966, in the Brands Hatch 500-mile (800km) production event. Tommy Robb and Chris Vincent came home ninth overall and

1966 T20/T21 Specifications (T21 in brackets where different)	
Engine	Air-cooled parallel twin, two-stroke, with piston–port induction, slightly inclined cylinders, alloy heads and barrels, the latter with replaceable liners, caged roller small- and big-ends, horizontally split aluminium crankcases
Bore	54mm
Stroke	54mm
Displacement	247cc
Compression ratio	7.3:1 (7.8:1)
Lubrication	Pump
Ignition	Battery/coil, alternator, 12-volt
Carburettor	2 × Mikuni VM24SH 24mm
Primary drive	Gears, 22/59
Final drive	Chain, 14/41
Gearbox	Six-speed, foot-change
Frame	Duplex, full cradle, all-steel construction
Front suspension	Telescopic forks, exposed springs
Rear suspension	Swinging-arm, with three-way adjustable shock absorbers
Front brake	200mm full-width alloy drum, 2LS
Rear brake	200mm full-width alloy drum, SLS
Tyres	Front 2.75 × 18; rear 3.00 × 18

General specifications

Wheelbase	50.4in (1,280mm)
Ground clearance	6.5in (165mm)
Seat height	30in (762mm)
Fuel tank capacity	3gal (14ltr)
Dry weight	298lb (135kg)
Maximum power	29bhp @ 7,500rpm (30.5bhp @ 8,000rpm)
Top speed	T20 98mph (158km/h); T21 100mph (161km/h)

second in class, completing 179 laps in 6 hours 22 minutes 21.8 seconds. Reg Everett and Peter

Inchley, the winners of the 250cc category, finished seventh overall and completed 180 laps. However, their machine was a Colton Conquest – essentially a pukka racer with lights!

By the following year most serious contenders were using the T20. Besides direct entries via Suzuki GB, the other early entrants of the T20 were Eddie Crooks and Harrogate dealer Harry Thompson.

Controversy surrounded the 1967 Isle of Man Production TT (the first year this class was staged), when the Bultaco Metrallas were allowed to compete with open expansion chambers, this gave them a performance advantage and they went on to take the first two places. The Thompson Suzukis of Australians Barry Smith and Kel Carruthers finished a creditable third and fifth respectively, sandwiching Frank Whiteway on a Crooks T20. Eddie Crooks came ninth, behind Chris Vincent on the Suzuki GB bike. Probably the best performance came from Carruthers in the Lightweight (250cc) TT. Riding a fully equipped roadster, he finished twelfth, averaging 83.36mph (133.88km/h), having completed in excess of fifty laps of the fearsome 37.73 mile (60.70km) mountain course.

ABOVE: *Harrogate dealer, Harry Thompson, pictured in 1968 with the two T20s he entered in the production TT that year, ridden by Barry Smith (75) and Kel Carruthers (76). They finished third and seventh respectively.*

RIGHT: *Barry Smith with the Thompson Suzuki T20 racer, now owned by Mick Oliver.*

Former Manx Grand Prix winner and Barrow-in-Furness dealer Eddie Crooks was responsible for preparing a T20, which, in 1968, set a record in the 350cc class. The record still stands today. Together with his parts manager Frank Whiteway, Suzuki works rider Hans Georg Anscheidt, and road racer Brian Ball, Crooks piloted a machine overbored to 256cc for twenty-four hours at Monza. Besides the larger-bore pistons, the T20 was equipped with Crooks' customizing goodies, but otherwise mechanically stock. Despite torrential rain in the final half-hour, which cut lap times dramatically, the team still managed a highly impressive 24-hour average of 91.055mph (146.48km/h), over a distance of 2,129 miles (3,425km).

ABOVE: Norfolk rider Tony Collison with his beautifully prepared home-built T20 racer, negotiating the old Hairpin at Snetterton, summer 1971.

LEFT: The ex-Barry Smith Thompson T20 Suzuki at Scarborough Gold Cup Pastmasters, 17 September 2006, with Mick Oliver (left) and Bill Robertson. Mick has owned the machine since 1978 and restored it to 'as new' condition during 2004/5. He achieved a lifetime ambition by riding in the 2006 TT parade.

A similar machine, but with the standard 247cc engine size, running in the 250cc category under the Suzuki (GB) banner, was less fortunate. It suffered a seizure when the oil pump cable became disconnected after some fourteen hours around the bumpy Italian track. Even so, it had already taken three records: the 1,000km, and the 6- and 12-hours, at speeds of almost 95mph (153km/h).

Several T20s were converted into pukka racers, mainly for use in club events and the Manx Grand Prix. The T20 was also employed in other fields of competition (*see* Chapter 8), including trials (six-day events) and as a proto-type motocrosser, whilst a number of engines were used in kart racing.

Today, the T20 is still seen in sporting events, via the classic racing scene, achieving victory in the very first Classic Manx Grand Prix, with Richard Fitzsimmons aboard. Stewart McDiarmid was also the historic winner of the first Classic TT.

Road Tests

With its class-leading performance and racer-like handling, it is hardly surprising that the T20 proved a favourite among the road testers of the day.

John Stoddart, assisted by road racer Joe Dunphy, did a three-page feature on the speedy Suzuki two-fifty twin in the September 1966 issue of *Motor Cyclist Illustrated*. Stoddart found it to be 'a machine with a very pleasant dual personality', equally suitable, in his opinion, 'for riding to work thanks to its absolutely perfect road manners', while being able to 'two-stroke reliably down to 2,000rpm'. Perhaps most impressive of all, and unusual for a high performance two-stroke, was the fact that during the *MCI* test it could achieve 'exactly 70mpg [4ltr/100km]' over a 'mixed' 1,200 miles (almost 1,930km). Stoddart felt that that figure 'might be improved upon if the rider is prepared to keep his right hand in check'.

Stoddart had a number of comments to make about the gearbox:

The clutch is smooth in operation, although it engages rather fiercely from a standstill…it is almost impossible to get into first gear without a clonk, and the change from first to second could

also be noisy unless the engine revs were just right, but the other four changes are as perfect as it is possible to get, the best results coming when upward or downward changes were made without touching the clutch.

While its forerunner, the T10, was a substantial, heavy bike, the T20 was just the reverse; perhaps 'finesse' was a good word to describe what it had. John Stoddart did an excellent job of conveying to the reader what it was all about:

The roadholding is excellent. This must surely be road racer handling on a road machine: the Super Six steers better, corners better than any motorcycle I have owned or ridden. Many other machines have similar duplex cradle frames, why should this one be so much better? Size, perhaps. When you sit astride the T20 for the first time it appears no bigger than a 125. Petrol tank frontal area has been reduced to the absolute minimum and the motor is slim in comparison with other 250 twins… The Suzuki has short, well-damped, telescopic front forks and the swinging-arm rear suspension has three load positions… a steering damper is fitted but I found it unnecessary.

He had very few criticisms to make. The steering was considered 'a little heavy under 20mph (32km/h)', while he did not like the 'small plastic tube mounted at the front of the petrol tank and intended to serve as a fuel level indicator… this can be dismissed as a gimmick… because you cannot see it when sitting in the saddle, and when the machine is pointing downhill, it gives an optimistically false reading.' Concern was also expressed about the Japanese-made tyres, which 'seem to be of the non-cling variety and the rear wheel breaks away all too readily when cornering in the wet'.

As for Joe Dunphy, he enthusiastically summed up the T20 quite simply: 'Fantastic acceleration, excellent brakes, superb roadholding, a six-speed close ratio gearbox… and a real beauty to look at.'

Motorcycle Mechanics were equally impressed in their December 1966 issue: 'Never before has a learner rider had the chance to ride such an exciting bike as the new six-speed Suzuki… this latest development of the Japanese line incorporates a list of good ideas as impressive and forward-looking as any bike has ever had.'

The following are just some of the key features that the *Motorcycle Mechanics* test pointed out to its readers:

- Both centre and side stands are fitted as standard equipment.
- A magnetic plug was fitted in the exit pipe of the oil tank, thus keeping the lubricant free of any metal particles. Oil level checked by a window.
- A warning light comes on when ignition is turned on with the bike in neutral.
- Engine idling speed is set by a knurled screw set on top of carb by the throttle cable. Carbs are covered with waterproof tops.
- Both wheels are balanced by the factory with weights.
- Twin carburettors breathe through the air cleaner fitted inside the toolbox. Tool roll must not foul air intake when it is put into its retaining clip in cover.
- Brake cams and kickstart lever equipped with grease nipples.
- All control cables have guide loops where they pass a frame tube.

Although the T20 did not feature an electric start, it retained a 12-volt electrical system, with an AC generator (alternator); the system was also protected by a series of 15-amp fuses. As *MCM* described, the 'headlamp gave a really bright light and a useful pattern, which meant that the bike could be ridden well into the seventies at night without any frights'.

Although it was 'learner-legal' (on British roads), the T20 could potentially cause problems for the inexperienced and in some cases experienced riders, as *MCM* revealed:

The T20's Nippon-Denso ignition, showing twin contact breakers and condensers.

We were not familiar with the bike, and its fierce take-off from a standstill ended in a couple of rear-wheel snaking sessions [probably not helped by the standard-issue Japanese rubber!]. Another couple of attempts had the front wheel so high in the air that the rider nearly slid from the saddle! A lot of experience is needed to get the bike to accelerate properly. The motor is so powerful and coupled with a low bottom gear, the result can be terrifying.

One owner who was experienced enough to get the best out of his T20 was Val Ward, who wrote an article in *Motorcycle Sport* in August 1974:

What qualities make a modern classic? Rarity value? General excellence with perhaps a quirk or two to make a machine endearing? I am not sure these parameters are fair or reasonable, but I am fairly certain that when the current craze for childish frills and two-wheeled elephants fades, the plain and purposeful lightweights of a few years ago will become sought after. Among them deserves to be the Suzuki Super Six, easily the best of the 22 machines I have owned to date.

Val Ward put forward a number of arguments in favour of the Suzuki:

> The Six, in my view, had everything. It looked the part, not being handsome like the YDS3 (Yamaha) but 'pretty'. The design – especially when compared with its successors, Hustler onwards – was beautifully neat. The Posi-Force oil pump, utterly reliable and fully waterproof, hid behind a simple cover blending with the engine casing. Speedo and rev-counter were combined under one glass, king-size exhaust pipes and silencers were individual items, and leak-proof sight gauges graced both petrol and oil tanks. An instantly fillable oil tank – no seat-lifting nonsense to cause problems if you were heavily loaded. Not too much chrome to go rusty. It made sense. The great thing was it seemed a logical development of what had gone before, a clear step forward in motorcycle evolution.… All the essentials of the Six were first-class and, unlike some machines I could name, the Six was good enough straight out of the showroom.

But was there a downside? Val Ward thought so:

> Was it too good? I often wonder. Look what follows: versions with features that seemed calculated to please dealers more than customers and bump up profit margins on spares – one-piece exhaust systems, completely plated mudguards, fragile turn-indicators… daft features – like ignition keys under tanks, which by some strange reasoning suddenly became smaller. More weight, less speed. Out-of-proportion back lights. Disc brakes, dodgy in the rain, indicating rushed development. And Ram-Air. Who do they think they are kidding? For riders of later 250s, lugging another 50lb [27kg] of fanciful gadgets, the secret of the Six was its power-to-weight ratio.

T200 Invader

For the 1967 model year, following in the tyre tracks of its larger brother the T20, came the T200. The newcomer was 'only' a two hundred, not a two-fifty, but it should not be assumed that it was simply a sleeved-down, cheaper version of the T20, as many people may think. Far from it. In fact, the T200 learnt lessons from its older brother and corrected many of its weaknesses, to produce, as Don Leeson once explained, 'a very sweet package, perfectly scaled down in all major areas'. Unless the two bikes were standing side by side, it was hard to tell the difference in displacement.

The heart of the T200 was the twin-cylinder engine, which maintained the square bore and stroke dimensions, now being 50 × 50mm, giving 196cc. There was a T125 twin for some

Clearly modelled on the existing T20, the T200 arrived for the 1967 model year. It displaced 196cc (50 × 50mm), and there were a number of other notable differences between it and its older, larger brother, including one less gear ratio and improved lubrication, as well as 22mm carbs that were now equipped with a new type of vacuum-operated control valve.

markets (not to be confused with the T125 Stinger). It had a three-main-bearing crankshaft, with roller bearings at both ends of the connecting rods, and two-ring pistons, the latter with chrome-faced rings, in the new 'keystone' profile, which was designed to prevent gumming in the grooves. Steel liners cast into the forward-sloping individual alloy cylinders allowed for rebores out to three over-sizes.

Oiling

Oiling on the Invader was an improvement over the Super Six. The earlier bike featured a pair of oil lines feeding lubricant to the outer main bearings only, and thence by splash to the bores. On the T200 – and subsequent twins – each main line split into two. One half fed the outer mains as before, the other half supplied oil to the top end of the engine, via a drilling at the base of the relevant barrel. Lubrication of the centre main bearing was handled in Suzuki's usual manner, via a weir fed from oil thrown up by the gearbox pinions – one good reason for keeping the gearbox oil level up! A rapidly falling gearbox oil level, with no sign of external leaks, is a sure sign of centre crankshaft oil seal failure, with the gearbox oil being sucked through into the engine and burned.

A Five-Speed 'Box

The gearbox of the T200 was a five-speeder (hence the American designation 'X5'), a redesign of the six-speed 'box of the T20 and superior to the earlier one. Use of an additional shaft to mount one of the three selector forks allowed each of the forks to have a wider base, leading to smoother operation and less chance of missed gears. Apart from the kickstart gear and a few bushes and washers, none of the gearbox components were interchangeable with the T20 – to the great disappointment of many boy racers of the day, who imagined a quick and cheap upgrade might be possible.

The clutch design was also new, with a unit of a smaller diameter, and springs retained in

position by pins rather than screws, as on the larger model. Mounting was still on the offside (right) end of the countershaft, with helical gear primary drive. Operation was changed, however, with pushrod operation through the hollow shaft and a quick worm arrangement in the nearside (left) engine cover. This arrangement exposed the nearside pushrod to road muck, thrown at it by the 525 drive chain, and this led to rapid wear of the rod where it entered the oil seal, allowing oil to drip out when the bike was on its side stand. Strangely, it was the steel rod rather than the rubber seal that seemed to wear. There were two identical pushrods employed, and turning each one over provided a total of four bearing surfaces to get through before replacement was necessary!

Carburation Revisions

Two Mikuni VM22SH carburettors were fitted to the Invader. These featured a new type of vacuum-operated control valve, which was incorporated into the single fuel tap. Switching on the fuel supply involved turning the tap to the 'prime' position and, once the engine had warmed up, the control lever could be moved to the 'on' position. This piece of Japanese ingenuity did away with the necessity of turning off the fuel when parking, and thus eliminated the risk of crankcase flooding.

The carburation was also more sophisticated on the T200, with improved throttle response at low speeds due to higher gas speeds. Over and above that, what were referred to by Suzuki as 'Homo-pressure' drillings between the float and mixing chambers reduced the tendency to run rich at low speed, and also provided a measure of altitude compensation – a useful sales feature for the American market.

Carb maintenance chores had also not been ignored either; getting at the inner mounting nuts on the T20 carburettors had proved a particular nuisance, even for owners with small fingers. The reduced clearance on the T200 would have made it even worse to replace the instruments had the mounting flanges not been slotted on the inside face of each carb. This allowed the inside nuts to remain in position on the ends of the studs while the carbs were slipped off and on again.

Other Features

One area deemed not in need of redesign was the electrical system. The twin contact-breaker ignition/generator assembly mounted on the nearside (left) crankshaft end was identical to the T20 system, as were the front and rear lights and headlamp shell-mounted ignition switch and speedo/tacho unit. Indicators were added to the Invader, with an additional lever; otherwise the hand controls were identical to those of the T20.

The front forks and wheels were visually similar, although they had been slimmed down in all dimensions; they were in fact identical to the components fitted to the 150cc S32-2, a model largely intended for the Japanese domestic market. The exposed spring rear shocks were identical to the Super Six, and were thus well up to the task of controlling the 269lb (122.25kg) dry weight of the smaller bike. Wheels were 2.75 × 18 front and rear, with smaller brake hubs – 160mm 2LS front and 150mm SLS rear.

Cost savings were evident on some of the smaller fitments. For example, the same gear lever and chainguard as the T20 were treated to zinc plate and silver paint, rather than the more expensive chrome finish. Welding the front header pipes to the silencers saved on clamps and seals (but made a replacement much more expensive for the owner!). Also, although stopping any potential leaks, it meant that removing a build-up of carbon deposits was much harder to achieve.

The finish, however, was certainly up to the standard of its bigger brother. The front and rear mudguards were silver, while the double cradle frame was in black. The chrome-panelled 2.6-gal (12ltr) fuel tank, oil tank and side-cover, headlamp and forks were available in a choice of black, candy red or candy blue shades.

1967 T200 Specification

Engine	Air-cooled parallel twin, two-stroke, with piston-port induction, slightly inclined cylinders, alloy heads and barrels, the latter with replaceable liners, caged roller small- and big-ends, horizontally split aluminium crankcases
Bore	50mm
Stroke	50mm
Displacement	196cc
Compression ratio	7:1
Lubrication	Pump
Ignition	Battery/coil, alternator, 12-volt
Carburettor	2 x Mikuni VM20PH 22mm
Primary drive	Gears, 20/59
Final drive	Chain, 14/37
Gearbox	Five-speed, foot-change
Frame	Duplex, full cradle, all-steel construction
Front suspension	Telescopic forks, exposed springs
Rear suspension	Swinging-arm, with three-way adjustable shock absorbers
Front brake	160mm full-width drum, 2LS
Rear brake	150mm full-width drum, SLS
Tyres	2.75 × 18 front and rear

General specifications

Wheelbase	49.4in (1,254mm)
Ground clearance	5.7in (145mm)
Seat height	29.5in (749mm)
Fuel tank capacity	2.6gal (12ltr)
Dry weight	269lb (122kg)
Maximum power	23bhp @ 7,500rpm
Top speed	80mph (129km/h)

As with the TC250 Street Scrambler, a TC200 version was offered, but very few came to the UK; *see* Chapter 5.

Obviously, the 23bhp (6bhp less than the T20) was not as attractive to the road-racing

ABOVE: *Arch Suzuki enthusiast Heidi Cockerton with her superbly restored 1965 S32 150 twin (1963–67). The 149.6cc (46 × 45mm) engine produced 12bhp at 7,000rpm and its specification included an electric start.*

TOP RIGHT: *The S32 engine with alloy heads and barrels, nicely polished engine casings and twin Mikuni carbs; note the pressed-steel frame with single front downtube.*

MIDDLE RIGHT: *The S32 was very much a cross between the T10 (four speeds and petroil lubrication) and the T20 (styling and basic engine design).*

BOTTOM RIGHT: *The T20 (Super Six) marked a milestone in Suzuki's evolution. Not only was it the first to sport a six-speed gearbox, but it also introduced Posi-Force lubrication to the marque's twin-cylinder range, a duplex tubular steel frame, sports-type suspension, a twin leading shoe front brake, and much more.*

Although only a two hundred, the T200 could still outrun most other makers' full two-fifties, with a top speed approaching 90mph (152km/h) and sparkling acceleration to match.

fraternity as the full two-fifty, but in Scotland and Ireland, which both had vibrant 200cc class events, the Invader enjoyed considerable success. Ulsterman Courtney Junk was particularly outstanding, scoring many victories. The power unit was also used extensively in karting events during the late 1960s, when the top capacity limit was 200cc.

Testing the Invader

My old friend, the late Alan Aspel (brother to television presenter Michael Aspel), tested an Invader, and published his report in September 1967. He was certainly impressed, calling the little Suzuki 'incredible' and 'as near perfection as it was possible to get'. Collecting the machine from Suzuki's new home in Fazeley Street, Birmingham, Alan Aspel headed up north to the hills of Derbyshire, where he put the 'handling and gearbox to the test through the many bends and gradients… the joy of playing a tune through the five speeds was such that it was difficult not to laugh out loud.'

Alan Aspel ended his test report with a bold statement:

I'm going to stick my neck out and say that the Suzuki Invader is currently the finest machine of its size in this country – or probably any other – and it would be difficult to imagine anything better. At £234 17s 6d any 16-year-old can have a machine almost as quick as bikes of more than twice the capacity, and at only a fraction of the insurance and running costs.

To many hard-core Suzuki enthusiasts, the T10, T20 and T200 were in their own ways the finest of the breed. The T10 was the luxury model, an almost over-engineered de luxe tourer, whilst the T20 and T200 were true super sports bikes, offering outstanding performance for their day. The subsequent twins of various sizes (*see* Chapter 10) were later developments, but they failed to match the brilliance of the originals – that is, until the pocket rocket X7 arrived, late in the 1970s. The T10, T20 and T200 are true classics – and this compliment comes from the heart of someone who has ridden all three over considerable miles, in the UK and overseas, and then gone on to sell, service and ride the Suzuki twins of the 1970s as an official Suzuki dealer.

4 Racing

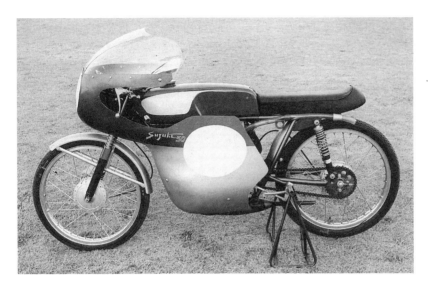

The very first over-the-counter racing motorcycle to be offered by Suzuki was the TR50 in 1963. Unfortunately, unlike the fantastic works GP bikes of the day, it was piston-port rather than disc-valve – and was both unreliable and underpowered.

BELOW: TR50 Kokusan racing magneto; suitably small for an equally small motorcycle.

In common with its Japanese rivals, Honda and Yamaha, Suzuki built and raced quite a few over-the-counter racers and production-based works machines during the 1960s and 1970s.

The TR50

The first such racer was the TR50 of 1963, which was very loosely based on the disc-valve RM62 works single of 1962, although, in truth, Suzuki missed a golden opportunity to pass on its GP success to paying customers. Instead, the 49.48cc (41 × 37.5mm) single-cylinder TR50 used conventional piston-port induction and produced a claimed 8.5bhp at 11,000rpm. The sandcast crankcases were split horizontally and contained a diminutive crankshaft and equally microscopic six-speed gearbox. One of the most unusual aspects of the whole machine was the ignition system – a half-engine-speed magneto running off the top of the clutch primary-drive gear, firing twice per revolution and

supplying a high-tension coil mounted under the 1.25gal (5.3ltr) fuel tank. Another interesting feature was the gearchange shaft, which was splined at both ends, allowing the choice of right- or left-foot gear operation.

The aluminium cylinder barrel was fitted with a cast-iron liner, but unusually no oversize pistons were available! A couple of micro-size pistons were offered, to compensate for wear, but the lack of oversize items meant that the owner was unable to rebore in the conventional manner.

The engine was fed by a Mikuni V22 remote-float carburettor with a massive bell mouth. The clutch was a wet multi-plate affair, and this was to prove the toughest part in the engine unit.

The TR50's career was destined to be blighted by mechanical glitches, with gearbox and piston seizures, as well as con-rod breakages (just below the small-end if over-revved) and occasional big-end failure. An improved TR50 did appear in 1967, but, although it was more reliable than its predecessor, it still could not match up to its main threat, Honda's dohc CR110.

TR250 and X6

If the TR50 was a flop, Suzuki's next effort was the reverse. In 1966, the company had launched the highly successful T20 (*see* Chapter 3), a 247cc (54 × 54mm) piston-port twin with exceptional performance. Right from the start, the T20, or Super Six as it was more commonly known in Britain, dominated the production class in events such as the Brands Hatch 500-mile race. The natural progression from this was

ABOVE: 1967 TR50 engine: 49.48cc (41 × 37.5mm), six speeds, duplex frame, alloy head and barrel, and horizontally split crankcases.

RIGHT: The 1967 TR50 with which Englishman Peter Kersey set a number of class speed records in 1969. For his efforts he received a congratulations telegram from Suzuki Japan.

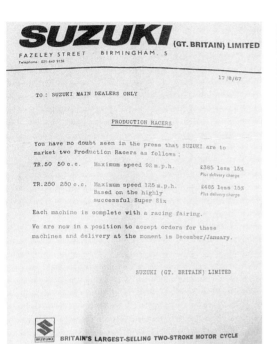

ABOVE: *An official Suzuki GB letter, regarding the TR50 and TR250 racing motorcycles, to its dealer network; dated 17 August 1967.*

ABOVE RIGHT: *Rod Gould at Suzuki GB's Birmingham headquarters trying one of the TR50s for size in 1967.*

RIGHT: *A brand-new TR250 in Birmingham during September 1967 – a useful photograph for enthusiasts and restorers alike as the machine is minus its fairing.*

ABOVE: *A Crooks TR250 prepared for the Isle of Man with a large main tank in aluminium, together with a smaller tank incorporated in the seat tail; circa 1968.*

LEFT: *Don Leeson with his TR250, Manx Grand Prix, circa mid-1990.*

undoubtedly a pukka racing version. Suzuki responded by building the TR250 and X6. The former was expressly a European machine intended to match Yamaha's TD1C. Unfortunately, although it was an excellent motorcycle, its 1968 model year launch was too late, as Yamaha's racing line was not only fully established but also shortly to announce the all-conquering TD2. The TR250 produced 35bhp at 9,000rpm, the TD2 44bhp at 10,500 – enough said!

One of the TR250's few successes was victory in the 1968 Manx Grand Prix by Frank Whiteway on an Eddie Crooks machine.

In the USA, Suzuki was quicker off the mark, with the X6 appearing a couple of years earlier, in 1966. The X6 shared the square 54 × 54mm bore and stroke and 247.34cc displacement with the TR250 (and T20). With a pair of Mikuni VM26 carbs and 7.61:1 compression ratio, it produced 33bhp at 10,500rpm. Besides its special engine bits, which included totally hand-worked pistons, with one 1.5mm piston ring located 4mm down from the top,

the porting of the X6 was entirely different from that of the TR250. The TR250 was more suitable for short-circuit racing than the X6; its exhaust port was narrower by 4mm and far shallower. This difference between the X6 and TR250 engine units, although they were similar externally, explains the marked difference in peak power figures: 9,500rpm for the TR250 and 10,500rpm for the X6.

The concept behind the two machines was also different. Whereas the TR250 was expressly designed as a pukka over-the-counter racer, the X6 was built to demonstrate to the Americans the durability of the standard Suzuki roadster.

The TR500

Suzuki launched its 492cc (70 × 64mm) T500 twin in 1967 (*see* Chapter 6) and soon realized its potential as a pukka racer, with the TR500 (code-named 'XR05') arriving in 1968. This produced 63.5bhp at 8,000rpm and was capable of 135mph (217km/h).

An American X6, which predated the TR250 by several months and had made its debut at Daytona on 26 March 1966; Dick Hammer finished runner-up in the 250cc event.

In 1968 Suzuki introduced its first TR500 (coded 'XR05'). This is a 1970 model with larger 34mm carbs, producing 70.5bhp and capable of over 150mph (241km/h).

In converting the five-hundred twin into a racing bike there were a number of important changes. These included a Kokusan magneto, Mikuni VM32SC carbs, 7.2:1 compression ratio pistons, close-ratio gears, revised porting, Fontana drum brakes (double-sided at the front), a full duplex frame, Ceriani suspension and a lower dry weight figure of 297lb (135kg).

Works riders Ron Grant and Mitsuo Itoh took their TR500s to the famous 200-mile event at Daytona on 17 March 1968, bringing them home fifth and ninth respectively.

For 1969, more tuning took place, raising power output to 64.5bhp, and Art Baumann proved the competitiveness of the latest TR500 by taking the machine to its first US National Championship victory at Sears Point on 7 September.

For 1970, larger VM34 carburettors were fitted and the compression was raised to 7.34:1. This, combined with a number of other more minor changes, resulted in a shade over 70bhp (still at the 8,000rpm bloodline). Meanwhile, Ceriani had replaced Fontana in the braking department, maximum speed having reached 152mph (245km/h). The highlight of the year was Ron Grant's victory in the US Grand Prix.

For the 1971 season power was up again to 71.5bhp, resulting in an additional 2mph

(3km/h) at the top end. Besides the Stateside team of Jody Nicolas, Art Baumann, Ron Grant and Ron Pierce, the TR500 also made its European debut. The year culminated in Suzuki taking runner-up spot in the manufacturer's class of the 1971 500cc World Championship series, the leading riders being Rob Bron, Jack Findlay and Keith Turner. In the same year, former Suzuki works star Frank Perris campaigned a Seeley-framed TR500 and gained a rostrum (third) finish in the Isle of Man Senior TT. In the individual 500cc World Championship series, Keith Turner finished runner-up (behind title winner Giacomo Agostini on an Italian MV Agusta), Rob Bron was third, Jack Findlay fifth and Frank Perris eleventh. Considering these were production-based machines, this was a fantastic achievement.

Jack Findlay had the honour of scoring Suzuki's first-ever 500 GP victory, with a win in the Ulster round, staged at Dundrod. He had switched to two-stroke power after many years of riding four-strokes (mainly British single-cylinder machines), and was given a choice between a pair of roadster-based models – Kawasaki's three-cylinder HI-R or the TR500. He later explained, 'I chose the Suzuki because it was lighter, more compact, less complicated and produced peak power at lower rpm.'

Eddie Crooks (left, holding bike number 20) at the TT during the early 1970s, with a pair of Seeley-framed TR500 machines.

The TR500II and TR500III

In 1972 the TR500 became the TR500II, although the specification remained essentially the same. For 1973 it became the TR500III, and this time the specification had been upgraded. The most important changes concerned the introduction of liquid-cooling of the engine and improved braking performance via triple discs (two at the front, one at the rear). There was also additional tuning, including larger 36mm carbs, which took the power output up to 73bhp and the maximum speed to 157mph (253km/h). It is also worth noting that some special (works) engines had six instead of five speeds for the first time.

The Hi-Tac Effort

Suzuki were not the first to use water-cooling. In late 1971, the British Hi-Tac team, run by Peter Inchley and Frank Higley, had employed a T500 roadster crankcase assembly, a jacketed, light-alloy cylinder block, 14:1 heads, a close-ratio five-speed gear cluster and electronic ignition. The engine was fitted into a Seeley chassis and Barry Sheene was closely involved in much of the early track testing. Sheene already had close links with Suzuki, having just finished runner-up in the 1971 125cc World Championship on his ex-factory Suzuki twin. That same year, he had ridden an air-cooled TR500 with considerable success.

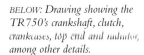

BELOW: *Drawing showing the TR750's crankshaft, clutch, crankcases, top end and rotator, among other details.*

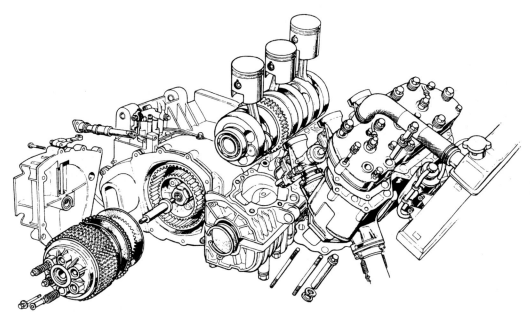

The TR750

For the 1972 Daytona 200, Suzuki created the TR750 (XR11), nicknamed the 'flexy flier' on account of its huge power and less impressive handling abilities. This 738.9cc (70 × 64mm) liquid-cooled, three-cylinder, piston-port two-stroke was derived directly from the series production GT750 sports/tourer (*see* Chapter 9). Like the street bike, the TR750 had a five-speed gearbox. It also had triple hydraulically operated disc brakes. With 100bhp and over 175mph (282km/h), the TR750 looked like a serious challenger to the Hondas, Harley-Davidsons and Kawasakis; certainly in North American racing.

Art Baumann qualified in the Daytona 200 at 171.75mph (276.34km/h), creating a new track record and achieving the first 170mph (274km/h) average around the Daytona speed bowl. There is no doubt that the new Suzukis were the quickest machines at Daytona that year.

Unfortunately, speed is not everything and the team was hit by a series of problems: tyres throwing their treads, clutches that burnt out too quickly and even magneto troubles. The result was that every single TR750 was forced to retire from the race and a Yamaha TR3 three-fifty twin emerged as the winner. The Harley-Davidson and Kawasaki works teams also failed to score *en masse*.

In 1973 Barry Sheene rejoined Suzuki GB with Stan Woods as team-mate. An ex-American TR750 engine was fitted into a Seeley

ABOVE: The TR750's three carburettors and braced top-frame tubing.

BELOW: Details of the Suzuki GB TR750 with which Barry Sheene garnered so much success in 1973, ending the season with the coveted Motor Cycle News *'Man of the Year' award.*

chassis for Sheene, while Woods received a brand new TR750. Sheene went on to win both the FIM Formula 750 Cup series (in effect the 750cc World Championship) and the British

MCN Superbike title, showing the sort of form that would mark him out as a future legend. TR750 riders largely dominated the F750 series, with Jack Findlay third, Woods fourth,

Guido Mandracchi fifth and Paul Smart seventh. Meanwhile, Australian rider Findlay had won the 1973 Senior (500cc) TT with his TR500III, and also finished the year fifth in the World Championship.

In early 1975, Sheene was to survive a fearsome 170mph (274km/h) crash on a TR750, during practice for the Daytona 200. However, he was to make a truly amazing recovery and was back in action later that year.

ABOVE: Barry Sheene lifting the front wheel of his TR750 at Cadwell Park Mountain section at Cadwell Park, September 1974.

RIGHT: Don Leeson with one of the ex-Heron Suzuki TR750s; note the layout of the exhaust system.

BELOW: Australian Jack Findlay on his way to victory riding the prototype RG500 (XR14) in the Isle of Man Senior TT, June 1974; he is shown at the Waterworks section.

The RG500 (XR14)

The new four-cylinder RG500 (XR14) arrived in 1974. At first, only works GP models were raced, and it was to be some two years before replicas were finally released for sale to private customers. By then, both the twin-cylinder TR500 and three-cylinder TR750 had been axed. Their final year was 1975, at which time the TR500 was producing 80bhp at 8,900rpm, the six-speed, liquid-cooled engine being

RG500 Evolution

Mark 1 (1976) Distinguishing features include lay-down twin-shock rear suspension and facility to put oil in frame. In practice, oil pump in engine removed and oil mixed in fuel; disc-valve covers, which were to feed the oil, blanked off. Designed to incorporate seventh gear, although this was removed. Early Suzuki brake cal-lipers closely resembled Lockheed versions of the time. Mark 1 also sported open pipes, or 'stingers' as they became known. Forks were 35mm and had no air assis-tance. Wheels spoked (wire) 18in front and rear. Four 34mm Mikuni carbs in magnesium. 56 × 50.5mm bore and stroke. Frame of tubular steel with square-section steel swinging arm.

Mark II (1977) Similar to Mark I; shocks more vertical, although still fairly laid forward. Expansion chambers featured integral pre-formed silencer to conform with noise regulations. Frames no longer had oil tank facility and disc-valve covers were cast blanked off. Overall appearance still similar to Mark I, with flip-up tail on seat. Wheels spoked, 18in front and rear.

Mark III (1978) Many cosmetic changes to fairing and seat, with seat style going to a pointed-tail type – a familiar feature on subsequent models. Front forks now with pneumatic assistance and brakes upgraded. Rear shock now featured undivided gas reservoirs.

Mark IV (1979) Main change in bore and stroke, from previous 56 × 50.5mm to square 54 × 54mm, widening power delivery. Changes in expansion chambers, and pressed-type silencers replaced with longer cylindrical steel ends. Forks upgraded to 37mm and Campagnolo 18in magnesium wheels fitted as standard.

Mark V (1980) Very similar to Mark IV but with braced swinging arm, better expansion chambers and modified cosmetics to fairing and seat.

Mark VI (1981) An up-rated version of Mark V, featur-ing anti-dive fitted to the front forks and modified fair-ing and improved expansion chambers.

Mark VII (1982) Main change was introduction of stepped engine with its magnesium crankcase (often proving fragile and subject to some modification). Now two cranks instead of four, as on previous six marks. Larger 36mm carbs improved performance. New aero-dynamic fairing and seat. Twin shocks replaced by monoshock and stronger 40mm forks.

Mark VIII (1983) Very little change except minor cos-metics and paintwork.

Mark IX (1984) Suzuki's last complete RG500 over-the-counter racer; at last, aluminium box-section frame similar to Suzuki's latest works GP bikes. Fairing again revised. 16in front and 18in rear magnesium wheel and different headstock.

Marks X to XII Suzuki's alternative to selling complete over-the-counter Grand Prix machines was to supply an up-rated engine with power valves and the comple-menting expansion chambers via Padgett's of Batley. Padgett's, in conjunction with Harris Performance Products of Hertford, produced a complete racing bike. Its main drawback was that it reverted to a steel frame and the engine had to be removed for even minor mechanical work. Spondon of Derby produced a beam frame, which allowed the engine to be dropped and cylinders removed in situ.

The final RG engine, the Mark XII. All Marks from VII featured magnesium 'stepped' crankcases, as illustrated here.

Ronnie Russell about to have his first-ever outing on Hector Neill's RG500 Mark III in the 1978 Ulster Grand Prix.

BELOW: Norman Brown during the 1983 TT, where he set a new outright lap record on his RG500 at 116.19mph (187km/h).

capable of propelling the bike to almost 160mph (258km/h). The final TR750, also with six gears, pumped out 116bhp at 8,250rpm and could reach 180mph (290km/h).

The first three marks of the RG500 used bore and stroke dimensions of 56 × 50.5mm, thereafter switching to the square 54 × 54mm figures. Likewise, the first six marks had twin-shock rear suspension, and monoshock thereafter.

The first production RG500 (1976) produced 103bhp, whilst the last (the Mark XII of 1987) put out 120bhp. Other major differences related to carburettor and wheel sizes, aluminium or magnesium crankcases, whilst the front fork stanchion diameter grew from 35 to 40mm.

With the advent of first the GS and later the GSX series, four-stroke development replaced two-stroke technology at Suzuki. There were countless riders taking part in production and open-class racing at both club and national level, and the works (via their various importers) also campaigned production-based four-strokes from the end of the 1970s. In Britain, stars such as Mick Grant, John Newbold, Roger Marshall and Graeme Crosby all won major races on either 1000 or 1100cc Suzuki dohc fours. The 750 four made a major impact in endurance

racing, this ultimately leading to the mould-breaking GSX-R750 of 1985. It was a major milestone in sports-bike development, but its story is outside the scope of this book.

5 Trail Bikes and Street Scramblers

The very first on-/off-road models from Suzuki were largely built for the US market and were closely based on existing series production roadsters. These included the TC250 twin (essentially a T20, but with raised exhausts) and the K11T (trail version of the 80cc K11 single).

The B105P

The first really new, purpose-built Suzuki trail bike, the B105P, arrived at the end of 1965 (for the 1966 model year) and was to share much of its design with the much better-known B100P commuter model. According to Don Leeson, the B105P Bearcat 'was to prove a forerunner for a new class of motorcycle'. Today, this early attempt to produce Suzuki's first real dual-purpose model may seem naïve, but, as Don also pointed out, it does 'serve to illustrate how quickly the Japanese adapted designs to get them right!'

The spine frame and engine were left unchanged, which meant the two major components of the B100P and its trail version, the B105P, were the same. This kept down development time and costs.

So, what was changed? Immediately obvious was the exhaust, with a raised system being fitted in place of the original low-level type, while the engine's crankcases were protected by a steel sump guard. With no obvious mounting points at the front of the engine, a chrome-plated steel brace provided the appearance of a

front downtube – and also acted as a front support for the engine's bash plate. The Suzuki engineering team had also come up with a new offside (right) engine casing, which was intended to ensure that the gearbox oil filler did not foul the equally new exhaust system.

The modifications to create a 'trail' bike continued with folding footrests, a short front mudguard mounted directly under the steering column, and an abbreviated dual seat (covered in a suede-effect vinyl), designed to make room for a comprehensive rear carrier. And, of course, since this machine was intended for going off-road, it was also given knobbly tyres and a braced handlebar.

Alongside these changes, it was the task of providing suitable gearing for both on- and off-road use that was the priority. It was achieved by the fitment of two rear sprockets and an additional length of chain – a most un-Japanese engineering solution, which had already been adopted by the Ducati factory a couple of years earlier, on its 90cc Mountaineer model. On the Suzuki, a 31-tooth 'road' and 50-tooth 'power' sprocket were permanently installed on the rear (like the Ducati set-up), and a slightly wider swinging arm was provided to achieve the clearance (with a chrome-plated top-run chainguard). A short spacer between the frame and left-hand shock absorber kept the unit aligned. The chain was left to take care of itself in true 'Heath Robinson' fashion, running out of true once the additional length was inserted and the larger sprocket was brought into play on reaching an off-road section. As Don Leeson explained: 'Despite the affront to mechanical sympathy implied by this arrangement, no problems of chain jumping or undue wear are reported by VJMC member, Chris Merret, who still has one of these models in regular use both on and off road.'

Dual-Range Gearbox

Of course, messing around with changing chain lengths – particularly after coming back on to the tarmac – hardly fitted in with Japanese marketing plans, and the B105P was soon to be overtaken with a far more technically efficient, if more costly, solution. Suzuki's next move was a series of machines with what is described as the 'dual-range' gearbox. These models were the KT120, TC90, TC100, TC120, TC125 and TC185.

The whole concept of the dual-range gearbox was to provide the rider with a choice of ratios greater than the existing four-speed 'box found on the roadster singles of the time. Essentially, instead of four gears there were two sets of three – one for (high) road use, the other

(low) for the trail. Later, on some models this was increased to sets of four, and even five on the 185.

Suzuki engineers cleverly managed to squeeze the total of six speeds (or eight or ten) into the same area as the original four-speed or five-speed cluster. Described by one commentator as 'a cunning design', it was achieved by coupling a three-speed box with a two-speed assembly and arranging the gear ratios to give three low and three high – and correspondingly more speeds/ratios with later models.

The detail design retained Suzuki's existing all-indirect crossover set-up so the drive entered the gearbox on one shaft from the offside (right) and left on the other shaft on the nearside (left).

On the original models, the KT120 and TC120, there were four gears on each shaft and the three on the offside were laid out as in a three-speed gearbox. This meant that the middle gear on the input shaft could slide to the nearside to engage top gear and a dog slid between first and second gears on the output shaft to select them.

The fourth gear pair of the left operated with the one next to it to provide the two-speed gearbox – one pair of gears provided for

TC90 with disc-valve 89.9cc (47 × 51.8mm) engine, dual-range gearbox (two sets of three speeds, giving a total of six) and knobbly tyres. With a power output of 11bhp, maximum speed was around 65mph (104km/h) in high ratio.

both 'boxes. The two end gears on the input shaft were manufactured in one unit to run freely on the shaft. The end gear on the output also ran free, but on a separate sprocket shaft that supported the gearbox sprocket and ran free in the output shaft. Notably, this sprocket shaft was cross-drilled with ball bearings set in the holes, and the balls being pushed out proud of the shaft by way of a plunger rod. The balls engaged with each end gear, thus locking in the additional gear reduction, or top gear on the output shaft to provide a direct drive.

The plunger rod operated in a hole bored into the sprocket shaft from the nearside and was enlarged at the end so it could force the balls outwards as it moved in or out. The larger-diameter section was of a length so as to only move one set of balls at a time and

thus by moving in or out another gear was obtained.

The actual selection process was achieved by way of a lever mounted externally of the gearbox outboard of the final-drive chain. Roy Bacon reported that 'riders soon became adept at moving this with their left foot rather than by hand'.

In theory, it may sound somewhat over-complicated, but in practice the dual-range gearbox worked well. However, in time Suzuki went on to develop five- and six-speed 'boxes and so the concept of two-speed units was consigned to history.

TC120 Trail Cat

The only dual-range gearbox model to be offi-cially imported into the UK for general sale was the TC120 Trail Cat. When it first arrived, in 1970, it had been available for some time in the USA. Bruce Preston tested an example and began his article in the December 1970 issue of *Motorcycle Sport* with the headline 'A superb dual-purpose machine'.

The report was complimentary:

> A glance at the photograph of the Trail Cat will show that it has cobby good looks. It is small, neat, well made – has an air of elegance despite its ruggedness… I had not ridden the TC120 far before I knew that I was going to like it… The rid-ing position is unashamedly sit up and beg. Sitting on the bike gave one the feeling that hours could be spent in the saddle without discomfort. So it was to be. The relationship of handlebars, seat and footrests was ideal. Normally when the in-the-saddle position is comfortable, standing on the rests over difficult going is less so. Happily, Suzuki have overcome this and the machine feels right whether one is standing or sitting.

The TC120's engine employed conventional piston-port induction and, like other Suzukis of the late 1960s and early 1970s, the marque's

A December 1970 advertisement for the newly imported TC120 Trail Cat by new British importers, Suzuki (GB) Ltd, Trojan Works, Purley Way, Croydon, Surrey.

well-known Posi-Force lubrication. For its 118cc (52 × 56mm) displacement, the Trail Cat's 12bhp at 7,500rpm and maximum torque of

8.67lb ft at 7,000rpm were pretty impressive figures. However, as Bruce Preston pointed out, 'It is a figure which suggests that at low revs the engine wouldn't pull the skin off a rice pudding, which would be misleading for once the motor was spinning at about 3,000rpm there was a surprising amount of life in it.'

Weighing in at only 209lb (94.8kg) the TC120 could truthfully be described as a genuine lightweight. A ground clearance of 8in (200mm), together with a crankcase protection plate, meant that it was well capable of tackling most off-road hazards. Suspension was by courtesy of three-way adjustable twin rear shocks and oil-damped telescopic front forks with sensible rubber gaiters for protection. Knobbly competition-type rubber also helped on the dirt.

At the end of the *Motorcycle Sport* test, Bruce Preston summed up the T120 with some favourable words:

> The Suzuki Trail Cat is sold as a dual-purpose machine and it fulfils this to perfection. On the road it was comfortable, handled well and, with good brakes and lights, could be used with confidence day or night. On the rough it was sure-footed and reliable with its optional gearbox providing a ratio for all conditions. It is one of the most desirable machines that I have ridden for a long time and at £240, it could be a bargain for the rider who wants the best of both worlds.

The final variants of the TC range, the TC125 with 123cc (56 × 50mm) and TC185, 183cc (64 × 57mm), were finally deleted from the Suzuki range in the mid-1970s, never having been imported into the UK, together with the TC100 (97.7cc, 49 × 51.8mm).

The RV Series

The models of the RV series – the RV50 (1973), RV75 (1974), RV90 (1971) and RV125 (1973) – were all notable for their balloon tyres, and best described as a cross between a

---

1967 TC120 Specification

Engine	Air-cooled single with piston-port induction, alloy head and barrel, caged needle roller small- and big-ends, vertically split aluminium crankcases
Bore	52mm
Stroke	56mm
Displacement	118cc
Compression ratio	7.2:1
Lubrication	Pump
Ignition	Flywheel magneto; 6-volt
Carburettor	Mikuni 18mm
Primary drive	Gears, 16/50
Final drive	Chain, 13/35
Gearbox	Six-speed. Only three ratios in operation at same time, high and low, changed by lever
Frame	Full cradle, steel tubing
Front suspension	Telescopic hydraulically damped forks
Rear suspension	Swinging-arm, with three-way adjustable shock absorbers
Front brake	140mm full-width drum; SLS
Rear brake	140mm full-width drum; SLS
Tyres	Front 2.75 × 17; rear 3.00 × 17

General specifications

Wheelbase	47in (1,193mm)
Ground clearance	8in (200mm)
Seat height	29in (736mm)
Fuel tank capacity	1.5gal (7ltr)
Dry weight	209lb (95kg)
Maximum power	12bhp @ 7,500rpm
Top speed	Low ratio 60mph (96km/h) High ratio 70mph (112km/h)

An RV90J (1972) with 88.4cc (50 × 45mm) reed-valve engine and near-horizontal cylinder, 8bhp, four speeds and 10in wheels. Like other RV series machines, it was classed as an all-terrain vehicle.

Suzuki RV125, built 1973–77: 123cc (56 × 50mm) piston-port engine, five gears, 10bhp at 6,000rpm, and 14in front / 12in rear wheels.

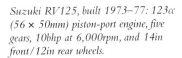

mini-bike and a trail bike – something of a two-wheel beach buggy!

The American *Motorcyclist* magazine tested an example of the RV125 in its November 1973 issue. They quickly discovered that it was a two-wheeler that could not be pigeonholed. Even Suzuki got caught out. They had assumed that the RV125 would appeal to teenagers but, in fact, in its main market, the USA, it sold to a surprisingly large percentage of people 'in the fifty-year-bracket' (*Motorcyclist*).

Weighing in at 244lb (111kg), the RV125 was quite heavy for its size. Some of this, of

course, could be put down to the tyres (5.40 × 14 front and 6.70 × 12 rear).

The engine was from the TS125 (released 1971) rather than the TC125. The *Motorcyclist* tester was somewhat confused:

Looking at the specs and comparing it with the other 125 Suzis can make you wonder what this bike is all about. Compression ratio is down to 6.3 from 6.7 of the others, and the carburettor is a 22mm size instead of 24. The TS and TC125s claim 13bhp at 7000rpm, whilst the RV claims 10bhp at 6000rpm. This seems reasonable for the differences in otherwise identical engines, but for the difference of one tooth in the wheel sprockets, the RV125 has the same gearing as the TS125 Duster... If this was to be a trail bike, why didn't Suzuki install the four-by-two gearbox of the TC125 Prespector?

We found out in riding it that the recommended 9psi in the tyres gives this bike such a footprint that utilizing wheel spin for hillside starts is virtually impossible. A lower overall gear ratio in the neighbourhood of 50:1 would allow it to crawl over anything with ease, yet the high gear range provided by the TC auxiliary gears would give it the same cruising ability.

Perhaps most amazing of all, although low speed manoeuvring could be, according to the *Motorcyclist* reporter, 'somewhat hazardous', high speed stability and riding comfort were something else:

Although the engine was running crisply, and throughout our riding never coughed, the top speed that could be indicated was 60mph [96.5km/h] on a slight downgrade of paved road. Even at this breakneck speed, and at the regular cruising speed of 50, the machine never reared its head or wagged its tail, and corners could be taken like a road racer. The washboard sections and embedded rocks of graded roads were taken by the tires and suspension as though the bike were always on smooth asphalt. The ride was just like a plush limousine.

The RV50, 75 and 90 models lasted until 1976, with the RV125 disappearing from Suzuki's model line-up a year later. Only the largest-engined version was sold in the UK.

The TS Series

The TS series began around the same time as the RV range (all except the original model, the TS250), at the beginning of the 1970s. Like the RV, the TS range was offered in various engine sizes: the TS50 (1971), TS75 (1974), TS90

1973 RV125 Specification	
Engine	Air-cooled single with piston-port induction
Bore	56mm
Stroke	50mm
Displacement	123cc
Compression ratio	6.3:1
Lubrication	Pump
Ignition	Flywheel magneto; 6-volt
Carburettor	Mikuni 22mm
Primary drive	Gears; 16/57
Final drive	Chain; 15/51
Gearbox	Five-speed; foot-change
Frame	Tubular steel, single loop, double cradle
Front suspension	Telescopic fork, with exposed stanchions
Rear suspension	Swinging-arm, with three-way adjustable shock absorbers
Front brake	110mm full-width drum; SLS
Rear brake	130mm full-width drum; SLS
Tyres	Front 5.40 × 14; rear 6.70 × 12

General specifications

Wheelbase	51.4in (1,305mm)
Ground clearance	7.7in (195mm)
Seat height	26in (660mm)
Fuel tank capacity	1.034gal (4.5ltr)
Dry weight	244lb (110kg)
Maximum power	10bhp @ 6,000rpm
Top speed	60mph (97km/h)

(1970), TS100 (1973), TS125 (1971), TS185 (1971), TS250 (1969) and TS400 (1972). Like most of Suzuki's models of the time, the TS250 was given a name, the 'Savage'. It was aimed squarely at the burgeoning American street-scrambler market, described by *Cycle* magazine as the arena of 'the compromised street-legal dirt bike'. And, in truth, the TS250 was the best of the breed.

The TS series began in 1969 with the 250 (called the Savage). This 1973 K version was very similar to the original with its 246cc piston-port engine, alloy head and barrel, five speeds, 6-volt flywheel mag electrics, and 19in front/18in rear tyres.

The TS range encompassed 50, 75, 90 (a 1972 J series machine shown here), 100, 125, 185, 250 and 400 engine sizes.

The biggest TS model was the 400. Offered from 1972 to 1976, its 396cc (82 × 75mm) piston-port engine produced 34bhp (reduced to 33bhp from 1975 model year). This is the original 1972 J model; first displayed at the Tokyo Show in November 1971.

TS250

Over the years the 250 was destined to prove the most popular of the TS series. In original form, the 246cc piston-port single, with bore and stroke dimensions of 70 × 64mm (later utilized on both the TM motocross and RL trials models), produced 23bhp at 6,500rpm. Other features of its specification included alloy head and barrel, Posi-Force lubrication, a five-speed gearbox, wet multi-plate clutch, flywheel magneto ignition and 6-volt electrics. There were 3.25 × 19 (changed to a 2.75 × 21 from the 1974 model year) front and 3.50 × 18 rear tyres, 150mm full width alloy drum brakes and a dry weight of 280lb (127kg).

It has to be said straight away that the TS250 was much more of a street bike than its rivals from either Yamaha or Kawasaki, or even Honda's four-valve XL250. Indeed, this was what most buyers needed. They wanted – and got – a bike that *looked* like a dirt bike, but was actually a roadster. The TS250's suitability for tarmac duties was fully displayed during the mid-late 1970s when London dealer Vic Camp

ABOVE: *Like all Suzuki TS models, the 250 employed Posi-Force (pump) lubrication.*

BELOW: *The TS250 engine, showing all the components; it was even used as a road racer.*

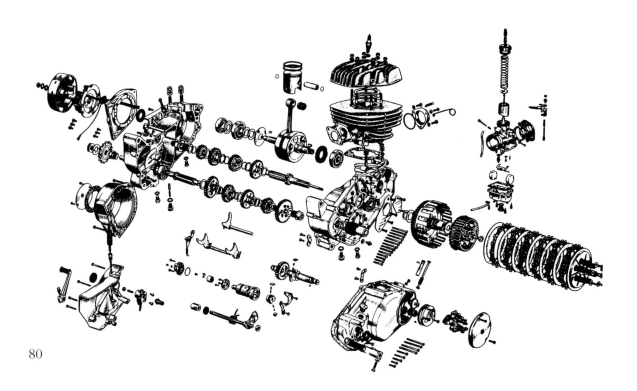

RIGHT: *Classic racer Robert Saunders, pictured by the author at the CRMC Mallory Park meeting, 10 April 2005, with his 1978 Vic Camp TS250 racer.*

1976 TS250L Specification

Engine	Air-cooled single with piston-port induction
Bore	70mm
Stroke	64mm
Displacement	246cc
Compression ratio	6.7:1
Lubrication	Pump
Ignition	PEI (Pointless Electronic Ignition) 6-volt
Carburettor	Mikuni VM28SH
Primary drive	Gears 23/71
Final drive	Chain 15/39
Gearbox	Five-speed
Frame	Tubular steel, with single downtube, branching into two under engine unit
Front suspension	Telescopic fork, exposed stanchions
Rear suspension	Swinging-arm, five-way adjustable shock absorbers
Front brake	Full-width drum, SLS
Rear brake	Full-width drum, SLS
Tyres	Front 3.00 × 21; rear 4.00 × 18

General specifications

Wheelbase	55.7in (1,414mm)
Ground clearance	9.8in (249mm)
Seat height	30in (762mm)
Fuel tank capacity	2gal (9ltr)
Dry weight	245lb (111kg)
Maximum power	22bhp @ 6,500rpm
Top speed	80mph (129km/h)

(earlier associated with Ducati) converted and sold a series of racing bikes – yes, road racing, not motocross! The Camp conversion was to prove a successful and reliable machine, and a race winner in the right hands.

The series production TS250 was also something of a bargain. For example, in 1973 the latest TS250K cost £392, compared with Kawasaki's F-11 at £521. The Kawasaki may have been more suitable on the dirt, but the Suzuki was not only cheaper, but more powerful and lighter.

Motorcycle Sport tested the TS250K and pronounced it 'a very good motorcycle' – except when it went off-road! Their question was, 'What is the Suzuki good for, then?' The answer they gave was telling:

> For a start it is a terrific road bike! Its 246cc single-cylinder engine comes as a welcome change from the twins that we are accustomed to from this stable. Smooth as the twins are, there is something very attractive about the Suzuki single. Power was very much greater than one would expect, and the tickover was a steady, reliable 800rpm, never varying even when the engine was a little hotter than usual. Certainly on the road or the rough this was a real asset, to shut the throttle and know the engine would keep going.

TS125/185

Like their bigger brother, both the TS125 and TS185 were most at home on the tarmac. *Cycle* reported in June 1973 that 'on urban streets and rural roads, the TS125 is a marvel. With its trail-patterned semi-dirt tires (both

Bridgestone Trail Wing: 2.75 × 19 front, 3.25 × 18 rear) inflated to 20 psi in the front and 28 psi in the rear, the little bike darts about with quiet, surefooted precision.' In the final analysis, the tester felt that the TS125 was 'a good road bike and a mediocre dirt bike'.

The 185 slotted into a gap between the 125 and the 250, being more powerful and flexible than the former, but not as bulky as the latter. The 183cc (64 × 57mm) five-speed engine put out a claimed 17bhp at 7,000rpm.

TS ER

For the 1980 model year, Suzuki brought out the TS ER series. Radically restyled from the outgoing TS machines, the ER versions benefited from several improvements that were aimed at making the balance more equal between street and dirt. Previously, the percentage of street/dirt would have been around 80/20; now it was more like 60/40.

The earlier TS series had been decent motorcycles, except for going off-road. Even though Suzuki later provided a larger 21in instead of 19in together with a less close-fitting front guard, plus more suitable (higher-clearance) exhaust along the way, until the arrival of the ER there remained several unresolved pitfalls for those wishing to take their Suzuki trail bike off-road, or something a touch more serious.

Not only did the ER bring a much more modern style to things, but it was also given a number of dirt-bike-friendly innovations by the Suzuki design team. There was a trendy box-section swinging arm, as well as genuine signs that some thought had gone into weight reduction and practicality. The handlebars (and the entire engine) were lacquered rather than chrome, and

LEFT: Another TS, the 125. This is a 1971 (R) bike (first year of production). The model ran from then until 1979, when it was replaced by the ER version for the 1980 model year.

BELOW LEFT: 1973 TS125L with matching speedo and tacho, plus centrally located ignition switch.

ABOVE: A 1976 TS185A – much as before, but with revised exhaust (from 1973) and 21in front wheel (from 1974).

painted instead of polished aluminium, respectively. Rubber-mounted indicators replaced the rigid, accident-prone components of yesteryear. There were motocross-type serrated, folding footrests, plastic for the mudguards and side panels and so on, a tuck-in hi-level MX-type exhaust, and quickly detachable mirrors. Smaller components such as the brake and clutch levers, so often the province of after-market suppliers, were now of high quality, being very slim and light. Other areas of control were equally well thought out. In addition, Bridgestone had come up with tyres of a new type, with a tread pattern that worked equally well on dirt or dry roads.

Another perennial problem of the TS since its inception had been its brakes. The dilemma was that brakes powerful enough for the road were too much for dirt. Reducing weight to a minimum on the ER – by using clever design, plus lightweight materials – meant that the new smaller 5in (6in on 250) conical hub brakes were, to quote *Bike*, 'more than adequate for the road without overtaxing the cohesive qualities of loose earth'. Both front and rear assemblies provided 'bags of feel and good progressive actions'.

For 1980 Suzuki introduced the much-improved TS ER series; an official Heron Suzuki brochure shows that year's TS100 model.

The 1980 TS185ER had a useful amount of ground clearance. This, together with square-section swinging-arm, plastic mudguards, flexibly mounted indicators, conical brake hubs and more modern styling, helped put the TS range back on buyers' lists.

1980 TS185ER Specification

Engine	Air-cooled single with reed-valve induction
Bore	64mm
Stroke	57mm
Displacement	183cc
Compression ratio	6.4:1
Lubrication	Pump
Ignition	Flywheel magneto, CDI, 6-volt
Carburettor	Mikuni 29mm
Primary drive	Gears
Final drive	Chain
Gearbox	Five-speed, foot-change
Frame	Full cradle, with twin front downtubes
Front suspension	Telescopic fork, with rubber gaiters
Rear suspension	Swinging-arm, with twin shock absorbers
Front brake	130mm drum, SLS
Rear brake	130mm drum, SLS
Tyres	Front 2.75 × 21; rear 4.10 × 18

General specifications

Wheelbase	53in (1,346mm)
Ground clearance	9in (228mm)
Seat height	32in (812mm)
Fuel tank capacity	1.5gal (7ltr)
Dry weight	230lb (104kg)
Maximum power	18bhp @ 7,500rpm
Top speed	74mph (119km/h)

Except for the '50' logo, the engine on the TS50ER gives the impression of being much bigger than it actually is. Note the full-loop frame, square-section swinging arm and neatly tucked-in exhaust.

The ERs were offered in 50, 125, 185 and 250cc engine sizes, the bigger ones benefiting additionally from a switch to reed instead of piston–port induction, usefully widening the power band.

The Suzuki trail bike range moved smoothly into the 1980s, an almost perfect mix of both on- and off-road ability in equal doses. The TS ER range particularly benefited both from its recent technical updates and from the marque's continuing success in off-road sport.

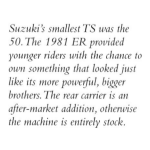

Suzuki's smallest TS was the 50. The 1981 ER provided younger riders with the chance to own something that looked just like its more powerful, bigger brothers. The rear carrier is an after-market addition, otherwise the machine is entirely stock.

6 T/GT500

With a production run spanning a decade from the end of 1967 through to the end of 1977, Suzuki's five-hundred twin, the T/GT500, was described by one commentator as 'one of the most under-rated models of all time'.

T500

The T500, first marketed as the 500/Five in the USA, was incorrectly described by the Suzuki publicity machine as 'the world's first 500cc dual-stroke'. In fact, a certain Alfred Angus Scott had already created a 500cc two-stroke twin – back at the turn of the twentieth century! What Suzuki should have said was that their new bike was the first *modern* five-hundred twin-cylinder 'stroker'. (Two decades later, another generation of Suzuki's PR department was to get it wrong in a similar fashion by claiming a first with the alloy-framed GSX-R750 in 1985; the truth was that the German firm Ardie had beaten them to it back in 1930.)

Simplicity of Design

The work of Masanao Shimizu (who had also designed the legendary T20 Super Six), Suzuki's new big displacement twin was an excellent design; it was both simple and very robust in its construction. The engine, of full unit layout like its smaller 250/305/350 brothers, was air-cooled with its cylinders slanted slightly forward.

Bore and stroke dimensions of 70 × 64mm (later utilized on the marque's two-fifty singles, the TS, TM and RL) gave a capacity of 492cc.

Factory image of the original T500 (known as the 500/Five in the USA), 1968 model.

T/GT500

BELOW: 1970 T500 Series II engine unit.

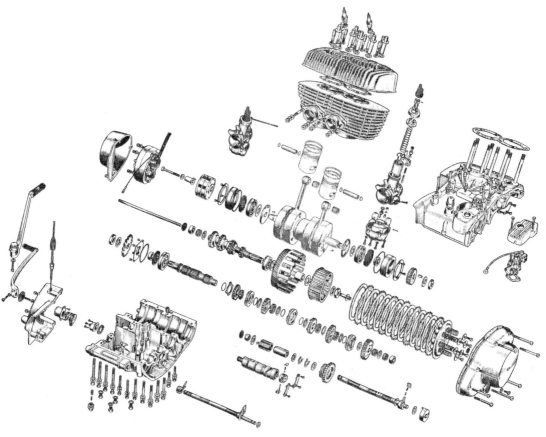

The crankshaft was equipped with a trio of main bearings of massive proportions and, partly thanks to the Posi-Force lubrication system, proved virtually bullet-proof. The 12-volt Kukusan Denki EF39 alternator rotor was keyed on to the nearside (left) end of the crank, the 26-/65-tooth primary gears for the fourteen-plate wet clutch being on the offside (right).

Cycle World reported the world's first test of the new Suzuki in its December 1967 issue, pointing out that, apart from having a larger engine, 'the 500/Five doesn't depart from current, common design practice. It simply has all the accepted items – in spades.'

Clutch Lubrication

The T500 featured horizontally split crankcases with O-ring seals, which prevented oil from seeping between the bearing recesses and the outer races into the clutch and electrical compartments.

In the smaller Suzuki twins, adequate clutch lubrication was guaranteed by routing oil from the gearbox into a reservoir, which supplied oil to the centre main bearing, into the clutch chamber where it was returned to the transmission; at least, that was the theory, and most of the time it functioned well. However, occasionally the clutch compartment could find itself with more oil than it needed, while the top-mounted gears in the transmission ran high and dry for want of a sufficiently high oil level. On the new five-hundred twin, the Suzuki design team set out to rectify this glitch. Although transmission oil was still used to lubricate the centre main bearing, now, instead of routing the oil into the clutch chamber, it was returned directly to the transmission. The clutch was supplied via a passage from the gearbox, ensuring that both systems received just the right amount of lubricant, rather than more or less, as before.

Gearbox

The development team, rightly, considered a six-speed 'box a waste on the much more torquey

Martyn Ashwood, sixth finisher in the 1971 500cc Production TT in the Isle of Man, with his T500; he averaged 85.33mph (137.29km/h).

five-hundred, so they opted for a five-speed cluster, retaining a modern vein, but not going overboard. The design departed noticeably, but not drastically, from what Suzuki had already done with its smaller twins. The key change involved the gear selector drum assembly, which, instead of employing encircling forks on the drum, used stubby half forks, mounted on an independent shaft. These had nubs that engaged with indexing slots on the drum. Suzuki claimed that this innovation reduced the fork-to-drum contact area, thus reducing wear.

The chief characteristic of the transmission was its robust nature, with wider gears, needle bearings inboard of the shafts, and rollers supporting the ends. The gearbox also had an additional and unfamiliar function on this machine: a worm gear on the 'lazy' end of the countershaft driving the oil pump. The one downside of this layout was that neither the pump nor the tachometer operated when the clutch was disengaged. However, in reality, this was not a problem, unless the engine was to run at high speeds with the clutch pulled in for a lengthy period of time. Another feature (on the early T500 gearbox only) was that neutral was obtained via a positive stop. Changing up from first with a full throw bypassed neutral. Later 'boxes required a half throw in either direction to illuminate the tachometer-mounted neutral light.

Throughout the T500's engine/transmission/clutch unit there was an underlying strength of design. Typical were the caged needle roller-bearing assemblies at both the small- and big-ends of the connecting rods. Both were lubricated by oil mist, which was created when the neat oil from the Posi-Force lubrication system passed through the outer main bearings and into the crank chambers, where it was mixed with the incoming fuel/air mixture. The connecting rods, around the big-ends, were 'split' to expose the middles of the needle-bearing assemblies to the oil-mist atmosphere in the crank chambers.

Examining the Pistons

The pistons employed windows, rather than notches, for port control. This design was quite uncommon at the time of the T500's launch, as manufacturing costs were higher. The full-

circumference skirts were stronger than notched ones, and quieter, as the 'bridges' between the solid portions of the skirt served to dampen, to a great degree, the rattling operating noise that is common in notched-skirt pistons. Both the heads and cylinder barrels were heavily finned and of cast aluminium, the latter being equipped with a pair of steel liners. Suzuki announced that replacement pistons would be made available in not only Standard, but also 1st and 2nd oversizes, so that the barrels could be rebored

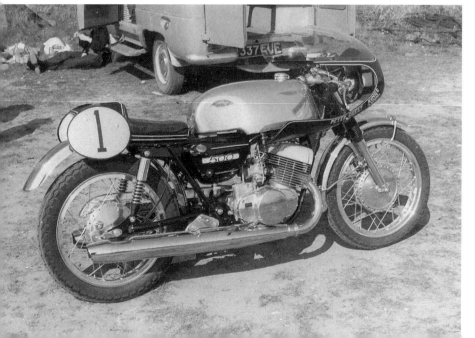

ABOVE: *Dutchman Piet Hogervorst and his Crooks-T500 production racer, circa 1973. Hogervorst rode this and other Suzukis in international sports production races such as the Barcelona 24 Hours and Thruxton 500-mile.*

LEFT: *Tony Collison's 1973 T500L in production race trim, Snetterton 1974.*

twice, before the cylinders needed to be refitted with fresh liners of the original dimensions.

As initially supplied, the engine produced 46bhp at 7,000rpm, giving a maximum speed with full silencing of around 108mph (174km/h). However, the state of tune was relatively low and as *Cycle World* commented, 'Porting is not as generous as might be expected of an engine that performs as strongly as this one… although abundant material around the ports promises good potential to the performance-minded enthusiast.' This was one feature that was to be exploited not only by private tuners on both sides of the Atlantic, but ultimately by Suzuki themselves, with the TR500 full-blown racer (*see* Chapter 4).

The Chassis
The Suzuki family resemblance – particularly to the T20 – was notable in the frame design; the T500 was effectively a scaled-up version of the smaller machine's duplex cradle design. The frame was described by *Cycle World* as being 'constructed of heavy-wall tubing, fabricated gussets, fine welding, and satisfying triangulation'. The swinging arm was equally robust, with reinforced gusseting aft of the pivot tube.

Braking was courtesy of drum brakes front and rear, of 200mm and 180mm respectively. Both were of the full-width alloy type; the front with twin-leading shoe operation. According to *Cycle World*, the brakes were 'superb with predictable action and high fade resistance'. The brakes really were that good, particularly at the front.

The report in *Cycle World* was generally complimentary, but the tester reckoned that the machine could be 'faulted on… one point': 'Unfortunately, for a motorcycle as fast as this one, poor suspension is a grievous shortcoming. The entire suspension system is not to be harshly criticized. However, the rear spring-shock units are well applied to their duties with spring rates that suit the weight and purpose of the motorcycle and damping that cannot be

disparaged. The front fork assembly is another matter. It is plagued with a set of too-soft springs and cursed with dampers that would scarcely be missed if they were left at home.' However, Suzuki was said to be looking for an answer.

Electrical Equipment
Although it did not feature an electric starter, the electrical specification of the new five-hundred Suzuki twin was well up to the standard set by the Japanese industry of the day. While the vast majority of British and European motorcycles were still wedded to the inferior 6-volt output, the T500 had a 12-volt system.

Ignition was by twin coil and contact breakers, whilst the battery was a 7-amp hour device; lighting being supplied via the alternator.

Direction indicators were part of the standard equipment package, but the tester writing for *Motorcycle Mechanics* was not entirely impressed with this feature: 'I have yet to find a machine fitted with a control switch which gives positive action. The Suzuki switch is no exception and it was necessary to fiddle about for some time when on the move to centralize the three-position switch to turn off the indicator.'

Arrival in the UK
The first production examples of the 500/Five, more commonly known as the 'T500 Mark 1', arrived in the UK during early April 1968.

Ivan Norris pictured at Mallory Park on his Difazio T500 special (with hub steering), 28 May 1972.

1968 T500 Mk I Specification

Engine	Air-cooled parallel twin two-stroke, with piston–port induction, alloy head and barrel assemblies, the latter with pressed-in steel liners, three main bearings, caged needle-roller small- and big-end bearings, horizontally split aluminium crankcases
Bore	70mm
Stroke	64mm
Displacement	492cc
Compression ratio	6.6:1
Lubrication	Pump
Ignition	Battery/twin coils and contact breaker, Kukusan Denki EF39 alternator, 12-volt
Carburettor	2 × Mikuni VM34SC 34mm (Mark II onwards VM32SC)
Primary drive	Gears, 26/65
Final drive	Chain, 14/33
Gearbox	Five-speed, foot-change
Frame	Duplex, cradle, all-steel tubular construction
Front suspension	Telescopic forks, with rubber gaiters
Rear suspension	Swinging-arm
Front brake	200mm, full-width drum, 2LS
Rear brake	180mm, full-width drum, SLS
Tyres	Front 3.25 × 19; rear 4.00 × 18

General specifications

Wheelbase	56.1in (1,424mm)
Ground clearance	6.3in (160mm)
Seat height	31in (787mm)
Fuel tank capacity	3gal (14ltr)
Dry weight	403lb (183kg)
Maximum power	46bhp @ 7,000rpm; 47bhp from Mk II (number 20,001)
Top speed	108mph (174km/h)

However, British enthusiasts had heard news of the impending newcomer in the previous year, in the 6 September 1967 issue of *Motor Cycle*: 'Star exhibit on the Suzuki stand at the Earls Court Show, which opens on Saturday, September 16, will be one of the prototype 500cc twin-cylinder Suzuki machines now being developed for the American market.' Suzuki GB's sales director Alan Kimber was quoted as saying, 'Suzuki has promised to fly us one of the prototype machines over for the Show, but I'm afraid that no one will be allowed to ride it. We have had to promise to send it straight back when the exhibition closes.' At that time the big Suzuki was not yet on sale anywhere in the world and no price had been fixed.

During the first week of April 1968, the T500 (known as the 'Cobra' in the British market) went on sale, priced at £423 10s 4d. The T20 Super Six cost £289 and the Triumph T120 Bonneville six-fifty could be had for £355 – some 20 per cent less – so most aspiring owners could only wish. This meant that Suzuki's new range leader was reserved, in the UK at least, for the privileged few.

The new T500 tried its best to justify its hyper-price, with a specification of twin 34mm Mikuni VM34SC carburetors (featuring in-built mixture-strength compensators), a fuel tap that embodied a diaphragm linked by tubing to the inlet tract, separate rev counter and speedometer (in an era when Japanese bikes had a combined one-piece assembly in the headlamp shell), and a mass of chrome (mudguards, tank panels, exhaust and much more), as well as a choice of colours (Polychromatic Gold or Metallic Blue).

First UK Test

Motor Cycle's David Dixon brought British readers the first real test of the T500 Cobra, published in the same issue (3 April) as the official launch. The report began with a bold statement: 'Road-burning types who consider it

*Silverstone, circa 1976: George
Fogarty (father of Carl) T500
(95), inside Neil Tuxworth (43)
Honda CB400F, during
Production Race at Becketts.*

*BELOW: Don Leeson with his
immaculate and original 1968
T500 Cobra; Stanford Hall,
summer 1983.*

beneath their dignity to straddle anything
smaller than six-fifties had better take a long
hard look at the Suzuki T500, or prepare to be
blown off in a big way.'

According to Dixon, the engine, which had
'a claimed power output of almost as much as a
Manx Norton or G50 Matchless... could, if the
gearbox was used properly, accelerate like a
rocket'. But, in his opinion, it was 'the manner
in which the bike performed which endeared it
to everyone who rode it'. As for power delivery,
this was 'beefy' from 2,000 to 4,500rpm; the
'real power surge' began at 5,000rpm, 'the revs
rocketing' from 5,500 to 7,000rpm maximum
in the gears.

Dixon detected 'a period of slight roughness
between 3,400 and 4,000rpm', but considered
the unit to be 'delightfully smooth right up to
5,600rpm. Then vibration became apparent
through the handlebar and footrests and
increased in intensity to maximum.' Vibes were
kept under control thanks to rubber-mounted
handlebars, large-diameter, soft grips, and a
rubber-mounted fuel tank.

The *Motor Cycle* test could not find fault
with the suspension, commenting that it was
'sufficiently soft to provide a featherbed ride
while pottering... while dealing with rough
surfaces taken at high speeds extremely well.'

Mark II

The Mark II version did not reach Britain until quite late in 1969, although it had already gone on sale in North America earlier that year. There was also a name change – from Cobra to Titan – but most people, press and public alike, referred to the bike simply as the T500.

Although Suzuki claimed that the power had risen by 1bhp to 47, the carburettor size had been reduced from 34 to 32mm.

The styling change applied to the Mark II led to what Don Leeson described as a more 'Europeanized look'; the rounded chrome-panelled tank had given way to an all painted, more angular version. At the same time, the mudguards, although still chrome-plated, became less effective – in this respect, it was a case of fashion winning over function.

When Charles Deane tested one of the Mark II machines for *Motorcycle Mechanics*, in its March 1970 issue, he compared it to Triumph's T100T Daytona. Both were twin-carb five hundreds, with a similar top speed, but Deane felt that 'where the two-stroke does and must score is in acceleration… With a power stroke every revolution, as compared with one every

two revs on a four-stroke, the T500 must win hands down until the upper limits are reached.'

Little Change

From the Mark II onwards – through the Mark III, the Mark IIIR, J, K, L and M variants – in all major aspects other than graphics and colours, the T500 series was to remain unchanged over the next six years. A hint of Triumph influence appeared, with the tank-top parcel grid of the Mark III, and reappeared in the chrome side-panel embellishments of the J; the latter were vaguely reminiscent of the eyebrow tank badges of the British marque, and condemned by Don Leeson as 'grotesque'.

The GT Series

For the new GT series, there were to be few changes either to the mechanics or to the cycle components. Any modifications were to be largely reserved for the very start of the series (the Mark I Cobra) and the final models, the GT500A (1976) and B (1977) machines.

By then, the five-hundred twin had changed its role, from that of expensive range

1976 GT500A with single disc brake and detuned engine.

leader to a bargain-basement workhorse; this was reflected in a price of £660, which made it less expensive than virtually any similar machine from rival manufacturers. One example was the latest Triumph Bonneville, which had risen in cost to the £1,000 mark.

The most significant differences between the GT series and what had gone before centred around the styling (components coming from the GT250, 380 and 750), the use of a 280mm single-disc front brake (the rear drum remaining unchanged), exposed fork stanchions, revised bracketry on the front mudguard and, perhaps most notably of all, electronic ignition. Suzuki used the initials 'PEI' (Pointless Electronic Ignition) to describe its new system. As a test report of the new GT500A in the April 1976 issue of *Cycle World* told potential buyers, 'There are no points to adjust or replace and ignition timing remains constant.'

Compared with earlier versions, the GT models were detuned to provide 'only' 44bhp. However, although it seemed to lack the crispness of the earlier bikes, *Cycle World* were able to report that the GT500A 'certainly dispels the last vestiges of the myth that a two-stroke engine can't be torquey. This one pulls smartly without bucking from just under 2,000rpm and signs off abruptly at 6,500. The machine is more comfortable if left in a higher gear under load, rather than buzzing along with the engine not pulling.'

Another change was the axing of the paper element air filter; this having been changed over to a double foam element complete with a newly designed airbox unit. *Cycle World* suspected that this contributed to the quieter intake roar at larger throttle openings.

Potential Problems

Whilst the T/GT500 series were generally strong in design, there were one or two points that could present problems. One was the gearbox. Not only could the engine's substantial

1976 GT500A Specification	
Engine	Air-cooled parallel twin two-stroke, with piston-port induction, alloy head and barrel assemblies, the latter with pressed-in steel liners, three main bearings, caged needle roller small- and big-end bearings, horizontally split aluminium crankcases
Bore	70mm
Stroke	64mm
Displacement	492cc
Compression ratio	6.6:1
Lubrication	Pump
Ignition	Electronic, with alternator, 12-volt
Carburettor	2 × Mikuni VM32SC 32mm
Primary drive	Gears, 26/45
Final drive	Chain, 15/33
Gearbox	Five-speed
Frame	Duplex, cradle, all-steel tubular construction
Front suspension	Telescopic forks, with exposed stanchions
Rear suspension	Swinging-arm, five-way adjustable shock absorber
Front brake	275mm hydraulically operated disc
Rear brake	180mm, full-width drum, SLS
Tyres	Front 3.25 × 19; rear 4.00 × 18

General specifications

Wheelbase	57.2in (1,452mm)
Ground clearance	6.3in (160mm)
Seat height	31in (787mm)
Fuel tank capacity	3.5gal (17ltr)
Dry weight	395lb (180kg)
Maximum power	44bhp @ 7,000rpm
Top speed	105mph (169km/h)

torque put strain on the gears themselves, but a potentially serious fault also lay with the fact that earlier crankcases were marked '1200cc' (oil quantity), whereas later ones read '1400'. However, the level screw was *not* moved along

with the recommendation to increase the quantity! As a result, it is essential not only to measure the oil in, but also to use EP90.

Cylinder heads have been known to crack, while small-ends need to be in good health, otherwise crankshafts will prove a let-down. Swinging-arm bushes (made of fibre) are a known weakness and grease should be applied on a regular basis. Front brake hubs (drum) can crack on the inside around the strengthening ribs, particularly when they have been fitted with Ferodo AM4 racing linings.

Finally, clutch rattle can occur on high-mileage engines, while the problem of rotting mudguards is one shared with other Japanese machines of the same era.

Despite all these drawbacks, Don Leeson, writing in the December 1986 issue of *Motorcycle Enthusiast*, came to the following conclusion: 'All I can say is that if I was to be restricted to just one bike it would be a T500 – others may do certain things better, but for a single machine, which is happy practically anywhere, it's hard to beat.'

T/GT500 Model Evolution

T500 Mark I (1968) Launched with drum brake, 2LS at front, 34mm carburettors, contact breakers, chrome tank panels, rubber knee grips, fork gaiters, enclosed rear shocks, 46bhp at 7,000rpm, compression ratio 6.6:1. Initially known as 500/Five in USA. Ran from 10,000 to 16,038.

T500 Mark II (1969) 32mm carburettors, 47bhp, all-painted fuel tank, chrome-plated headlamp shell and headlamp brackets. Ran from 20,938 to 23,937.

T500 Mark III (1970) Tank-top parcel grid. Ran from 23,938 to 31,294.

T500 Mark III R (1971) Ran from 31,295 onwards.

T500 J (1972) Chrome side panels.

T500 K (1973) Candy Wine Red or Bright Blue metallic.

T500 L (1974) Red and Gold.

T500 M (1975) Offered in metallic blue only.

GT500 A (1976) Disc front brake, GT750 style tank, GT250 instruments, exposed fork stanchions, electronic ignition (PEI, or Pointless Electronic Ignition), new wiring system, 44bhp.

GT500 B (1977) Black side panels.

7 GT380/550

How's this for a wheelie? American Pat Hennen pops one on a GT380 at the Guthrie Memorial during his inaugural visit to learn the TT course in 1977. He finished third in his first TT.

The first news of newly developed Suzuki air-cooled three-cylinder models in Great Britain was published by *Motor Cycle* in its 13 October 1971 issue, when it was announced that the bikes would be 'on sale in America next year'. This came some twelve months after the prototype liquid-cooled GT750 triple had made its dramatic debut at the Tokyo Show, at the beginning of November 1970 (*see* Chapter 9).

The first of the smaller triples to appear was the GT380, which was displayed on the Suzuki stand at the 18th Tokyo Show during the first week of November 1971.

GT380

Engine

The 371cc engine of the GT380 (using the 54 × 54mm bore and stroke dimensions from the existing two-fifty twin) employed heavily finned horizontally split crankcases, a six-speed gearbox, wet multi-plate clutch, six main bearings, four oil seals, needle roller small- and big-ends, and two-ring pistons featuring a keystone top and plain bottom rings with a compression ratio of 6.7:1 and developing a claimed 38bhp at 7,500rpm. Lubrication, as was to be expected, was by Suzuki's by now well-known Posi-Force (pump) system.

A notable feature at the time (although it was later also used on the twin-cylinder 185/250 models, among others) was the new Ram Air system, which was in reality a light alloy sheet suitably bent and bolted to the cylinder-head fins. The fitment of Ram Air to the twins was

generally agreed to have been a marketing gimmick, but on the GT380 (and on its larger 550 brother) the system could at least be claimed to help cool the middle cylinder.

There were a trio of Mikuni 24mmVM24SC carburettors, while the exhaust pipe from the central cylinder divided into two, giving one large and one small silencer on each side. The rationale behind this set-up was to distance Suzuki from one of their main rivals – at least in the Japanese industry. Kawasaki had originally come up with the air-cooled across-the-frame three-cylinder two-stroke formula, and Suzuki did not want to be seen to be following

GT380 engine with Suzuki Ram Air cooling system (essentially an aluminium plate bolted to the cylinder head).

their lead. Cleverly, by having a four-cylinder-type set of mufflers and their Ram Air cooling they did set themselves apart from Kawasaki. In any case, the two marques' efforts were, except for cylinder layout, quite different in temperament – Suzuki's were just a tad more civilized!

The GT380's carburettors featured cold-start jets and there was a diaphragm-lock fuel-tank tap; the air-filtration system featured an oil-soaked foam element.

Transmission

Besides the six speeds, the transmission of the GT380 (the first year's production being coded 'J') featured helical primary-drive gears (24/68), giving a primary reduction ratio of 2.833:1. As for the final drive, this was by chain, with front and rear sprockets of 14/42 respectively. The overall ratios were 19.82, 12.74, 9.83, 7.68, 6.64 and 6.01:1.

Clutch adjustment (and access to the alternator) was gained by removing the two near-side (left) outer engine covers. As for the clutch itself, this comprised six each of friction and steel plates, plus springs.

Electrical Equipment

Ignition was by a 12-volt 7-amp hour battery and a trio of coils (the latter being housed under the fuel tank) and three sets of contact breakers that lived under the circular alloy cover on the offside of the engine. The lack of electric starter helped to keep down both weight and price, but other features that buyers now expected of Japanese bikes, including direction indicators, warning lights and decent switchgear, were all evident in the new GT380.

Chassis

The substantial duplex cradle frame closely followed that of the GT750 (and, when it arrived, the GT550). Although the *Motor Cycle* test published in August 1972 adjudged it to feel 'lighter than its weight' and to have a 'good turning lock and light, responsive steering', the 'laden seat height was high for an average-size rider'. The origins of the GT750 frame design were still somewhat evident in the smaller-capacity, lighter 380.

The same could be said, but for a different reason, of the front brake, which was the same

The T10 of 1963 was a direct descendant of the TA250 Twin Ace model of 1960. It featured a 246cc engine with bore and stroke dimensions of 52 × 58mm, as well as four speeds, electric start and petroil lubrication.

One of the first batch of models imported via AMC (Associated Motor Cycles) into Britain during October 1963 was the 50cc M12 Super Sport.

INSET RIGHT: Checking the fuel level of the M30; the round sticker shows recommended ratios of fuel and oil.

Introduced in mid-1964, the M30 'Step-thru' featured a three-speed gearbox and automatic clutch.

1965 S32 150 twin, with four speeds and electric start – something of a cross between the T10 and T20.

The ground-breaking T20 Super Six arrived for the 1966 model year, offering square 54 × 54mm bore and stroke dimensions, six speeds, Posi-Force lubrication and breathtaking performance.

OPPOSITE PAGE: *1967/1968 K15 Trial 80, developed from the earlier K11T. The K15 was visually very similar to the KT120 built during the same period.*

Stuart Addie's T20 racer pictured at the Bob McIntyre Memorial meeting, East Fortune, 18/19 June 2005.

SUZUKI
TRAIL 80
MODEL K15

For new adventures off the beaten path

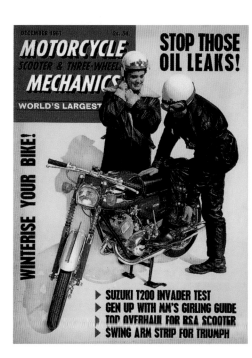

Front cover of the December 1967 Motorcycle Mechanics *magazine, showing the T200 Invader that was tested in the same issue.*

OPPOSITE PAGE: *The first Suzuki over-the-counter customer motocrossers were the TM models (1973 125, 250 and 400 shown here). Suzuki pushed the 'straight-out-of-the-crate' theme in its sales blurb. Unfortunately, performance failed to match up to the hype.*

A GT750J dating from 1972 (first year of production). The liquid-cooled triple came with drum brake front and rear. Later models sported hydraulically operated discs up front.

1974 TS125L trail bike underslung exhaust; note the black-finished protection guard for both engine crankcases and exhaust.

The GT380 triple with Ram Air System was a popular model during the mid-1970s. This is a 1974 'L'.

Much was expected from Suzuki's revolutionary RE5 Wankel-engined Rotary. The engine layout was a complex one, as can be seen on this 1974 model.

For 1975 the GT750 (coded 'M') gained increased ground clearance for the silencers, porting modifications, more power and revised gearing.

A 1976 GT550A. Like the smaller 380 version, the 550 triple was air-cooled and came with the controversial Ram Air cooling.

SUZUKI
GS750
BREATHTAKING PERFORMANCE
SUPERB RELIABILITY

DOHC 4 FOUR STROKE

Launched for the 1977 model year (together with the GS400 twin), the GS750 was Suzuki's first modern four-stroke design.

In spring 1978, Suzuki introduced the GT250X7, which, with its new reed-valve engine, electronic ignition, and much more, moved the company back to number one in the two-fifty performance stakes.

The new 'Ton-up' Suzuki GT 250 X
A 250 has never looked so good

The latest Suzuki 250 doesn't exactly hang about. It's top speed is around 100mph.
But speed is only half the story.
Like superb handling. (Back at the factory, Suzuki engineers have got weight distribution down to a fine art).
What else?
An all-new "Power Reed" engine.
Pointless ignition.

Spot-on braking with beefy discs up front.
6-speed gearbox.
Lightweight frame.
Totally new styling.
See the quickest-ever 250 at your Suzuki Dealer. And get away from the pack.
Yes, you can believe your eyes.
The getaway bike has never looked so good.
Or performed so well.

Superbly balanced frame.
Lightweight yet very strong

Alloy wheels

Pointless ignition
for faultless performance

6-speed gearbox

All-new "Power Reed" 2-stroke twin

TEXACO HERON TEAM SUZUKI
HERON SUZUKI

the getaway bike

GSX750E

For 1980 the Suzuki four-stroke twins and fours went from GS (2-valves) to GSX (4-valves). The GSX 1100 and 750 (750 shown here) offered class-leading performance.

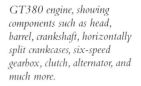

GT380 engine, showing components such as head, barrel, crankshaft, horizontally split crankcases, six-speed gearbox, clutch, alternator, and much more.

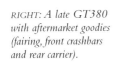

RIGHT: *A late GT380 with aftermarket goodies (fairing, front crashbars and rear carrier).*

assembly used on the two-fifty twin. While the 180mm 2LS drum was quite suitable for the smaller machine, on the 380 it proved to be a really weak point. It was to last only for the J series, being replaced by a disc thereafter.

The front and rear suspension were quite soft, but most testers (and, more importantly, owners) found that it provided a very comfortable ride, at the same time giving good, safe roadholding. It was not perhaps in the road

racer class, but it was still good. Perhaps the only complaint (particularly with a passenger) was that the centre stand tended to ground too easily, certainly on bumpy bends. The rear shocks had five-position adjustment, whilst the front forks benefited from rubber gaiters to protect the stanchions (and therefore the seals).

Most also agreed that a six-speed gearbox was not really necessary and that top was more like an overdrive. According to *Motorcycle*

Mechanics, in their June 1972 issue, 'buzzing in fifth gear proved more economical on fuel than an overloaded sixth. Something to remember on those long motorway hauls where headwinds and long inclines make themselves felt on a heavily laden machine.'

Detailed Refinements

The *MCM* test of June 1972 also pointed out that 'the Suzuki GT380, like the majority of third-generation Japanese machines, abounds with detailed refinements'. For example, Suzuki had found that many of its warranty claims came from fuel troubles, which could be blamed upon 'all manner of things finding their way into the tank', to rectify this, they had fitted a neat, lockable fuel cap, operated by the ignition key.

The ignition switch had on/off and park positions and was placed between the speedometer and tachometer. Lights were controlled entirely from the nearside (left) handlebar with a dual control switch for on/off, dip/side and main beams. The indicator button was below these two switches and the horn button below the trafficator switch. As with other Suzuki switches of the period, the buttons were deemed 'difficult to operate' when wearing normal riding gloves.

Test Report

Charles Deane reported on his test of a GT380J in the May 1972 *Motorcycle Mechanics*:

> It's turbine-like smooth with incredible flexibility. It has a wide, useful power band that not only offers very good about-town riding but has sufficient steam to maintain an 80mph (129km/h) cruising speed if required... The beauty of the GT380 is that it's not too GT to be scary in nervous hands and not too 380 to make a fool who want a 500. A top speed of just over 100mph (161km/h) is enough for most and the thought that one can trickle along at just over 30mph (48km/h) in top should satisfy the rest.

The UK price at the launch of the GT380J in spring 1972 was £499.95, including tax. As for colours, it was offered in either Candy Red or Candy Turquoise. The colour was applied to the fuel tank, side panels, headlamp shell and headlamp brackets.

Suzuki specialists Apple Motorcycles built this very special GT380, the 482cc engine size obtained using 315cc twin-cylinder pistons; it was used in the 500cc class of the Avon Tyres production racing series.

This view shows not only the finning for the head and barrel of the 550, but also the crankcases.

BELOW: Carburettor operating linkages on the GT550.

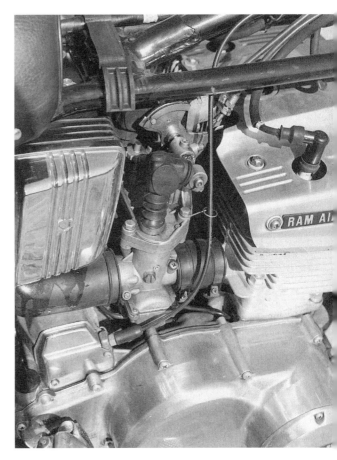

The GT550

Engine Development

In concept at least, the GT550J that followed shortly after the arrival of the 380 was developed from the GT750. However, whereas the Suzuki engineers merely grafted another cylinder, con-rod and piston on to their existing two–fifty and created the smaller triple, things were not quite as simple with the 550. Using the 316cc T350 Rebel as a basis would have meant a triple of 474cc, if they had followed the same formula as with the GT380, but that would have produced a bike that competed directly with their existing T500 model – at a much higher price.

By utilizing the same 61mm bore (and there-fore the same piston as the T350), but increasing the stroke from 54mm to 62mm, the Suzuki design team managed to increase the displacement to 544cc. This way, they avoided too much additional cost, to say nothing of increased development time, as they did not have to construct a completely new set of internals.

The result was an excellent engine, running on a relatively low compression (6.8:1), but providing wide torque, free revving and a considerable increase in maximum power (50bhp at 6,500rpm) over the GT380.

Testing

Motor Cycle published a report in its issue of 23 August 1972:

> In some respects looking superficially like a mixture of the others [the 750 and 380], the GT550 combines their best attributes. It has the untiring high-speed capability of the seven-fifty, the highly efficient Ram Air cooling of the three-eighty, and low fuel consumption in relation to engine size of both… The GT550 gobbles up the miles well. The torque range is usefully wide, with ample urge from as low as about 3,500rpm; the engine is tractable enough for traffic crawling, and the bike feels nimble when being ridden very slowly… The electric starter motor, mounted beneath the gearbox, invariably got the engine firing, hot or cold, almost at once. So did the kickstarter.

Performance wise, *Motor Cycle* electronically achieved a mean maximum speed of 107mph (172km/h) and a fastest one-way (albeit with a strong tail wind) of 112mph (180km/h). These figures were some 10mph (16km/h) up on the 380 and virtually the equal of the 750!

Differences Between the 550 and 380

Besides the addition of push-button starting and a five- instead of six-speed gearbox, there were a number of other notable differences between the 550 and 380.

Probably the most important of all was the front brake – essentially a 200mm double side 2LS (making it a four leading shoe device in total) lifted straight off the GT750 – along with the rear brake, wheel and tyre sizes (3.25 × 19 front and 4.00 × 18 rear). Since it had a dry weight of some 60lb (27kg) less than the seven-fifty, this meant that of the three triples the original 550J had by far the better stopping abilities of that year's models. In the opinion of the *Motor Cycle* tester, 'both brakes were sensitive, grab-free and showed no signs of fade when repeated crash stops were made'. From personal experience, I would rate the 1972

GT550J's brakes as about the best drums I have ever found on a production roadster and in many ways the equal of any disc of the era… and considerably better in the wet.

Technically, the construction of the 550 followed that of the 380, as did the alternator. However, the ignition cam drive was different, as was the drive to the tachometer and oil pump; even the clutch-release mechanism was not the same between the 380 and 550. Also there were larger 28mm carbs.

The 550 had the following overall gear ratios: 15.2, 9.35, 7.35, 6.05 and 5.17.

As there were only five speeds in the gearbox, there were only three selectors (four on the 380). Whereas the 380 had a primary kickstarter (being able to be started in gear), on the 550 the kickstart gear meshed with first, so the 'box had to be in neutral prior to the kickstarter being operated.

The chassis of the 550 was very similar to that of the 380, but not exactly the same. Although the two bikes looked similar, both lengths and wheelbases were different. In addition, both had 19in front and 18in rear tyres, but those on the 380 were smaller-section.

All three bikes – the 550, the 380 and the 750 – shared the same rear drum brake, but with different rear sprockets.

In the USA, the 380 was known as the 'Sebring', while the 550 was the 'Indy'. In the UK, the bikes were referred to simply as GT380 or 550, plus the year code letter.

Various Developments

For the 1973 model year (K series) all three triples were given disc front brakes – single on the 380/550 and twin on the 750. In all cases the disc diameter was 295mm and the hydraulic operation was applied via twin piston calipers. The discs were fine in the dry (*see* Chapter 9), but could be found wanting in the wet. Suzuki even applied a fork sticker that read, 'Caution – braking performance at beginning of the

1976 GT380A/GT550A Specifications
(550 in brackets where different)

Engine	Air-cooled across-the-frame two-stroke triple, with piston-port induction, one-piece alloy head, one-piece alloy barrel, six main bearings, roller bearing small-and big-ends, horizontally split aluminium crankcase, Ram Air cooling
Bore	54mm (61mm)
Stroke	54mm (62mm)
Displacement	371cc (544cc)
Compression ratio	7:1 (6.8:1)
Lubrication	Pump
Ignition	Battery/coil with triple contact breakers; 12-volt
Carburettor	3 × Mikuni 24mm (28mm)
Primary drive	Gears, 24/68 (33/74)
Final drive	Chain, 14/41 (15/36)
Gearbox	Six-speed, foot-change (five-speed)
Frame	Duplex, full cradle, steel tubular
Front suspension	Telescopic forks with exposed stanchions
Rear suspension	Swinging-arm, with five-position adjustable shock absorber
Front brake	275mm hydraulically operated disc (295mm)
Rear brake	180mm full-width drum, SLS
Tyres	Front 3.00 × 19; rear 3.50 × 18 (front 3.25 × 19; rear 4.00 × 18)

General specifications

Wheelbase	GT380 54.3in (1,379mm); GT550 55.3in (1,404mm)
Ground clearance	GT380 6.1in (154mm); GT550 5.9 in (150mm)
Seat height	31in (787mm)
Fuel tank capacity	3.3gal (15ltr)
Dry weight	GT380 377lb (171kg); GT550 441lb (200kg)
Maximum power	37bhp @ 7,500rpm (53bhp @ 7,500rpm)
Top speed	GT380 101mph (162km/h); GT550 110mph (177km/h)

This interesting GT380-based liquid-cooled three-cylinder special was seen at the 1974 Isle of Man TT. Built by Terry Hart of Barton Engineering, the cylinder block was replaced by a water-cooled one with larger cylinder bores, 61mm instead of 54mm; the engine displaced 472cc. The man in the car is Rex White, Heron Suzuki's race team manager.

application may change with wet brake disc.' It was hardly a vote of confidence in its own product!

For the L series (1974) the carburettors were changed to the CV (Constant Velocity) type; while from the M series (1975) the 550 was fitted with new cylinder barrels with chrome-plate bores; claimed power output rose to 53bhp at the higher 7,500rpm figure. In the same year the front forks lost their protective gaiters.

The 1976 model year ushered in the A series; the 380 now cost £649, the 550 £889 (both including VAT).

In 1977 Suzuki introduced the B series, which was to be the last for the 550 (and the GT750), as Suzuki was about to enter the fray with its brand-new range of GS four-strokes (*see* Chapter 12). As 1978 dawned, the GT380 was the final remaining triple. It continued, in unaltered form, until the end of 1979, by then very much a bargain-basement offering, with a low price tag.

Like the Kawasaki triples, the Suzuki three-cylinder two-strokes had been pensioned off due to a combination of rising fuel costs and ever-tighter emission controls, notably in North America. It has to be said that the Suzukis represented a much more civilized, owner-friendly breed than the rip-snorting, fire-breathing 'Big K' offerings. Certainly, as far as that magic word 'torque' goes, the GT380 and 550 (and of course the GT750) were at least the equal of other Japanese manufacturer's four-stroke machines. The triples were also notable for having character, each of them providing its own personal brand of riding pleasure.

ABOVE: *Barry Sheene with Suzuki GB sales director Maurice Knight, and new GT550K, circa 1973.*

RIGHT: *A 1974 GT550L out on the road. Many considered the 550 the best compromise between lightweight and performance of the three Suzuki triples.*

8 Off-Road Sport

Of all the Japanese manufacturers it was Suzuki that made all the early running in the world of motocross, most notably during an entire decade of complete control in the 125cc World Championship series, between 1975 and 1984.

World Championship Success

The first-ever 125cc world series was held in 1975. Suzuki promptly took the title thanks to a combination of the most competitive bike

One of Suzuki's first motocross efforts, the two-fifty RH67, which had twin expansion chambers.

Suzuki RN71 works motocrosser. The works efforts won world titles and the technology was progressively transferred to the production machines.

and the excellent capabilities of Belgian rider Gaston Rahier. Rahier retained the crown for Suzuki in 1976 and 1977, then defected in a big-money deal to rivals Yamaha.

Suzuki continued winning without Rahier. The new champion was the Japanese national title holder Akira Watanabe, with Rahier runner-up. For 1979 Suzuki took former 250cc World Champion Harry Everts into the squad and the Belgian totally dominated the class for the next three seasons, before handing over to fellow countryman Eric Geboers, in 1982. Geboers held on to the crown in 1983, then, in a topsy-turvy 1984 season, Italian star Michele Rinaldi grabbed Suzuki's tenth consecutive title at the final Grand Prix of the year!

At that time Suzuki's success in the 250 and 500cc World Championship made it the most successful marque in the history of motocross, with no fewer than twenty-one individual world titles in just fifteen years. Suzuki was also the only factory to have won a world crown in each capacity class.

Customer Bikes

Suzuki was determined to cash in on its huge and much-publicized success on the world stage, and was engaged in a ceaseless drive to offer paying customers 'over-the-counter' production motocross racers.

It has to be said that the very early production motocrossers, coded 'TM', were not too successful. The first, the TM400 (Cyclone), arrived in 1971, followed by the TM250 (Champion) in 1972. The 250 followed the lines of the 400, and both were based on the existing TS400 and TS250 trail bikes. The TM125 (Challenger) followed for 1973, using a new engine, but retaining some of the 400's features. The TM125 displaced 123cc (56 × 50mm) and, running on a compression ratio of 7.5:1, produced 20bhp (or 18bhp with a silencer). Gearbox, as on the other TM models, was Suzuki's usual five-speed, all-indirect,

Roger de Coster taking part in the 1972 500cc World Championship.

cross-over drive type, with the output sprocket on the nearside (left). On the offside (right) was an additional pair of cogs, which meshed with the kickstart and oil pump shaft at the rear and were coupled to the clutch drum at the front, to provide primary starting (in gear if required) and to keep the pump turning all the while the engine was running.

In the same year, 1973, Suzuki also introduced a 75cc model, and a 100cc version followed for 1974.

Even though Suzuki was starting to gain some results at international level, the TM series was soon seen for what it was: essentially tarted-up and tuned TS trail bikes, minus lighting equipment. Something better was needed.

RM Series

The something that was needed was the RM series, the first of which, the 'A' range, arrived for the 1976 model year.

A typical example of the new breed, the RM100, was extensively tested by the American *Cycle World* for its April 1976 issue. Essentially, it was a scaled-down version of the new RM125. *Cycle World* was right to point out that, in catering for the 100 class, 'in the late '60s the people at Hodaka made a fortune', as had Harley-Davidson with its Baja model (produced at the Aermacchi plant in Italy). However, the category was now back in Japanese hands and, according to *Cycle World*, 'the current bikes to beat were Suzuki's RM100 and Yamaha's 100cc Monoshock'.

In converting the 125 to a 100, the biggest problem was the 125's 35.5in (900mm) seat height, which was reduced by 3in (76mm). There were new fork yokes to adapt the 1³⁄₁₆in (30mm) diameter TM100 forks, and shorter gas/oil rear shocks. The TM forks were not known for their damping qualities, so Suzuki engineers spent some time modifying the internals. Damper rod diameter was increased so that compression damping could be softened up. Together with other changes, this modification helped to make the fork much more suitable for the task at hand. Together with the rear shocks, suspension was the 1976 RM100's weakest point – but the set-up was still a massive improvement over what had gone before.

Suzuki's engineering team avoided simply updating the existing TM100 powerplant.

Instead they took the crankshaft, connecting-rod, transmission and clutch from the new RM125 and installed them in what were essentially TM100 crankcases.

To this bottom end they added an all-new cylinder barrel with six transfer ports (compared with the four of the TM). There was a good reason for this: the increase in transfer ports was to keep the engine's cylinder full of fuel without having to resort to radical inlet or exhaust timing, providing an excellent compromise between outright power and good torque.

The new barrel was accompanied by a redesigned head, a 28mm Mikuni VM carburettor, and a new exhaust system. Suzuki claimed these changes gave a maximum output of 17bhp at 10,000rpm. The very first RM100s had helical-cut primary gears, but straight-cut components were specified thereafter.

In an attempt to keep the final-drive chain on its sprockets (a problem on the TM series), Suzuki provided the RM100 with two chain guides. One was located just ahead of the rear sprocket, the other just rearward of the gear-

Centre of attention in the paddock.

box sprocket. They featured small rubber runners to prevent the chain from rubbing against the swinging arm.

The drum brakes – a full-width hub at the front and a conical rear – were adjudged by *Cycle World* to be 'excellent'. This could not be said of the outgoing TM's stoppers, in particular the rear assembly, which had caused real problems. Although the old hub did not break up entirely, a bushing in the hub wore out very quickly. No such bushing existed on the new RM.

Another major redesign on the RM100 concerned the airbox. *Cycle World* described the new set-up:

> Access is afforded by the removal of the seat (two 10mm bolts). A single wing nut removes the foam element. The airbox itself is steel and is designed to draw air in from under the seat. When you realize what this system replaces, you can fully appreciate it. Ineffectual best describes the TM's unit. Getting the filter out was practically impossible and too much dirt reached the filtering element.

The remainder of the bike was taken directly from other RM machines. The aluminium fuel tank was from the 125. The mudguards and the seat were common to all 1976 RMs, from the 370 downwards. The same applied to components such as control levers and the like.

Overall, *Cycle World* praised the RM100 as 'a fast, light bike. We liked the ease of control. It steers well, yet still has the ability to slide turns. We found the suspension to be a good compromise between wheel travel and the overall height of the machine. But perhaps most importantly, the RM100 is competitive.' That was certainly something that could not have been said of its predecessor. The Suzuki RM series was now a bike for novice and expert alike.

RM125A

The RM125A represented an equally giant leap from the TM, with its all-new engine, which included a power reed-valve (open port

to cylinder, reed to crankcase), six transfer ports (as on the 100) and larger 32mm carburettor. The frame was also new and constructed from chrome-moly tubing (as on the works models). Also there were now six speeds as opposed to five on the TM. The front forks were also new, with no less than 7.8in (198mm) of travel; those of the smaller RM had been modified TM components. The laid-down forward-mounted gas/oil rear shocks had three load settings and 8.4in (213mm) of travel.

Suzuki had just won their first-ever 125cc world motocross title the previous season, so the company's customers were benefiting by being able to buy a truly competitive production model, developed in the heat of battle at the highest level.

The B Series

When the RM B series arrived for the 1977 season, *Cycle World* saw it as 'an upgrade of an already good thing', going on to comment that, externally, 'the sharp-eyed motocross connoisseur will immediately detect giveaways proclaiming the bike as a B, such as rubber fork gaiters, chain tensioner, offset axle forks with air caps, conical front hub and reservoir shocks, to name the most obvious'.

Taking the 125 as an example, it was very much a case of improvement, rather than wholesale change, although numerous major changes had taken place between the TM and RM125A, including the new crankcase-reed induction engine and new chassis. The most important development were hidden away inside the engine unit and came direct from Suzuki's factory race shop and its championship-winning machinery. For example, Gaston Rahier's RA works model had square cylinder dimensions of 54 × 54mm, and these had been transferred to the RM125B. Other changes for 1977 matched the new displacement configuration.

All ports were taller, and there were four transfers, two booster ports, a reed port and a bridged dual exhaust port. As one commentator of the day put it, it added up to 'lots of holes in a tiny cylinder'. The reed valve had been modified to close more quickly under positive pressure; Suzuki claimed that this prevented blowback during induction.

The revised engine employed a new, lighter piston with a 14mm gudgeon pin instead of the 16mm component of the A model. Coupled with larger, stronger crankshaft flywheels, this helped to reduce the engine's vibration level significantly.

The B forks looked quite different from those on previous versions. Like the GP bikes, the production models now carried a set of spring-air combination forks, which, together with the forward-mounted axle and equally new Kayaba remote reservoir rear shocks, were not only more efficient but also had the disadvantage of increasing seat height – to a whopping 36in (914.4mm).

Cycle World had some advice for its reader:

If you're interested in buying an RM125B for casual play riding or fooling-around racing, don't bother. This is as serious a race machine as one can come up with and when it's doing anything but a full-on charge around a motocross track, it's out of its environment and going to waste. This is the big difference between the A and B versions. The A can be ridden casually and used for a hot play bike. The B is so pippy and raceworthy that it just doesn't work for anything but business.

The C Series

The B series was as near a full GP racer as makes no difference, and this presented the problem that only a top rider could get the best out of it. This caveat applied equally to the 125 and the 250. Only bigger or smaller RM models (100 and 370) could be handled by riders of lesser ability in the 1977 season.

In 1978, Suzuki launched the new C series. The engineers had not been resting on their laurels; the new 125 and 250 machines benefited not only from a broader spread of power,

but suspension changes also made them much easier to ride than the outgoing B bikes. This applied particularly to the two-fifty, which for the first time used the air fork that had already proved its value on the 125.

1978 RM 250C Specification

Engine	Air-cooled single with crankcase reed-valve induction, bridged exhaust port, six transfer ports, alloy head barrel, the latter with iron sleeve, vertically split crankcases, magnesium side covers
Bore	67mm
Stroke	70mm
Displacement	246cc
Compression ratio	7.8:1
Lubrication	Petroil; mix 20:1
Ignition	Electronic
Carburettor	Mikuni VM 36mm
Primary drive	Gears 22/60
Final drive	Chain 13/50
Gearbox	Five-speed
Frame	Chrome-steel moly tubing, single front downtube
Front suspension	Leading axle telescopic forks, air-charged, oil-damped
Rear suspension	Swinging-arm, twin shock absorbers
Front brake	Conical drum
Rear brake	Full-width drum
Tyres	Front 3.00 × 21; rear 4.50 × 18

General specifications

Wheelbase	57in (1,447.8mm)
Ground clearance	12in (305mm)
Seat height	35.25in (895.4mm)
Fuel tank capacity	1.8gal (8ltr)
Dry weight	205lb (93kg)
Maximum power	32.2bhp @ 7,500rpm
Top speed	80mph (129km/h)

The RM250C displaced 246cc (67 × 70mm), the same as that used on the earlier RM, and also the TM, TS and TL singles. However, like the RM125 motocrosser, it was equipped with crankcase reed induction. Other features included a five-speed gearbox, electronic ignition, a 36mm Mikuni VM carb, and an exhaust expansion chamber which passed through the frame. Maximum power was quoted at 32.2bhp at 7,500rpm.

With the C series, Suzuki really come of age, and during 1979 and 1980 far fewer radical changes were made to the RM line-up. However, with the 1981 model year ('X' series), Suzuki, in common with the rest of the Japanese manufacturers, began a switchover from air- to water-cooling and twin shock to monoshock rear suspension. The full story is outside the scope of this book, but the first engine to switch from air to water was the RM125 – a replica of Suzuki's 1980 World championship winner.

The PE Series

The PE range of enduro machines was developed from the RM motocrossers, and incorporated many race-proven components.

As an example, the PE250 used the basic RM250 engine with its crankcase reed-induction system. Other motocross items included chrome-moly steel frame, box-type swinging arm, laid-down gas/oil shocks and leading axle forks, while the enduro requirements included special (larger-capacity) fuel tank, speedometer with resettable trip meter, protected (chromed wire) headlamp grill, and steel sump bash guard.

There was also a PE175 (172cc, 62 × 57mm), and for the 1980 model year the wealth of experience gained was used to create the PE400.

For 1981 Suzuki created its 'X' series; by then the 175 was putting out 28bhp, the 250, 35bhp and the 400, 42bhp. All three machines still retained the air-cooling and twin-shock rear suspension. A year later Suzuki's 'Full Floater' monoshock rear suspension was adopted (again

Suzuki offered the PE in 175 (shown), 250 and 400 versions. A 1982 model is shown with 'Full Floater' monoshock rear suspension.

TRY OUR PE-250 ON THE ROCKS.

Or in mud. Or sand. Or streams. Or anywhere else that other bikes fear to tread.

Go ahead. Because this gritty enduro bike is made to take on the toughest terrain that Mother Nature makes.

If you harbor doubts, take a close look at the PE-250. As you will see, it incorporates many of Suzuki's durable RM motocross components.

For instance, power is supplied by the proven RM-250 Power Reed™ induction engine. Extensively refined, of course, for rugged enduro use.

Other hardy motocross items include a chrome-moly steel frame, box-type swing arm, laid-down gas/oil shocks and leading-axle front forks. All of which contribute to its agile handling as well as toughness.

Naturally, it packs a full complement of enduro necessities. Like a big 3-gallon tank, speedometer with resettable tripmeter, protected headlight and steel skid plate.

Add it all up and you've got an enduro bike that's as nimble as a MXer.

And as hard as a rock.

SUZUKI

Ride safely: wear a helmet, eye protection and appropriate riding apparel.

CIRCLE NO. 29 ON READER SERVICE PAGE.

American Suzuki advertisement for 1979 PE250 enduro bike, incorporating many components from the RM motocross model.

pioneered on the motorcrossers), but otherwise most of the features of the PE series remained much as before, including their air-cooled engines.

As was the case with both the motocross (RM) and trails (RL) models, PE imports for the UK were handled by a separate company, headed by Graham Beamish in Portslade, Brighton, Sussex.

The RL Series

The RL series began with the 250 model, which arrived at the beginning of 1974 (coded M). It was intended for one-day trials (unlike Suzuki's earlier efforts, which had been converted roadsters, both twins and singles, and had taken part in events such as the International Six Days during the mid-late 1960s). There is no doubt that Suzuki was influenced in its design of the RL250 by the Spanish, notably Bultaco.

1979 PE175 Specification	
Engine	Air-cooled single with reed-valve induction alloy head and barrel, the latter with a steel liner, inlet and exhaust ports bridged, plus six transfer ports, unit construction, vertically split crankcases
Bore	62mm
Stroke	57mm
Displacement	172cc
Compression ratio	7.6:1
Lubrication	Petroil
Ignition	Flywheel magneto, with CDI; no battery
Carburettor	Mikuni 32mm
Primary drive	Gear
Final drive	Chain
Gearbox	Six-speed; foot-change
Frame	Full cradle, single downtube, all-steel construction
Front suspension	Telescopic forks with exposed stanchions
Rear suspension	Swinging-arm, with twin Kayaba gas/oil shock absorbers
Front brake	130mm drum, SLS
Rear brake	150mm drum, SLS
Tyres	Front 3.00 × 21; rear 4.00 × 18

General specifications

Wheelbase	56in (1,422mm)
Ground clearance	8.5in (216mm)
Seat height	36.5in (927mm)
Fuel tank capacity	2.6gal (12ltr)
Dry weight	220lb (100kg)
Maximum power	26bhp @ 9,500rpm
Top speed	85mph (137km/h)

For a first effort it was an excellent little bike. Weighing in at 199lb (90kg) dry, the RL250M was a purposeful-looking piece of kit. Its air-cooled 246cc (70 × 64mm), five-speed engine unit featured petroil mixture and produced a claimed 18bhp at 6,000rpm. Perhaps more relevant were the maximum torque figures of 16.6lb ft at 4,500rpm.

1975 Suzuki RL250 one-day trials model, with a dry weight of 199lb (90kg).

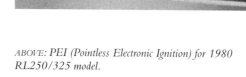

ABOVE: *PEI (Pointless Electronic Ignition) for 1980 RL250/325 model.*

LEFT: *Larger-capacity RL325 with 325cc (80 × 64mm) five-speed engine.*

With a ground clearance of 11.4in (290mm), oil-damped telescopic front forks, a neatly crafted frame, five-way adjustable twin-shock rear suspension and a well-tucked in exhaust system, the RL250 certainly looked pretty.

By the end of 1976, the RL250 had adopted the crankcase reed induction pioneered on the RM125/250 motocrossers. At the same time, the RL325 arrived, the larger engine size achieved by increasing the cylinder bore size to 80mm; the stroke remained unchanged at

64mm. Running on a compression ratio of 7.5:1 (the 250 being 6.7:1) the '325' put out 24bhp at 6,500rpm.

Generally, the RL325 was simply a larger-bore RL250. Again, it was something Suzuki had copied from the Spanish. At 201lb (91.3kg), the newcomer was only slightly heavier than the original, but it offered a considerable improvement in its power-to-weight ratio.

Later still, with a combination of British craftsmanship and Japanese technology, the two RL models were further improved. The centre of this Anglo-Japanese effort was the well-known Whitlock frame, manufactured from lightweight Reynolds 531 aircraft tubing, bronze-welded and finished in hard chrome.

The 250's engine output also increased, to 19bhp, from the 1980 model year.

1981 RL325 (and RL250), which used the British Whitlock frame, manufactured from lightweight Reynolds 531 tubing, bronze-welded and finished in hard chrome.

1970 Alta TC120 Trials Specification

Engine	Air-cooled single, with piston-port induction, alloy head and barrel, caged needle-roller small- and big-ends; vertically split aluminium crankcases	Frame	Spine type with twin downtube; auxiliary bracing, material T45, 16-gauge tubing
Bore	52mm	Front suspension	REH hydraulically damped telescopic fork
Stroke	56mm	Rear suspension	Swinging-arm, with twin Girling three-way shock absorbers, silentbloc swinging-arm bushes
Displacement	118mm		
Compression ratio	11:1	Front brake	4.5in (114mm) SLS
Lubrication	Pump (oil carried in frame-top tube)	Rear brake	4.5in (114mm) SLS
		Tyres	Front 2.75 × 21; rear 4.00 × 18
Ignition	Flywheel magneto		
Carburettor	Mikuni 22mm	*General specifications*	
Primary drive	Gear		
Final drive	Chain	Wheelbase	50in (1,270mm)
Gearbox	Six-speed. Only three ratios in operation at same time; high and low changed by lever on crankcase	Ground clearance	12in (304mm)
		Seat height	28in (711mm)
		Fuel tank capacity	1gal (4.5ltr)
		Dry weight	142lb (64kg)
		Maximum power	12.3bhp @ 7,000rpm
		Top speed	Depending upon gearing

1979 RL325/RL250 Specifications
(RL250 where different in brackets)

Engine	Air-cooled single, with crankcase reed-valve induction alloy head and barrel, the latter with steel liner, vertically split aluminium crankcases	Front suspension	Telescopic air-oil-damped
		Rear suspension	Swinging-arm, twin oil-damped shock absorbers
Bore	80mm (70mm)	Front brake	5in (127mm)
Stroke	64mm	Rear brake	5in (127mm)
Displacement	322cc (246cc)	Tyres	Front 2.75 × 21; rear 4.00 × 18
Compression ratio	7.5:1		
Lubrication	Petroil mixture; 20:1 ratio	*General specifications*	
Ignition	PEI	Wheelbase	52in (1,320.8mm)
Carburettor	Mikuni 28mm	Ground clearance	13in (330.2mm)
Primary drive	Gear 17/72 (22/58)	Seat height	30.5in (774.2mm)
Final drive	Chain 15/54 (12/39)	Fuel tank capacity	1gal (4.5ltr)
Gearbox	Five-speed, foot change	Dry weight	RL325 201lb (91kg); RL250 194lb (88kg)
Frame	Reynolds 531 tubing, chromed and highly polished, with built-in rockguards, chain oiler and spring-loaded footrests	Maximum power	RL325 24bhp @ 6,500rpm; RL250 19bhp @ 6,000rpm
		Top speed	RL325 72mph (116km/h); RL250 68mph (109km/h)

NOTE: Early RL250 had piston-port induction

1970 Welsh-built Alta trials bike used Suzuki's TC120 engine unit and two-stage (six-speed) gearbox.

In all three disciplines of off-road motorcycle sport – motocross, enduro and trials – Suzuki more than often led the field. It was something of which the company could be justifiably proud, and from which customers benefited, being able to purchase bikes developed in competition by works participation in their respective sport.

112

9   GT750

The first production GT750 (1972 J series shown here) used a massive double-sided 2LS (making 4LS in total) drum front brake. If set up properly – and with the right linings – it was excellent, but it still came in for serious criticism.

Although Honda is generally credited with producing the first 'big bike' among the Japanese manufacturers with its 444cc CB450 dohc twin in 1966, it could be argued that this title should go to Suzuki with its T500 Cobra (*see* Chapter 6); the Honda lacked the physical size that was to prove an essential ingredient in marketing motorcycles to a new breed of customer in the export markets of the West, notably the USA. (Incidentally, Kawasaki's 650SS Commander, although big in size, suffered for different reasons – being too closely associated with its BSA origins.) The Suzuki effort, with its torquey twin-cylinder engine, a five-gear gearbox (the Honda only had four speeds), and a mixture of bright metal flake paintwork and abundance of chrome plate and polished alloy had been a big hit in the all-important US market.

The New GT750

In 1969 Honda launched its mould-breaking CB750 four-cylinder; the first of the modern superbikes. After the appearance of the Kawasaki Mach III, rumours began to surface of a counter-attack by both Suzuki and Yamaha via seven-fifty two-stroke multis. At the seventeenth Tokyo Show, held in November 1970, Suzuki was at last to prove that these rumours were founded on fact – its GT750 liquid-cooled three-cylinder machine was the star of the show. (Sadly, Yamaha's contender, the four-cylinder GL750, was never to enter production.)

Following the Tokyo Show, Suzuki organized a world tour, taking in both the USA and Europe, for its potential range leader, the show-bike prototype. In Europe, it made its first appearance in Germany before being flown into Britain on Christmas Day 1970, in readiness for a starring role at the London Olympia Show early in the New Year. Don Leeson recalled the event in *Motorcycle Enthusiast* in July 1986: 'Evidence of a hard life during its short existence was plain, with a dented tank clearly visible. The burning-out of the electric motor meant to drive the display turntable didn't help much either!'

Back in Japan, ever conscious of their reputation for reliability and sound engineering, the Suzuki engineering team undertook a rigorous development programme for the new range leader. However, it was not until early 1972 that the first supplies arrived in the UK. The launch price of £766.50 made it more costly than its rivals: the air-cooled Kawasaki H2 triple was £758, the Honda CB750 £761 and the British Triumph Trident £665. Like the Trident, the Suzuki GT750 was, in simple terms, 1½ of the relevant marque's 500cc twin; sharing as it did the T500's 70 × 64mm bore and stroke dimensions, to give a displacement of 738cc. Porting know-how from the T500/ TS250 trail bike helped explain the high torque and low-revving nature of the early versions.

Reducing Engine Width

To reduce engine width the Suzuki design team twisted the transfer port axis by around 60 degrees from the line of the crankshaft, as with the T500. Even so, with the 280-watt alternator mounted on the offside (right) and triple contact breakers on the nearside (left) end of the crankshaft, overall engine width was 19.7in (500mm). The points cam, although co-axial with the crankshaft, was mounted outboard of the starter clutch assembly. Driving the cam via a pin and groove arrangement, rubber buffers prevented vibrations reaching the unit. Don Leeson felt that this might well provide 'a side benefit... to save the crank being damaged if the machine was thrown down the road!'

Liquid-Cooling

The GT750 was Suzuki's first series production roadster engine to feature liquid-cooling.

This was a key feature of the machine, so its employment merits a detailed explanation.

The chief advantages included extra mechanical silence, a result of closer piston clearances being permitted by the maintenance of more even temperatures, the muffling effect of the water-jacketing, and a more consistent power output. As for drawbacks, these were additional complication and weight, and potential styling problems. It was not simply a case of finding a place to put the component parts for the cooling system, but also of overcoming the motorcyclists' legendary resistance to change. Impressively, on this last point Suzuki largely managed to achieve its goal.

At first sight, the fuel tank appeared to be a large 5gal (23ltr) one, but it actually 'only' held 3.75gal (17ltr); at its front, it accommodated the cooling header tank, which was cleverly hidden and accessible via a hinged flap. The cooling system, which had a capacity of some 1gal (4.5ltr), was operated by a vane-type pump housed in the crankcase. A thermostat maintained only a small quantity of water in

The 739cc (70 × 64mm) GT750 unit. To reduce engine width the transfer port axis was twisted by some 60 degrees from the line of the crankshaft. Even so, overall width was still 19.7in (500mm).

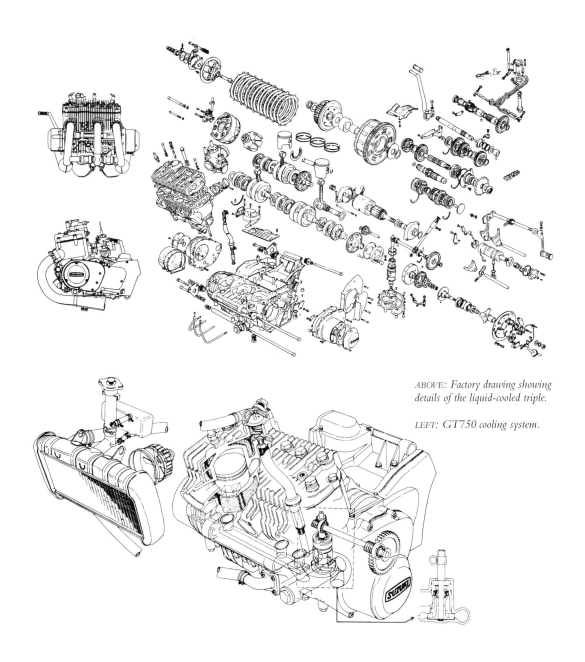

circulation until a temperature of 80°C was achieved. A small fan behind the radiator, which was barely visible and never heard, chimed in when the water's temperature rose to 105°C. My own experience with the GT750, albeit only in Great Britain, reveals that the temperature needle rarely got to within terms of the mid-way mark on the dial (86°C), and certainly never approached the 105°C mark.

Cylinder Block

Cast-iron liners were fitted into a one-piece alloy cylinder block, with two-ring pistons. The cylinder head was also a single casting, again in aluminium, while there were five main bearings. With its horizontally split crankcases, much of the balance was very Suzuki-like.

A couple of features require explanation. At around the time of the launch of the GT750, there was a bit of a Japanese craze for giving initials to any new marketing ploy; the buzz words associated with the GT750 were 'ECTS' and 'SRIS'.

ECTS represented 'Exhaust Coupler Tube System', which, Suzuki claimed, boosted low-down torque, while providing a quicker, deeper exhaust note. Three exhaust pipes were joined by short cross-tubes running at right-angles to them, just in front of the silencers. As Don Lee son commented, 'The resultant four joints were the source of much annoyance to many owners over the years.'

SRIS stood for 'Suzuki Recycle Injection System', which was intended to give a cleaner exhaust and minimize oil consumption. Oil accumulating in the crankcase bottom was forced into the scavenging port of an adjacent cylinder by pressure differences induced as part of the two-stroke cycle. The exact routing of the small bore pipes and mounting of the check valves changed from engine number 31252. However, the principle of using one cylinder to burn off another's excess oil remained unchanged.

A Comfortable Tourer

The original concept of the GT750 was very much that of a deluxe tourer, rather than a racer replica sports bike. This is not to say it was slow, but at 472lb (214kg) – rising to 507lb (230kg) from the K model – it was no lightweight. However, the GT750 was an impressive motorcycle. For a start the engine was ultra-smooth, such that *Motorcycle Sport* was able to comment in its June 1972 issue that 'a BMW seems in comparison like a Leyland diesel'. It was also, for a two-stroke, surprisingly economical, with 50 mpg (5.6ltr/100km) easily obtainable; a cautious right hand could achieve over 60mpg (4.7ltr/100km)! Reliability also proved truly

excellent, making the bike at least the equal of (if not better than) similar Japanese four-strokes.

Thanks to its water-cooling, it was also extremely quiet (mechanically and exhaust-wise), comfortable (solo or two up), and offered reasonable handling and roadholding (at least with decent tyres). Steering could be described as involving some effort when thrusting into tight corners, while the acceleration was strong without being of the neck-jerking variety, thanks to the near-linear torque curve provided by the power delivery. Official figures gave 55.7lb/ft (7.7kg/m) at 5,500rpm. The lights were also rated as 'good' (*Motorcycle Sport*), and my own experiences with the A and B variants of the model confirm this.

As for the cycle parts, these were pretty conventional, with a duplex cradle welded steel

GT750J engine; note the plain cylinders.

frame, swinging-arm twin-shock (five-way adjustable) rear suspension, oil-damped telescopic front forks, a dashboard with speedometer (including a trip), tachometer and centrally positioned, smaller-diameter water-temperature gauge. Centre and side stands, direction indicators, chrome-plated mudguards, an electric start (with a 500-watt motor), and a rear grab rail, together with high and wide handlebars, were all features that buyers had come to expect from the new crop of Japanese superbikes.

The five gears were all indirect, with the following ratios: 14.92, 9.09, 7.14, 5.89 and 4.48:1, equating to around 4,500rpm in top at 70mph (113km/h) on the standard gearing of 15/47 (final) and 49/82 (primary). It should be noted, however, that, although the latter figure did not change through production, the final-drive gearing was the subject of some modification. From the 1974 model year, it was revised to 16/43, and from 1976 onwards (beginning engine number 74191) it became 15/40.

Drum Unit – Good or Bad?

The *Motorcycle Sport* test published in June 1972 considered the 750 Suzuki to be 'at least 95 per cent right', but had to stop short of giving praise in one particular area:

> Well, yes, the brakes weren't so hot. The front, two 500 units back to back, giving four leading shoes and about 80sq in of swept braking area, was, quite simply, short of power; and the rear, a single drum unit, was so spongy in operation that one had almost to dislocate one's right ankle to get much effect.

Don Leeson shed some light on the drum front brake in *Motorcycle Enthusiast*, accepting that it generated criticism for 'fade and lack of power'. However, he went on to reveal that 'time spent in adjustment of the various linkages was repaid by an excellent stopper, which when fitted with Ferodo AM4s was more than capable of halting the machine from any speed'. Suzuki were stung by the comments of the

The GT750J's double-sided drum front stopper.

critics and in September 1974 a disc-brake update kit was made available for the J machines, at a UK cost of £89.50. This contained all the component parts necessary to convert the GT750J to the twin-disc set-up that had been introduced the previous year on the 1973 K model.

Wheel Removal

Another potential problem concerned the difficulties experienced by any owner who wished to remove the rear wheel. This was not only because of the exhaust system, but also because the GT750 was one of the very first motorcycles to be offered to the public fitted with an endless chain (without the conventional spring link); the bike also lacked a QD (Quickly Detachable) rear hub. With a bit of know-how, wheel removal was in fact quite easy. The swinging arm was detachable, allowing the entire wheel and sprocket assembly, complete with spindle, to be slid out. The chain could then be slipped off and on the sprocket by simply pushing the wheel forward with the adjusters swung down.

If removing the rear wheel was relatively easy, once the owner was familiar with the procedure, the same could not be said of the front. Don Leeson explained the problem in *Motorcycle Enthusiast*: 'Firstly, the bike is extremely nose-heavy when on the stand, and needs supporting under the engine. Secondly, the position of brake calipers (on models with discs), mudguard stays, etc, necessitates a major dismantling exercise before the wheel will come out.' It is worth pointing out that the stayless mudguard introduced with the final B model resolved most of these problems.

The Flexy Flier

If the power unit was the star turn of the GT750 triple, its weak point was its frame, certainly when it came to fast road work or racing. Not for nothing were the first TR750 racers (*see* Chapter 4) dubbed 'Flexy Fliers'. This weakness was so significant that a large number of special builders set to and came up with frame kits to tame the worst excesses of the original frame's bad behaviour, including Nico Bakker in Holland, Reimo in Germany and Englishman Dave Degens (under the Dresda name). The best-selling special retained the standard Suzuki frame and was in fact a very clever marketing feat; Don Leeson described the Paul Dunstall effort as 'a fibre-glass racer look-a-like kit, which added nothing apart from bulk!'

GT750J

Fitting a Sidecar

Several GT750s were to be fitted with sidecars, and the April 1973 issue of *Motorcycle Sport* published a test report of a J model hitched to a Blacknell San Remo double adult chair. Owned by Geoff Howell, the sidecar was attached at four points. At the front, spanning the downtubes as high as possible, was the traditional swan-neck

fitting. *Motorcycle Sport* pointed out that, 'to accommodate this has meant scrapping the cooling fan, as this was apparently considered superfluous even in the Nevada desert. It was felt England's chillier climate would be quite "safe". Suzuki themselves are happy enough with the idea.' The bottom front fitting was a short telescopic tube attached to the bottom nearside (left) front downtube.

At the rear, below the dual seat and just forward of the meeting place of the sub-frame tubes, came the top lean-out bar. Below this came what was described as 'the difficult one'. According to *Motorcycle Sport*, 'by shape it could also be defined as a swan neck, sweeping forward to meet the Suzuki just about where the rear pivoted fork pivots. It is held by a plate which is attached at two points. One of these is a clamp to the frame just above the pivot and the other actually utilizes the pivot spindle.'

Converting the big Suzuki for a third wheel was otherwise relatively simple:

- Japanese tyres changed for British Avons (original sizes retained);
- Girling shocks, with heavier springs;
- wider (32in) handlebars;
- Ferodo AM4 (green) brake linings;
- Renolds ⅜in rear-chain conversion;
- lower gearing (larger rear-wheel sprocket);
- finally, the stock front mudguard, which *Motorcycle Sport* described as a 'slim, useless affair', was replaced by one from a Norton Dominator.

With the lower gearing and the additional weight of the large double adult sidecar, fuel consumption dropped to an average 32mpg (8.85ltr/100km)

It is also worth mentioning that the Ferodo AM4 green linings received considerable praise. If only Suzuki had used linings like these on their models from the start, the potentially powerful double twin-leading shoe front brake would not have earned its reputation for

RIGHT: Black-finished end cones were a feature of the J and K series models.

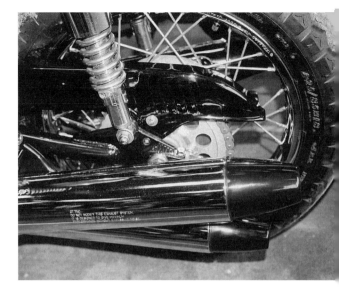

GT750J Specification

Engine	Liquid–cooled across-the-frame two–stroke triple, with piston-port induction, crankshaft supported by four ball race bearings, alloy heads and barrels, horizontally split aluminium crankcases
Bore	70mm
Stroke	64mm
Displacement	738cc
Compression ratio	6.7:1
Lubrication	Pump
Ignition	Battery/coil 12-volt; electric start, triple contact breakers, 280-watt alternator
Carburettor	3 × Mikuni VM32 32mm
Primary drive	Gears, 49/82
Final drive	Chain, 15/47
Gearbox	Five-speed, foot-change
Frame	Double cradle, tubular steel with a third bracing tube running from the top of the steering head
Front suspension	Telescopic, oil-damped, with rubber gaiters
Rear suspension	Swinging-arm, with twin oil-damped shock absorbers
Front brake	Double-sided 200mm drum, 4LS
Rear brake	180mm drum, SLS
Tyres	Front 3.25 × 19; rear 4.00 × 18

General specifications

Wheelbase	58in (1,473mm)
Ground clearance	5.2in (522mm)
Seat height	32in (812mm)
Fuel tank capacity	3.75gal (17ltr)
Dry weight	472lb (214kg)
Maximum power	67bhp @ 6,500rpm
Top speed	115mph (185km/h)

impotency. The *Motorcycle Sport* feature was complimentary: 'With Green Ferodos in, these brakes are nothing less than superb. In fact one has to take care not to take too large a handful of the front brake for the wheel would lock with a squeal without any effort. A real stopper.' Considering that the local weighbridge came up with a combined 952lb (432kg) for the GT750J and Blacknell San Remo chair (with an empty fuel tank!), the efficiency of the uprated braking cannot be disputed.

For chair work the Suzuki engine was given the 'thumbs up'. In the view of *Motorcycle Sport*, 'one of the delights of the engine is the wide power band'.

At the conclusion of the test report, there were very few criticisms of the machine, other than 'the electrical controls' and 'any form of generator light'.

More Testing

Another early GT750 test of the J version was published by *Motorcycle Mechanics* magazine in its October 1972 issue. Editor Charles Deane began by asking, 'Why water-cooled?', and went on to answer his own question:

There are several reasons; greater heat dispersion being the main one. Two-strokes always have a heat problem because they fire twice as often as a four-stroke. Excessive heat causes distortion of piston and rings, which has to be allowed for by making larger clearance between moving parts to avoid seizures. Large clearances are fine, but they make the engine noisy and aid power loss through blow-by past piston rings. A well-designed water-cooling system reduces these problems considerably.

The comments were quite valid – Suzuki claimed that the GT750 ran some 30 per cent cooler than any other series production two-stroke at that time. This enabled piston clearance to be set at 0.0019in, as against 0.0026in clearance on the air-cooled T500 (*see* Chapter 6). This, with the deadening effect of the cylinder's water jackets, contributed to the unit's impressive level of mechanical quietness.

Charles Deane was less impressed with the handling:

> The first slow bend I came to reminded me of a ride I had on a reluctant camel in the Middle East. It took two or three bends to decide who was master – this time I won… At very slow speeds, it seemed as if the head bearings were too tight, but as the knots increased, steering became light and precise.

Although he might not have been too happy with the roadholding, when it came to describing high-speed cruising, Charles Deane used words such as 'superb' and 'effortless': 'This really is a long-legged bike which loves to gobble miles. The quietness of the motor plus the large, comfortable seat helped to shorten the longest journey.'

Like *Motorcycle Sport*, *Motorcycle Mechanics* highlighted the handlebar switch gear, which, although 'impressive to view', was deemed difficult. The multi-purpose switch on the left was 'a pig to operate with a gloved hand'.

Although the speedometer and tachometer were 'well placed, vibration-free and well lit for

night riding', the oil filler 'has a small hole and you need a funnel to avoid making a mess when topping up. A minor criticism, but still a nuisance.' (The oil filler, along with the battery and tool bag, were accessed by lifting the dual seat.) Although final-drive chain stretch and tightspot (at 6,000 miles/9,650km), when handed back to Suzuki, probably contributed to a 'clonk' when selecting first gear and on subsequent upward changes, the clutch was light in operation. So, surprisingly, was the throttle twistgrip, which connected to the three Mikuni carburettors via a junction box with a single cable.

As for finish, this was adjudged by *MCM* to be 'excellent': 'The paintwork showed no deterioration and the chromium plating no rust, except on the front brake anchor arm and flashing indicator bolts.' The welding came in for comment and although it 'looked solid enough there must be a shortage of scurfing boards or files in Japan, as the welds had not been smoothed at all – just sprayed over.' However, Charles Deane considered that the 'main rust trap was the underside of the dual seat. Rust was eating away there with a vengeance and is not what you'd expect from a machine of this calibre under a year old.'

However, according to the report, 'the engine remained oil- and water-tight throughout the test. The finish of the engine castings and water jackets is absolutely first class.' However, a comment was made about 'a distinct whine' from the gearbox: 'Probably this noise would have gone unnoticed on most other bikes, but the mechanical quietness of the 750 was such that anything amiss was heard immediately.' The report came to a favourable conclusion: 'The Suzuki GT is one of the best bikes we have tested. It is extremely fast and comfortable, has impeccable road manners and really is terrific.'

GT750K and L

When the GT750K arrived for the 1973 model year, the major change in most markets,

A 1973 disc-braked GT750K factory brochure.

BELOW: *Phil Ryan of Wakefield with his immaculately restored GT750K at the Classic Motor Cycle Show, Stafford, April 2006.*

BELOW RIGHT: *From the 1974 L model, the cylinder block on the GT750 was given 'Liquid-Cooled' badges.*

including the UK, was the fitment of a twin-disc front brake to replace the somewhat controversial double-sided drum assembly. (Despite the doubts, the drum brake was retained on the K in some countries.) Other changes involved no more than minor cosmetic details, otherwise the bike remained as before. Colour choice was either Pearl Blue or Candy Gold (on the

Also from 1974, the instrument console incorporated a gear position indicator and warning lights for high beam, neutral and turn signals.

fuel tank, headlamp shell/brackets and side panels).

The L version arrived for 1974 and again it involved small changes rather than major modifications. However, the addition of CV (Constant Vacuum) carburettors was notable although power output remained unchanged.

Redefining the Model – GT750M

With the M version, the model was redefined from simply a comfortable, super-smooth tourer to a serious sports/tourer for the 1975 season. In retrospect, one of the reasons for this was related to the arrival of the RE5 Wankel (*see* Chapter 11), which was also liquid-cooled, a tourer and very heavy. With all its investment in the RE5 project to recoup, Suzuki felt that it needed to shift the GT750 to more of a sporting theme. This was provided thanks in part to the extensive racing programme undertaken by the factory with the TR750 (*see* Chapter 4).

The engineering team stripped the torque from the lower reaches of the power curve to make quite a drastic improvement higher up

the scale. The porting had been quite extensively altered, with several millimetres being carved from the timing on the exhaust port, and commensurate alterations all round. Although, on paper, there was a rise of just 3bhp to 70, this did not tell the full story. In fact, the engine felt much snappier, or crisper, than the original ultra-soft version.

The exact changes were as follows:

- raising the exhaust port by 2.5mm and dropping the inlet port by 5mm, decreasing the combustion capacity of each cylinder;
- increasing the compression ratio from 6.7:1 to 6.9:1 by thinning out the head gasket;
- changing the overall gearing from 15/47 tooth sprocket to 16/43; and
- replacing plastic resin clutch plates with aluminium components.

Motorcycle Mechanics tested one of the new M models in its October 1975 issue and in general terms the tester was impressed with the changes that had been made (which had not just been reserved for the engine):

The last time we tested a GT750 our complaint wasn't about low-speed handling, but what happened when the taps were opened. From about eighty miles an hour upwards the bike started to tie itself in knots. Our comment then was that there seemed to be a flexible coupling between the front and rear wheels… but, while handling and steering on the M series isn't perfect, at least the problems are reserved for high speed. When the bike is moving out into the three-figure bracket the front end starts to go light, and road surface imperfections can cause it to weave around, but at no time does the bike feel as though it is in charge of the rider.

Amazingly, as the *MCM* test pointed out, 'The only significant difference between the old and new models seems to be the front forks. They don't look that much different from outside but the construction is beefier and they appear to be stronger laterally.'

Slow-speed manoeuvres were described as 'outstanding' and 'for such a large, heavy machine to be able to tackle heavy traffic with such little strain, is a big bonus feature'.

The tester was also positive about the performance of the GT750M: 'Unlike the Kawasaki 750 triple, with which the GT must inevitably be compared, the Suzy spreads its power over a wide band. The more the throttle is twisted the more power there is available. The almost turbine-like performance can be deceptive and on more than one occasion I found myself going a lot faster than I realized.'

He also liked the dual front disc brake, which was described as 'superb': 'At low speeds up to 50mph, the double disc isn't any more efficient than a single disc, but from high speeds it hauls the heavy bike down to cruising speeds incredibly quickly.'

It was standard practice in those days for original-fit Japanese tyres to come in for some very stiff comment. According to *MCM*, the tyres fitted to the GT750 were no exception: 'They certainly feel as hard as plastic and give about as much grip… and both front and rear tyres wore out at an incredible rate… After riding the GT750 I am sure that there is a case for importing bikes without tyres and fitting either Michelin, Dunlop or Avon.'

By now the big Suzuki had been in service for over three years and its reliability was becoming legendary, with *MCM* commenting as follows: 'Check with any large dealer and he'll tell you that the Suzuki is one of the most reliable big bikes on the market. Everything seems to be almost over-engineered.' This is something with which I can concur – I was a Suzuki dealer during much of the 1970s, and we never had to strip a GT750 engine!

For 1975 (M model) the silencers were raised to improve ground clearance, ECTS was deleted, and porting modifications were carried out, which increased power output from 67 to 70bhp (with gearing altered to suit).

Price in late 1975 was also something of a bargain, at £969.50. The Honda CB750 was nearest, at £979, while the Triumph T160 was £1,215, the Moto Guzzi S3 £1,749, the Ducati 860GT £1,299 and Suzuki's new RE5 £1,195.

GT750A and B

For 1976 Suzuki introduced the A version. To begin with there was a larger fuel tank with a lockable flap over both fuel and water fillers. The B version, for 1977, was given a stayless front mudguard, as well as a number of other new features, including a square rear-light assembly, black headlamp shell and black side panels. The price (in 1976) had risen to £999 (including VAT).

The 1976 GT750A (top) introduced a larger tank with lockable flap (above) over fuel and water fillers.

In its April 1976 issue, *Bike* praised the technical and cosmetic changes that had been made during the four years of production of the GT750:

They have not only improved the Suzuki, but radically altered its once bland character… It's still the pleasant tourer we all knew it was anyway, but now it's also more of an all-round performance motorcycle than its weight and obese appearance would lead you to believe.

In 1977, the GT750 was taken out of production, its place on the Suzuki lines being taken by the newly released GS750 dohc four-cylinder (*see* Chapter 12).

Conclusions on the GT750

My old friend Graham Sanderson, one-time staff member for *Bike* and later *Motor Cycle*, and subsequently Honda UK's PR man, saw the liquid-cooled Suzuki like this:'Maybe trade, press and public alike expected too much and although the Suzuki was by no means a failure, it perhaps did not make the impact one might have expected.'

However, those who did buy one of the liquid-cooled triples were generally well pleased with their purchase. As Don Leeson was to recall, 'Evidence of the esteem in which the GT750 is held is clear from the range of nicknames applied and owners' clubs which have sprung up.' In the UK, the Suzuki Owners' Club lists the GT750 – commonly referred to as 'kettle' or 'hot water bottle' – as their most popular model. Stateside riders are catered for by the Le Mans Club of America, 'Le Mans' being the official US Suzuki name. In Germany, the bike

Don Leeson's immaculate 1976 GT750A, touring in Germany during the 1980s.

Jan Skelson/Paul Shaw-White GT750-powered outfit, pictured at the Third Festival of Sidecars, Mallory Park, 18 October 1998. Engine width had been decreased by removing the alternator, as per the TR750.

is called the 'Water Buffalo', and such is the enthusiasm of its supporters that they even arranged to have a real live buffalo, Hansi, as a mascot during the 1980s!

The GT750 was definitely one of Suzuki's finest, described (accurately, in my opinion) by *Motor Cycle* in August 1972 as 'The Gentleman's Superbike'.

GT750 Model Evolution

GT750J (1972) Launched with double-sided 2LS front brake, painted radiator side covers, radiator fan, bulbous side covers with 'Water-Cooled GT750' badges. Plain-sided cylinder block, slide carburettors and paper element air cleaner. Black-finished cones on ECTS mufflers, black chainguard, fork gaiters, power output 67bhp, compression ratio 6.7:1.

GT750K (1973) Dual hydraulically operated front disc brakes with metal lower brake pipes, chromed radiator side covers, chrome chainguard later in year.

GT750L (1974) Plastic grill to radiator, fan optional, slim 'square' side panels with 'GT750' badges, chrome sides to polyurethane air cleaner, CV carburettors, cylinder block with 'Liquid-Cooled' badge, silencer cones deleted. All hydraulic lines flexible hose, single-bulb tail-lamp, sealed-beam headlamp, gear indicator and combined seat helmet lock.

GT750M (1975) Silencers raised to improve ground clearance, ECTS deleted, porting modifications raising power from 67 to 70bhp (and compression ratio to 6.9:1), gearing altered to suit revised power output, bike now marketed as a 'sports/tourer'.

GT750A (1976) Larger fuel tank with lockable flap over fuel and water fillers.

GT750B (1977) Stayless front mudguard, square rear-light assembly, black headlamp unit and side panels.

NOTES:
The years given are model years, not calendar years.
The double-sided drum front brake of the J version was continued on to the K series in some markets.

10   X7 and Other Later Twins

With the T20 Super Six, Suzuki had produced an outstanding performance machine. It not only won countless sports machine races, but was also a World Speed Record holder and twice winner of the *Motor Cycle News* 'Machine of the Year' readers' poll.

However, the very ingredients which were to make it so successful – its small size and light weight – actually worked against it in one of Suzuki's most important markets – the USA. Although it was close to being ideal in Europe, and did enjoy reasonably good sales in the USA, it was generally considered too small to be, as the Americans needed 'a real man's machine'. In addition, non-mechanically-minded buyers of the T20 (or 'X6', as the Americans called it) found that it was not as robust as its forerunner, the T10, and that the gearbox in particular suffered from missed gears and a jerky clutch.

T250/T305

Suzuki's answer to the T20's problems was a complete redesign for the 1969 model year. The US Suzuki organization (now totally Japanese-owned, after a major legal wrangle with former Vice President and General Manager Jack McCormack) had provided continuing feedback to the factory. The message had come through loud and clear that the American market needed a beefier motorcycle all round, and Suzuki built not one but two new models – the T305 Raider and T250 Hustler. (The name of the latter was a bit confusing, as the T20-X6 had already been known as the Hustler in the USA.) Apart from a larger 60mm bore (the stroke remaining unchanged at 54mm), chrome-panelled fuel tank and suede-effect seat covering, the T305 was identical to the T250.

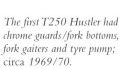

The first T250 Hustler had chrome guards/fork bottoms, fork gaiters and tyre pump; circa 1969/70.

Roy Simmonds riding the Vic Bates T250 Hustler to seventh position in the 1971 Isle of Man Production TT.

BELOW: Exploded view of the T250 engine unit; one major difference between this and the old T20 was that the oil pump was now mounted on top of the crankcase, rather than the side.

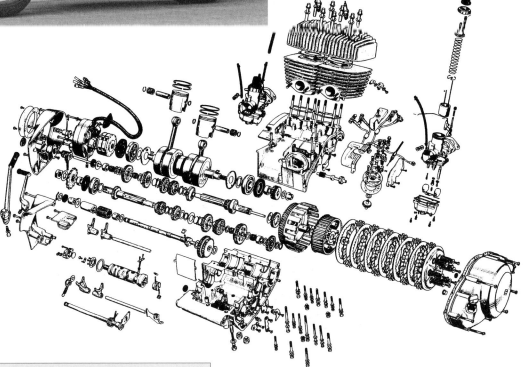

T20 or T250?

As described in Chapter 3, the 'T250' prefix had already been used in Japan on the later T20 series, so should not be confused with the mainstream T250. The instantly recognizable feature of the T250 distinguishing it from the T20 was the positioning of the oil pump. On the T250 this was mounted on top of the crankcase, whereas on the T20 it was to be found on the side of the engine, behind the clutch.

Following AMC's financial collapse, there were problems in deciding who would handle UK imports, and British enthusiasts did not see the T250 until late in 1969, and they did not see the T305 at all.

The basic GT250 introduced for the 1969 season employed essentially the same motor until being face-lifted to power the GT250L in 1973. To explain this further, following on from the initial T250 of 1969 came the T250-II (1970), T250R (1971), T250J (1972), the short-lived TT250 and the first disc-braked GT250K (1973).

The New Design

In designing the crankcases and crankshaft, the Suzuki engineering team took into consideration the need to harness the additional power and torque of the 305cc T305 (later 315cc T350) bigger brothers. Apart from bore sizes and gear ratios, the T305/T350 and T250 were virtually identical in terms of engine components.

The T250 engine retained the 54 × 54mm bore and stroke dimensions of the T20, but the individual iron-lined aluminium cylinder barrels were equipped with heavier-looking, squarer-shaped finning than on the T20.

The designers also set out to rectify what they saw as the weaknesses of the T20; as a result, the T250, although heavier than the machine it replaced, was to prove exceptionally robust. The horizontally split crankcase layout was retained, as were the shaft centres of the T20, and this contributed to keeping down tooling costs.

Individual iron-lined aluminium cylinder barrels were equipped with heavier-looking, squarer-shaped finning than on the T20. Internally, bore and stroke (on the T250) remained unchanged, at 54 × 54mm, giving a displacement of 247cc. The aluminium cylinder heads were given nicely polished outer fins, each being bolted down by a quartet of stud bolts on wider centres than those on the T20. A pair of chrome-plated 'keystone' rings were specified for each piston; with gudgeon pin and needle roller small-ends increased in diameter over the T20. With a nominal compression ratio of 7.5:1, the T250 produced a claimed 32bhp at 8,000rpm; carburation was via a pair of Mikuni VM24SH instruments. Later versions with their six-port barrels breathed through 26mm units, producing a claimed 33bhp. As for the T305 and T350, these were fitted with VM28SH and VM32SH assemblies respectively.

Improved Lubrication

Lubrication for the new engine was much improved over the T20. The Posi-Force system introduced with that model remained – to be renamed 'CCI' (for 'Cylinder Crankcase Injection') – from the T250R of 1971. Whatever the name, the principle remained the same: to supply oil directly to the engine according to speed and load, rather than via the less efficient induction tract method as on some rival versions (notably Yamaha). On the T20, feed was taken to each of the outer main bearings and thence to the cylinder bores and other components. On the T250, the system had been refined to include an additional feed to the cylinders, improving top-end oiling. Moving the pump to the top of the crankcase provided simpler maintenance, with access to the clutch now possible without disturbing the pump.

Gearbox Changes

As it was such a star feature of the T20, Suzuki naturally retained its pioneering six-speed transmission concept. However, this is not to say that it was not further developed. Far from it, in fact – not only were the gears beefed up, but also the engagement dog angles were undercut to prevent the previous tendency to give missed changes. In addition, the 'clonk' when engaging first gear was minimized thanks to the introduction of a neutral brake. This device applied a drag to the low-gear pinion while it was being engaged with the low gear, thus preventing grinding and ensuring a positive selection. The selection mechanism changed from three sets of forks encircling the change drum to a system of two pairs of forks running on parallel rails on either side of the drum. Ball or needle roller bearings were employed throughout.

The clutch also received an update. Its area was increased by some 12 per cent over the T20, and this was achieved by lifting the plates from the T500 (*see* Chapter 6). Operation was via a quick-thread arrangement mounted in the nearside (left) crankcase cover, with pushrods passing through the countershaft. This was something of a mixed blessing compared to the T20's direct-acting lever mounted in the clutch cover.

As with the T200 (*see* Chapter 3), on the positive side clutch-cable replacement was now a much simpler task. On the T20, this job had meant disturbing the clutch cover, with the consequent risk of damaging the gasket and thus causing an oil leak; the oil pump drive could even be damaged when the work was attempted by a really ham-fisted home mechanic. Changing the T250/T305/T350 cable was a totally 'dry' task. However, as with the T200, the drive chain threw dirt up on to the exposed pushrod, leading not only to wear on the rod but also to early failure of the oil seal.

Revised Ignition

The ignition was by a 12-volt twin contact-breaker system, which was based on the T500 set-up. It was mounted on the nearside (left) crankshaft by a key and taper. Access for timing purposes was provided by a circular chrome plate held by two screws. One change that was definitely not for the better was the transfer of the ignition switch from its previous, easily reached place on the headlamp housing of the T20, to a new location underneath the nearside (left) tank nose.

The frame closely followed that of the T20, being of the full-loop duplex cradle type, but with additional gusseting provided around the steering head. The cross-brace joining the front downtubes, just below the exhaust ports (introduced on later T20s to cure the problems experienced with a spate of broken front engine-mounting bolts), was retained. To make doubly sure, all engine bolts of the T250/T305/T350 were increased in size to 12mm diameter.

Ancillaries were supported in conventional fashion – with twin ignition coils under the fuel tank, a pleated-paper air filter element contained in a steel box to the rear of the carburettors (connected by rubber hosing), and the 12-volt, 5-amp hour battery to the rear of that. The filter assembly and battery were hidden from view behind the steel oil tank on the offside (right) and the matching tool box on the nearside (left).

Both front and rear wheels, including the drum brakes with 2LS front and SLS rear operation, were essentially straight from the T20.

Changing the Style

In many ways, in terms of styling at least, the new twins were closer to Honda's CB250/CB350 than to the outgoing T20. Besides the chrome-plated mudguards in place of the painted assemblies, Suzuki also abandoned the combined speedo/tacho as part of a plastic headlamp unit. In its place came the slab-sided separate instruments, introduced on the T500, which appeared absolutely identical except for

1971 T250/T350 Specifications
(T350 where different in brackets)

Engine	Air-cooled parallel twin, with 180-deg crankshaft, alloy head and barrel, needle roller small- and big-end bearings, horizontally split aluminium crankcases
Bore	54mm (61mm)
Stroke	54mm
Displacement	247cc (315cc)
Compression ratio	7.5:1 (6.94:1)
Lubrication	Pump
Ignition	Battery/coil, 12-volt
Carburettor	2 × Mikuni VM26SH (VM32SH)
Primary drive	Gears, 20/61
Final drive	Chain, 14/41
Gearbox	Six-speed, foot-change
Frame	Duplex, full cradle, all-steel construction
Front suspension	Telescopic fork, with rubber gaiters
Rear suspension	Swinging-arm, with twin shock absorbers
Front brake	180mm full-width drum, 2LS
Rear brake	180mm full-width drum, SLS
Tyres	GT250 front 2.75 × 18, rear 3.00 × 18; GT350 3.00 × 18, 3.25 × 18

General specifications

Wheelbase	50.8in (1,290mm)
Ground clearance	6.1in (155mm)
Seat height	30in (762mm)
Fuel tank capacity	2.6gal (12ltr)
Dry weight	GT250 283lb (128kg); GT350 285lb (129kg)
Maximum power	33bhp @ 8,000rpm (40bhp @ 7,500rpm)
Top speed	GT250 95mph (153km/h); GT350 98mph (158km/h

the placement of the red-line zone. These were used in conjunction with a separate chrome headlamp, the rim of which was entirely circular, with the former horseshoe profile.

The chrome-plated mudguards (as with all other assemblies on Japanese bikes of the period) proved to be rot-prone in service, and often pose a problem for present-day restorers. However, the chrome-plating of the lower fork legs was a better idea, preventing stone-chip damage, which was a problem with the T20's painted components. The forks were equipped with rubber gaiters.

Although welding the silencers (which were highly efficient) to the exhaust header pipes gave them a cleaner appearance, this alteration presented a problem on two counts: decoking and the extra cost when needing a replacement.

Exposed spring rear shock absorbers, indicator bodies, rear light unit, chain guard and the wide, motocross-type braced handlebars rounded off the chromework.

In its initial guise, the T250 (and T305) sported what is best described as a bulbous fuel tank, the knee recesses giving it a blunt arrowhead proform. Colour – a choice of either Candy Lime Green or Orange – was applied to the tanks and side covers, while the base of the fuel tank, headlamp brackets and frame were finished in black. The dual seat was notable for having a heavily quilted criss-cross pattern, and a line of chrome studs along its lower edge.

The initial price of the T250 when released on to the UK market at the tail end of 1969 was a hefty £355, £50 up on the T20 and within £10 of the 500cc Triumph Daytona or Velocette Venom! Suzuki's official UK marketing brochure attempted something of a hard sell:

> The sleek machine grips the road surface like hell at any of the six available speeds and turns the sharpest corner with surprising grace. The smell of gas fumes, thundering feeling of slicing into 100mph thick air-wall and a variety of manoeuvring ecstasies, hitherto red-taped within the prohibited circle of professional racers, are now all yours with Suzuki's T250!

Unfortunately the overall performance of the bike failed to match that of the departed T20. The quoted 10 per cent power boost over its older brother was not transferred into more performance, owing to the extra weight and the barn-door riding position imposed by those wide, motocross-type braced handlebars.

T250-II

Don Leeson described the new T250 model in the March 1988 issue of *Motorcycle Enthusiast* thus: 'If the Suzuki stylists had managed to make the first T250 look much more solid than the T20, when it came to the T250-II the result was decidedly pretty.' The front end had been transformed by the adoption of Ceriani-type forks, slim chrome-plated headlamp brackets and a much smaller headlamp with flat back shell. The instruments were now of a more rounded profile, with plastic-cased components, while the seat gained all-round stainless-steel trim and widthwise quilting. Setting this off was a new peanut-style tank. The Phlolina Yellow finish was particularly attractive, with thin blue, white and red stripes along the base of the fuel tank. Candy Corporate Blue was the other colour option.

Suzuki sources now claimed 33bhp at 8,000rpm. *Motorcyclist Illustrated* tested one of the T250-IIs in its September 1970 issue and was generally pretty impressed. The report began with the following headline: 'Suzuki MkII Hustler. Strong contender for the "world's fastest production 250", yet one of the sweetest-natured motorcycles we have experienced.'

Early on in the article, the tester expressed his surprise at 'the apparently low top speed of the machine – somewhere around 85mph'. However, he went on to explain that, 'before we accepted delivery of the Hustler, the speedometer had been replaced by a serviceable unit, but as was proved later, the clutch had not. During high-speed runs, maximum speeds deteriorated from a first time one of approximately 90mph down to 80mph and less.'

The problem was due partly to a slipping clutch, partly to the motocross handlebars. *MCI* replaced the latter with a flat T20-like handlebar. With the clutch and handlebar issues sorted, *MCI* took the bike to Snetterton race circuit in Norfolk, where they achieved 98mph (158km/h). An even higher figure of 102.3mph (198km/h) was posted following a change of the standard 41-tooth rear-wheel sprocket to a 39 item, together with a lighter (10-stone) rider.

Although many features of the Hustler Mark II were praised, it was the engine's ability to pull a higher gear than expected that was most appreciated: 'Unlike the Kawasaki Mach III, say, when, unless 6,000rpm was pulled, it all gasped to a growling halt in top gear, the Hustler kept purring out power enough to keep speed up in top, right down to the rider's whim.'

The *MCI* test summed up the Mk II with some complimentary words:

> From tickover at 1700rpm through the power band up to over 9000 the engine could not be faulted. Smooth, silky power all the way. Oil tight, gas tight. Nearly 300 mpp (miles per pint) of oil used by the Posi-Force system only. White exhaust pipes at the end of it all and most of all, a couple of very impressed, supremely satisfied journalists.

T350

In 1970 the American magazine *Cycle* did a comparison test of six 350cc class bikes: the Kawasaki A7 Avenger, Harley-Davidson (Aermacchi) Sprint, Bridgestone GTR, Yamaha R5, Honda CB350, and Suzuki's T350 Rebel. Even though the Yamaha was declared the ultimate winner, the Suzuki came top in the performance section, which was judged according to acceleration, braking and lap times. At 305lb (138kg), the T350 was the lightest of the group, and of course it was giving away displacement at only 315cc. Gear ratios were: 1st 19.26:1, 2nd 12.40:1, 3rd 9.59:1, 4th 7.48:1, 5th 6.45:1, 6th 5.87:1.

The 1972 T350J Rebel was distinguishable from the earlier T350R by way of its larger 3.8gal (17ltr) fuel tank, the same as fitted to the GT250K.

BELOW: A T350 engine modified by Terry Shepherd, with water-cooled heads and barrels, mounted in a Seeley-type chassis.

In the UK, *Motorcycle Mechanics* editor Charles Deane penned a pretty comprehensive test of the Rebel in the May 1971 issue.

Although the T350 was considerably more powerful at 40bhp (at 7,500rpm) than its two-fifty brother, maximum speed was not much different, although torque and acceleration were considerably improved; *MCM* achieved 14.5 seconds for the standing ¼-mile sprint. Charles Deane described the testing: 'With 3,500rpm showing on the tachometer, the Rebel would accelerate rapidly when the taps were opened. This meant useful performance between 3,500 and 5,500rpm without having to scream the motor to its 8,000 red-line peak.' By keeping to these intermediate revs, mechanical and exhaust noise was kept to a 'minimum'.

On the other hand, as Deane went on to explain, 'If you made use of the 6,000 to 8,000 front-wheel-lifting rpm band, the motor took on a semi-racing yow! Emitted clouds of blue smoke from the exhaust and the Rebel took off like a scalded cat.'

Three criticisms were levelled at the engine. First, 'quite loud piston slop was apparent during the warming-up period'; second, high-frequency vibration 'made itself apparent at engine speeds of over 5,500rpm', and finally, 'another reason for keeping revs down was fuel consumption', with the test going on to explain that, 'used gently, this 350 would be quite reasonable with a happy 65 to 70mph. But use the revs and performance and just over 40mpg was the penalty.'

Some of the features that had previously been praised on Suzuki twins, from the T20 onwards, such as handling and braking, were something of a let-down on the larger-engined model: 'Handling for average road speeds was good, but when forced the Rebel protested with a pitching motion'; the suspension 'would bottom when carrying a pillion passenger and riding over bumpy roads'; as for stopping, the 'twin-leading shoe front brake is good at low speeds, but could be improved for high speed use'.

By this time, British imports were being handled by the Lambretta concessionaires, run by Peter Agg in Purley Way, Croydon, Surrey. The T350 retailed at £399.50 including purchase tax.

T250J

By the time *Motorcycle Sport* ran a test of the T250J in its August 1972 issue, a new company (still with Peter Agg as Chairman), Suzuki (GB) Ltd, had moved to 87 Beddington Lane, Croydon. The cost of the T250J had risen to around the £350 mark.

Somehow, as the *Motorcycle Sport* test revealed, the sparkle seemed to be disappearing from Suzuki's two-fifty twin: 'The T250J, still known to many as the Hustler, had good looks, adequate performance and braking, gives reasonable economy and costs no more than comparable machines. On the debit side the machine seems to us to be less comfortable than the older model and marginally less quick.'

It was hardly a glowing recommendation, and the *Motorcycle Sport* tester was equally unimpressed with certain details:

> For years we seem to have been grumbling about the awkward position of the ignition key beneath the nose of the petrol tank. It is still there but the light switch has been moved to the handlebar, which makes things easier and safer. One still has to grope beneath the tank to stop the engine, though. Sad to relate that Suzuki have still some way to go with their light switch arrangement. The new position has the on/off switch on top of the combined clutch lever unit, with the dip switch and flasher switch one above the other, both working on the same plane. With heavy gloves both could easily be operated together and once or twice we found ourselves having to look down to choose the right switch. Back to the drawing board!

A comment was also made regarding the dual seat (repeated in other tests), with *Motorcyclist Illustrated* complaining that 'an "ample" seat, in our view, has 25in [63mm] of usable length. The seat on the T250 has 23in [58mm] available. It is not quite enough for two.' However, the report did say that the testers 'really appreciated being able to place both feet on the ground… We were beginning to think that our legs were getting shorter! The dual seat on the Suzuki must be one of the few around today that does not hinge.'

One particular remark in the *Motorcyclist Illustrated* article perhaps summed up the 1972 T250J: 'It is not an out-and-out racer, just a pleasant sports tourer.'

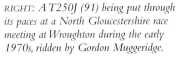

RIGHT: A T250J (91) being put through its paces at a North Gloucestershire race meeting at Wroughton during the early 1970s, ridden by Gordon Muggeridge.

LEFT: The 1972 T250J introduced a slimmer look, thanks to the abbreviated headlamp, Ceriani-type front forks (with exposed stanchions) and new tank shape.

BELOW: For 1973 Suzuki introduced the new GT250K with Ram Air System.

GT250K, L and M

For 1973 Suzuki introduced the GT250K model. What was new? The answer was Ram Air cooling and a front end that now included a disc front brake; plus revised styling and graphics. And what was the same? The frame, the six-speed 'box, and just about everything else. In truth, the GT250K and its successors for the next half a decade represented a 'holding' exercise, until the arrival of the brand-new X7, in 1978.

In the GT series of two-fifty twins, the descendant of the T20 and T250 had reached just about the summit of its development. *Motorcycle Sport* commented upon the GT250K's launch: 'As we have said before, once this peak has been reached it is the devil's own job to stay there; often, in the external search for that little bit extra, the machine can actually go downhill.'

And that in a way was to be the fate of the model.

There is absolutely no doubt that with the GT250K marketing hype took over from practicality. Many observers were moved to ask whether an 85mph (137km/h) top speed really

Ram Air

One feature of the K series was its Ram Air 'cooling' system. The benefits or otherwise of this system were debatable; after all, as one commentator of the period accurately described it, the system really only involved a 'metal deflector' shield atop the cylinder head. The concept was, according to Suzuki, 'to keep a stream of cooling air aimed in the right direction'. It might have helped the cylinder head remain cool, but it did little for the cylinder barrels; on a two-stroke, these were the components that were most affected by heat, together with the pistons that operated within them. If Suzuki had really been keen on cooling, the answer – as they knew from their racing experience – would have been to go the whole hog and use liquid, not air.

In truth the Ram Air System was more of a sales gimmick, but it provided Suzuki's twin with a visible update, if not any sort of performance boost.

needed a disc front brake. The answer might have been yes, provided it was better than the 2LS drum it replaced. Unfortunately, at least in the wet, it most definitely was not! The following extract from the *Motorcycle Sport* test of June 1973 highlights the problem:

> Of the brake we can have nothing but praise when it is used in the dry. Its hydraulic operation was sensitive, light and efficient. Then we took the Suzuki out in the wet. Did we get a fright! It was all right at first, not too grabbing, but it just happened that we went for a few miles without needing the front brake. Approaching a set of lights as they changed we braked in good time. Nothing. We braked harder, as cautiously as we could. Still nothing. We braked very hard, caution thrown to the winds. Everything. We didn't fall off but a large dent in the tank suggested that a predecessor may have been less lucky.

The *Motorcycle Sport* experience was not just a one-off – all GT250Ks suffered from the same, potentially dangerous problem. To be fair, it was not purely a Suzuki problem, but a Japanese one, caused by putting showroom glitter before on-road performance. These early discs were highly polished, usually of a stainless material, and their performance in wet-weather conditions was often abysmal.

In contrast, the new front fork was more substantial-looking than before, partly because it had been fitted with rubber gaiters; this proved to be a good idea, as it protected the previously exposed stanchions.

Another problem for the GT250K was weight, which had risen to 322lb (146kg) dry. The *Motorcycle Sport* tester put it quite succinctly: 'There is a great deal of motorcycle underneath one, for a 250, and one aspect of this is that a short rider has a job to reach the ground.'

Luckily, Suzuki had retained many of the features that had helped turn its predecessors into best-sellers. These included the excellent CCI pump lubrication, the full duplex cradle frame, and the basic, six-speed, largely vibration-

SUZUKI GT250

SPECIFICATIONS
Maximum Speed ....144~152 kph (90~95 mph)
Maximum Horsepower ...30.0 hp/7,000 rpm S.A.E. NET
Engine Type................2-stroke, ram air aluminum twin cylinder
Piston Displacement .....247 cc (15.1 cu-in)
Transmission ....6-speed, constant-mesh
Fuel Tank Capacity ....15 ltr (4.0/3.3 gal, US/Imp)
Lubrication ....Suzuki CCI
Overall Length ....2,045 mm (80.5 in)
Overall Width.............815 mm (32.1 in)
Overall Height.............1,130 mm (44.5 in)
Ground Clearance ....160 mm (6.3 in)
Tires, Front 3.00-18, 4PR
        Rear 3.25-18, 4PR
Dry Weight ....146 kg (322 lb)
Starter ....Primary kick
Color ....Serurian Blue Metallic
                Candy Tahiti Orange
*Specifications subject to change without notice.

SUZUKI CCI
SUZUKI MOTOR CO.,LTD.
300 Takatsuka, Hamamatsu, Japan

Printed in Japan

Tach/speedometer with tripmeter
Flip-up gas cap with key lock
Ram air cooling
Suzuki CCI lubrication
Hydraulic disc brake
Primary kick starter
6-speed transmission

1974 GT250L factory brochure illustration.

free engine unit. In fact, the rear shocks were a definite improvement, having solved the previous rear-end pitching experienced on the T250J and T350 Rebel models. In addition, the dual seat was a much-improved and more comfortable affair.

The L (1974) and M (1975) models did little to revive Suzuki's fortunes, which were by now flagging in the hotly contested 250cc class. The June 1975 issue of *Bike* gave the GT250M all the wrong sort of publicity, claiming that the model 'should have the British importers in receivership within a year'. Measured up against seven other two-fifties, it came across as a machine with a serious problem – *Bike* blamed its 'total lack of personality'. Suzuki needed to do something significant, and they did, indeed, bring in a revised bike for 1976.

GT250A

Suzuki may have introduced the 'A' suffix on the new model in an attempt to indicate that

they were starting with a clean sheet. However, at least on the surface, the only really noticeable difference between the outgoing M and the incoming A was the dropping of the Ram Air system on the quarter-litre model. When Peter Watson tested a GT250A in the February 1976 issue of *Bike*, he commented that 'a braver man than I had suggested to Suzuki GB that its [the Ram Air system's] deletion merely underlined the fact that the effect had always been more visual than actual'.

Mechanical Changes

Costing £529 (including the newly introduced VAT, or Value Added Tax) on the British market, the GT250A's major mechanical changes were a fairly radical revision of the porting, and the number of main bearings increased from two to three. The porting alterations meant that the power band was moved upwards, with a useful amount of power available as low as 4,000rpm. According to Peter Watson, 'Below that it really won't pull the skin off a tangerine, and above 5,000rpm things start to happen with gratifying rapidity all the way up to eight grand in every screaming gear.' *Bike* recorded an electronically timed 90.90mph (146km/h), which was over 6mph (10km/h) quicker than the bike it replaced, and declared the 'power delivery… very smooth, making this parallel twin one of the silkiest around'. However, it was the GT250A's acceleration that most impressed. The front brake was described as 'one of the best discs we've come across – strong, but with plenty of feel'. The same could not be said of the GT250A's fuel consumption figures, and *Bike* recorded an overall figure of just 33mpg (8.55ltr/100km).

In Service

The July 1978 issue of *Motorcycle Mechanics* carried out a 'Used Bike Test' of a 1976 GT250A with 12,000 miles (19,300km) on the clock, to see what the bike was like in service. According to tester Frank Melling, the mechanical changes (porting and an additional main bearing), in addition to Suzuki's CCI oil-injection system ('probably the most efficient of any mechanical two-stroke lubrication device'), 'gave the whole engine a reliability which borders on the miraculous'. Melling carried out his own investigation of the GT250A among dealers:

> Between three dealers, one of whom is a 100 per cent Suzuki main agent, there had only been one case of crankshaft failure, and that was caused by the owner leaving the petrol tap on for a period of months, during which time the crankcase filled up with fuel. When he came to start up the bike, hydraulic compression took place and bent the con-rod.

As for the subject of the 'Used Bike Test', 'its top half showed no signs of fatigue after 12,000 miles on the same pistons and rings. There was quite a lot of engine noise which equates more or less with piston slap but is more a result of there

Suzuki ditched its Ram Air System for the new 1976 model, which was coded GT250A. The revised engine also saw a change to the porting and the number of main bearings increased from two to three. Production finally ended in 1978 with the 'C' version.

being large holes in the barrels and very little metal to support the piston than were actually allowing the piston to flutter in the bore.'

Although the engine was generally considered bullet-proof, the same could not be said of certain aspects of the finish:

> The transparent lacquer which is used to protect the engine cases had suffered from the winter road grit and salt and the alloy beneath was beginning to pit. Similarly, the swinging arm, which for some reason is never painted thoroughly on Suzukis, was beginning to show signs of rusting. Traces of rust were also beginning to appear on the chrome front fork covers, just below the headlamp and on the fork stanchions themselves where they were not wiped by the sliders. The only mechanical defect, or rather potential defect, was in the rear brake which was showing signs of linings nearing the thin side of comfortable.

The Early and Mid-1970s

During the 1970s, Mick Walker Motorcycles sold the various Italian marques, including Ducati, Moto Guzzi, Benelli and MV Agusta, and was also a main Suzuki dealer. In my experience, the Japanese brand was generally a reliable one, with some more exciting bikes turning up towards the end of the decade. These included not only a series of new four-strokes, but also the sensational X7 two-fifty, which, until the advent of Yamaha's LC, was to put Suzuki back at the top of the two-fifty pile. However, before examining the X7 and its derivatives, it is important to review the smaller-capacity two-stroke twins built by Suzuki during the early and mid-1970s.

The Stinger

Although the company had offered 125 and 150cc twins during the early/mid-1960s, followed by the excellent T200 Invader and T125 parallel twins (the latter not to be confused with the T125 Stinger), which featured near-vertical cylinders and was imported into the

ABOVE: *T125 Stinger, built between 1969 and 1973. Its 124.9cc (43 × 43mm) engine featured near-horizontal cylinders. This Series II machine dates from 1972.*

BELOW: *Early Stinger Series I (1969) with flat instead of kinked front mudguard stay. A smaller 90cc version was sold in Japan.*

UK, albeit in relatively small numbers. Technically, the Stinger was an interesting design, being the only Suzuki to reach production status with this engine layout. In total, some 50,000 units were built between 1968 and the end of 1972; 4,000 of them went to the UK. Like the early T250 Hustler, they were manufactured in Series I and II.

With 'square' bore and stroke dimensions of 43 × 43mm, the Stinger's engine displaced 124.9cc with a compression ratio of 7.3:1; maximum power was 15.1bhp at 8,500rpm with 9.9lb/ft of torque. Weighing in at only 211lb (96kg), the Stinger could top 70mph (112km/h). The crankshaft featured needle roller bearings for both the big- and small-ends, the cylinder heads were of aluminium, the barrels cast-iron. The crank was supported by four main bearings, two ball race on the timing side, one ball race at the centre and another ball race on the drive side.

The Suzuki Posi-Force lubrication system supplied oil to the centre and nearside (left) main bearings and intake tracts from a pump driven off the kickstart pinion, regulated by the throttle, whilst the gearbox shafts ran in an oil bath that also supplied the offside (right) main bearings.

The fuel system was taken care of by a pair of Mikuni MD18 carburettors. Transmission was by a five-speed crossover gearbox with primary drive by helical gears and final drive by chain. The multi-plate clutch featured ten plates (five bonded and five steel) with six springs. Gear ratios were as follows: 1st 24.88:1, 2nd 16.20:1, 3rd 12.21:1, 4th 9.70:1, 5th 8.53:1.

Ignition was by a 6-volt, 7.5 amp-hour battery and twin coils. The battery was recharged via a crankshaft-mounted alternator (either Nippon-Denso or Kokusan-Denki) and a bridge-type rectifier.

Other details of this tiny machine's specification included telescopic forks, swinging-arm rear suspension, 140mm drum brakes front and rear (both SLS operation), and 18in wheels,

1969 T125 (Stinger) Specification

Engine	Air-cooled parallel twin with piston-port induction, near-horizontal cylinders, needle roller big- and small-ends, four main bearings (all ball race), horizontally split aluminium crankcases
Bore	43mm
Stroke	43mm
Displacement	124.9cc
Compression ratio	7.3:1
Lubrication	Pump
Ignition	Battery/coil 6-volt, Nippon-Denso or Kokusan-Denki alternator
Carburettor	2 × Mikuni MD18
Primary drive	Gears, 16/50
Final drive	Chain, 16/40
Gearbox	Five-speed, foot-change
Frame	Beam-type tubular construction, no front downtube or cradle
Front suspension	Telescopic fork with rubber gaiters
Rear suspension	Swinging-arm, twin shock absorbers
Front brake	140mm full-width drum, SLS
Rear brake	140mm full-width drum, SLS
Tyres	Front 2.50 × 18; rear 2.75 × 18

General specifications

Wheelbase	46.9in (1,191mm)
Ground clearance	6.7in (170mm)
Seat height	29in (736mm)
Fuel tank capacity	1.7gal (8ltr)
Dry weight	211lb (96kg)
Maximum power	15.1bhp @ 8,500rpm
Top speed	77mph (124km/h)

with 2.50 and 2.75 section tyres front and rear respectively. A 90cc (coded T90) version was sold at home on the Japanese market, but not

exported to the West. The 38 × 39.6mm dimension gave a precise displacement of 89.8cc with maximum power of 10.5bhp at 9,000rpm.

GT125/185

Next came the GT125/185 parallel twins. The larger model appeared first in K series form during 1973, with the 125 arriving shortly afterwards. Both employed vertical cylinders and a five-speed gearbox.

The 125 shared the same 'square' bore and stroke dimensions as the Stinger: 43 × 43mm = 124.9cc; the 185, 49 × 49mm = 184.8cc. It was not simply a case of Suzuki boring out the cylinders to create the larger bike. The smaller engine put out 16bhp at 9,500rpm, the 185, 21bhp at 7,500rpm. The original GT125/185

1974 GT185K with Ram Air System: 185.8cc (49 × 49mm), 20bhp and five speeds.

machines had Ram Air and drum brakes front and rear, with a twin-leading device at the front.

The 125 had twin 18mm Mikuni carburettors, the 185, 20mm instruments. The bottom half of both engines followed conventional Suzuki practice with needle roller big- and small-ends. However, in place of the usual three mains and four seals were four mains and three seals, the centre one acting as a double type. This change also affected the lubrication system, although the fundamentals remained the same. A major difference between the two lay in the electrics. The 125 had an alternator with a rectifier. It also had no electric start. These differences prevent engine swaps between the 125 and 185.

Both machines used a full cradle frame, where a single front downtube split into two under the engine and gearbox unit, 2.75 and 3.00 section 18in tyres and five-way adjustable rear shocks.

For the 1974 model year (coded 'K'), both bikes gained a 250mm disc front brake, lost their fork gaiters and were given new graphics for the tank. In addition, the power of the '185' dropped 1bhp.

Although the 125 was something of a buzz box, the 185 was a much better bike, with a wider spread of power and superior fuel economy – plus of course better electrics and push-button starting. Weighing in (dry) at 253lb (115kg), against the 125's 238lb (108kg), the 185 also had a significantly superior power to weight ratio.

The GT125/185 K series was offered in a choice of Candy Tahiti Orange, Bright Blue Metallic or Stardust Silver Metallic, with colour being applied to the petrol tank and side panels. The frame and swinging arm were black and the remainder was either polished alloy or bright chrome-plate (including the mudguards).

Although changes were made to cosmetic details as the decade unfolded, major changes were limited to moving the disc brake to the nearside left on the 125 (from the 1978 model year, C series), whilst the 185 was offered with

1975 GT125M, essentially a smaller version of the GT185, but not simply a larger bore; instead it retained the square dimensions (but in smaller sizes of 43 × 43mm). Power output was 16bhp at 9,500rpm.

1973 Suzuki GT185K/125K Specifications
(GT125K in brackets)

Engine	Air-cooled parallel twin, two-stroke, piston–port induction, alloy heads and barrels, Ram Air cooling, needle roller small- and big-ends, horizontally split aluminium crankcases	Front suspension	Telescopic forks with rubber gaiters★
		Rear suspension	Swinging-arm, with five-way adjustable twin shock absorbers
		Front brake	160mm full-width drum, 2LS★
Bore	49mm (43mm)	Rear brake	130mm full-width drum, SLS
Stroke	49mm (43mm)	Tyres	Front 2.75 × 18; rear 3.00 × 18
Displacement	184.8cc (124.9cc)		
Compression ratio	7:1 (6.8:1)	*General specifications*	
Lubrication	Pump	Wheelbase	50.6in (1,285mm)
Ignition	Battery/coil, with contact breaker, 12-volt electric start	Ground clearance	5.5in (140mm)
		Seat height	29in (736mm)
Carburettor	2 × Mikuni VM20SC 20mm (18mm)	Fuel tank capacity	2.2gal (10ltr)
		Dry weight	GT185K 253lb (115kg); GT125K 238lb (108kg)
Primary drive	Gears, 19/61		
Final drive	Chain, 14/40 (14/50)	Maximum power	21bhp @ 7,500rpm (16bhp @ 9,500rpm)
Gearbox	Five-speed, foot-change		
Frame	Full cradle, with single front downtube, branching into twin tubes under engine unit	Top speed	GT185K 80mph (129km/h); GT125K 74mph (119km/h)

★ 1974 onwards disc front brake and exposed stanchions

optional cast-alloy wheels, coded GT185EC. Both models were discontinued at the end of 1979.

New Technology

The Suzuki engineers in Japan had realized for some time that the GT250 series had reached the end of the road, partly because emission regulations, particularly relating to the American market, were becoming ever stricter. The final GT, the B, was produced in the 1977 model year.

The company had been actively developing a whole new breed of motorcycles using four-stroke engines with one, two and four cylinders (*see* Chapters 12, 13 and 14). However, with this trend towards four-strokes, why did Suzuki feel the need to continue to develop its twin-cylinder two-stroke? The answer was provided by Suzuki's chief engineer Kiyoshi Kushiya, in an interview during the summer of 1978. He explained that up to 250cc the two-stroke 'gives much better performance, while it is lighter and cheaper to make'. From 400cc upwards, Kushiya said there was no difference between the performance of the two engine types, although emissions of the four-stroke were lower.

X7

With the X7, Kiyoshi Kushiya and his design team went back to the formula that had been so successful with the T20 lightweight: function above glitz. As a result, the bike was designed down rather than up, and it ended up tipping the scales at 282lb (128kg) dry. The engine alone weighed 16lb (7kg) less than the GT unit.

Like the T20, the X7 was designed as a two-fifty, whereas the T250 (the forerunner of the GT) was created as both a two-fifty *and* a three-fifty. This meant that the cylinder spacing was more generous. In addition, other components, notably the transmission, had to be able to cope with the larger engine size. The X7 engine was narrower and lighter. The gearbox was also more compact. The result was that the X7's engine/transmission assembly weighed only 81lb (37kg) against 97lb (44kg) for the old one.

Factory brochure for the new 'ton-up' GT250X7; the first genuine 100mph (160km/h) 250cc production street bike.

Reed-Valve Induction

Apart from its low weight – which was also transferred into the chassis – what made the X7 much better than the old, outgoing bike was its use of reed-valve induction (Suzuki's Power Reed Dual Intake, or PRDI, system) in place of the less sophisticated piston-port type. On the new X7, the main difference was that the inlet opening period of the piston-controlled port was about 16 degrees *less* than on the GT250B. The precise timing of the ports on the two engines was as follows:

- Inlet timing: X7 64 deg BTDC to 64 deg ATDC; GT250B 74 deg BTDC to 74 deg ATDC;

- Transfer port timing: X7 59 deg BBDC/ABDC; GT250B 60 deg BBDC/ABDC;
- Exhaust timing: X7 89 deg BBDC/ABDC; GT250B 90 deg BBDC/ABDC.

The reed valve opened at around the same point as the piston-controlled port, and at 6,000–7,000rpm it closed at about 60 deg ATDC.

Besides its reed-valve induction (which gave much greater torque throughout the rev range), the X7 was also the first Suzuki production two-fifty twin to feature electronic ignition. Note also rubber stripes to prevent fin 'ringing'.

Power Reed Dual Intake (PRDI)

Developed from Suzuki motocross world championship winners, the company's new reed-valve induction system worked as follows. There was still the conventional inlet port, whose opening and closing was controlled by the piston. In addition, there was another port opening into the crankcase just below and behind the cylinder, which had a reed valve. The inlet port forked into two parts in the cylinder barrel.

The object of the exercise was to provide power lower down the scale, just as much as good peak power output. Normally, with a conventional piston-port system, it was very much a case of all or nothing. Having maximum power at the top end as a priority meant losing the bottom pull, or vice versa. Suzuki's Power Reed Dual Intake (PRDI) system was an early attempt to overcome that basic fact of life in a series production roadster engine.

The concept was that the piston-controlled port had fairly 'mild' timing, so as to provide good performance at low speeds. It would still work at higher speeds, but tended to run out of puff a bit. On the other hand, at low speeds, the reed valve hardly opened at all, so it had little effect on the performance characteristics. For the reed valve to open at all there had to be a reasonable depression in the crankcase to pull the reeds off their seats.

Of course, the reed valves remained opened until there was a positive pressure in the crankcase to close them. But, as engine speed increased, so the inertia of the column of gas passing through the reed valves increased. In other words, there was a column of gas moving into the crankcase, and gas at the rear tended to push that at the front. The effect of this was that, as the speed increased, so the reed valve remained open longer.

The distinctive expansion-chamber-type exhausts and cast-alloy rear wheel of the X7.

Peak power was developed at 8,000rpm, and at that speed the reed valve closed at around 70 deg ATDC.

The performance characteristics were also affected by the exhaust port timing and the exhaust system, and, although the timing was virtually identical to that of the GT250B, the expansion chambers of the X7 were more efficient. Official Suzuki power curves for the X7 showed that all the way up the speed range, as far as 8,000rpm, the X7 developed more actual power than the GT250B – even though the latter, on paper, produced 31bhp, compared with the 29bhp of the X7! Clearly, the X7 gave its rider much more *usable* power, particularly in the all-important mid-range sector.

Contactless Ignition

Besides the reed-valve induction, another major change was the use of contactless ignition. This not only had the advantage of eliminating certain maintenance chores, but, more importantly for optimum performance, also ensured consistent timing.

Why did Suzuki opt for capacitor discharge and not the transistorized type? Suzuki's official answer was simply a case of energy available at high speeds. With transistorized ignition, in which the conventional inductive coil was employed, the energy available at the spark plug fell off above 5,000rpm. On a two-stroke, the equivalent speed was only 2,500rpm, since the

sparks were needed twice as often, which is why the CD system was chosen.

Although the new engine looked completely different from the outgoing one, a surprising number of components were either the same or based on the same principle. The 'square' 54 × 54mm bore and stroke dimensions remained unchanged, giving the same capacity of 247cc. However, the engineering team had altered all the internal gear ratios, which were now as follows: 2.5, 1.63, 1.21, 1.0, 0.84 and 0.783:1. The reason for this was to reduce the previously over-wide gap between 1st and 2nd, while increasing the other gaps marginally. Change in the gearbox was to provide the ability to kickstart the engine into life in any ratio (by pulling the clutch lever, and using the kickstart lever); this system was referred to as a 'primary kick'.

The X7 employed a pair of Mikuni VM26SS carburettors with a polyurethane foam element air cleaner.

Cycle Parts

The chassis and its components saw at least as much change as, or more than, the engine unit. The frame was entirely new and, although only using a single front downtube, was a pretty rigid affair. At 26lb (12kg), it was 3lb (5kg) lighter than the GT250B duplex type. Needle roller bearings were used at the swinging-arm pivots.

Alloy wheels represented another significant change, being of 18in diameter and shod with 3.00 and 3.25 section tyres front and rear. The styling was also much more racy, with entirely new bodywork, including the 3.3gal (15ltr) fuel tank and racing-type dual seat. Potential owners had the choice of red, white or blue (all non-metallic) colours (for the tank, seat base and tail-light section and side panels). The engine was grey finished, which was something entirely new when the X7 hit the streets, in 1978. Black was applied to the frame and smaller components such as the stands, fork yokes and swinging arm.

1978 GT250X7 Specification

Engine	Air-cooled parallel twin with piston-port reed-valve to crankcase dual induction system, alloy heads, alloy barrels, the latter with iron liners, needle roller bearing for small- and big-ends, horizontally-split aluminium crankcases		Gearbox	Six-speed, foot-change
			Frame	Tubular steel, single downtube with duplex cradles under engine
			Front suspension	Oil damped telescopic fork
			Rear suspension	Swinging-arm, with twin, angled, rear shock absorbers
Bore	54mm		Front brake	10in (254mm) single front disc
Stroke	54mm		Rear brake	Drum, full-width, SLS
Displacement	247cc		Tyres	Front 3.00 × 18; rear 3.25 × 18
Compression ratio	6.7:1			
Lubrication	Pump (Suzuki CCI system)		*General specifications*	
Ignition	Contactless, CD (Capacitor Discharge), electronic, 12-volt battery		Wheelbase	51.6in (1,310mm)
			Ground clearance	6in (152mm)
			Seat height	30in (762mm)
			Fuel tank capacity	3.3gal (15ltr)
Carburettor	2 × Mikuni VM26SS		Dry weight	282lb (128kg)
Primary drive	Gears		Maximum power	29bhp @ 8,000rpm
Final drive	Chain		Top speed	105mph (169km/h)

Barry Utting putting a 1978 X7 through its paces in a Production race event, Snetterton, 1981. Except for rear shocks and handlebars, the bike is largely stock.

Other details included twin mirrors, a console to which both instruments were fitted, these flanking the warning lights (high beam, turn and neutral), ignition switch and a small circular Suzuki 'S' badge.

When the X7 went on sale in the UK during spring 1978, the price was £720, against £735 for a Yamaha RD250 and £799 for the four-stroke Honda CB250N. The last remaining GT250Bs were going for £657. But in truth the X7 was a much better buy.

90mph in Fifth

Having sponsored a couple of racers on X7s in 1978 and 1979, I know from personal experience that a standard, untuned model could achieve 105mph (169km/h) and 90mph (145km/h) in fifth gear. Pretty impressive figures! In addition, the reed valves (helped by the precise timing provided by the electronic ignition) meant that, even though the carbs were 2mm smaller than those on the GT250B, not only was maximum speed improved, but also the power band was much wider. The X7 would pull cleanly from 3,000rpm right through to its peak at 8,000 with only a slight surge at around 7,000rpm. The gearbox was now provided with near-ideal ratios, helping a fast road rider or racer always to be in the right gear.

Riding at high speeds was much easier than on the GT250B, because of the riding position adopted for the X7. It had shorter, flatter handlebars, as well as better-positioned footrests. There were a couple of problems, though: vibration (through the footrests) above 6,000rpm, and the skittish nature of the handling, at least on poorly surfaced roads. For racing this was not so much of a problem (except on road circuits such as the Isle of Man). Its light weight made it very flickable, certainly in comparison with the existing crop of Japanese rivals.

For general commuting the X7 was less successful. For a start it was really a solo bike, on which the rider crouched in order to get maximum performance at high speeds. Sitting up at near maximum speed could reduce the top figure by as much as 10mph (16km/h) or more, depending upon the conditions. However, on a race track, or when getting down to it (in one-piece leathers), the X7 could easily outperform any other series production two-fifty of its day. In truth, it was the first genuine 100mph (160km/h) two-fifty road bike.

A Pair of 200s

In spring 1979 Suzuki launched a pair of brand-new 200s: the GT200 (more commonly known as the X5) and the SB200N. Their engines and chassis were clearly based on the X7, but they could not have been more different in purpose. The GT200 was in effect a scaled-down X7, with its cast-alloy wheels, disc front stopper, five speeds and rakish lines, whereas the SB200N was not only considerably cheaper but also had a far less impressive specification, with its wire wheels, drum front brake, four speeds and less power.

Both engines used 50 × 50mm bore and stroke giving a capacity of 196cc. The GT200 X5 sportster ran a 7:1 compression, twin 22mm Mukunis and produced 20bhp at 8,000rpm, whereas its commuter/touring brother had a 6.5:1 ratio, twin 18mm carbs and put out 18.3bhp at a lower 7,500rpm. Surprisingly, the SB200 was some 14lb (6.35kg) lighter than the GT200X5. But, this did not help much when it came to performance figures, with *Bike* recording electronically 85.27mph (142km/h) for the X5 and 76.53mph (127km/h) for the SB200.

As one commentator of the day remarked, the two bikes were 'like chalk and cheese'. Even though the basic engine unit and main frame were the same, Suzuki's new two-hundreds were poles apart in terms of the level of tuning, equipment and, ultimately, price. *Bike* had plenty to say on the disparity:

> Assessing the SB after riding the X5 becomes a very illuminating exercise in realizing how two motorcycles sharing similar major components can be given two entirely different personalities… While the X5 wouldn't look out of place on the seafront at Cannes, the SB would be more at home hauling you out of the factory gates, with a sandwich tin and a flask strapped to the seat. It's not only the lack of a ratio in the gearbox and a detuned engine that accomplish the transition, but the differences in a whole list of minor fittings… There really is £100 worth of differences between the two bikes, and it shows.

That list of differences was a long one. A medium-rise handlebar provided the SB with a 'more homely' riding position. The front forks and rear shocks on the X5 were shrouded, the seat was a two-layer affair with thicker padding, and it not only had a locking filler cap (missing on the SB) but also matching separate speedo and tacho; the SB had a blob-like console housing a speedo only, plus warning lights and ignition switch. Polished engine cases on the SB contrasted with the matt grey finish of the X5.

Probably the most notable of the differences concerned the braking performance – or lack of it on the SB; its soggy single leading shoe front drum did it no favours, whereas the X5 had the same 10.25in (260mm) hydraulically operated disc brake found on the X7. Probably the SB's main redeeming feature, compared with its more sporting brother, was its much wider spread of power, this going some way to disguising the inadequacies of its four-speed gearbox, compared with the extra ratio on the X5.

Why did Suzuki produce the SB anyway, when so much was different? It must have been an expensive exercise for a limited market. Why two cylinders, two carbs, two exhaust systems for what was, after all, supposed to be a humble commuter bike? Surely, as *Bike* asked, 'A more functional, lighter, more enjoyable motorcycle could be made by adapting parts from Suzuki's single-cylinder trail-bike range and dressing them in roadster bodywork. With a five-speed gearbox and flat bars it should be about as fast as the SB and about the same price.' On 1 August 1979, the SB200 cost £574 and the X5, £674.

Liquid-Cooling

In October 1979, at the Paris Show, Yamaha stunned the motorcycle world – and Suzuki in particular – by launching its now-legendary LC (liquid-cooled) models, beginning with the RD350LC and RD250LC. At a stroke, the arrival of the RD250LC killed X7 sales stone dead; I know from personal experience, since I was a Suzuki dealer at the time!

For three years the LC ruled the roost as the top two-fifty sports bike, until Suzuki responded and, in creating its brand-new RG250 Gamma liquid-cooled parallel twin with mono-shock rear suspension, took Yamaha's crown. And it held the top position for the next decade, first with the RG, then, from the late 1980s, with its fabulous RGV v-twin model. Later still, when the RGV gave up its crown to the Aprilia concern, it was via an updated RGV engine!

1979 Suzuki GT200X5/SB200
Specifications
(SB200 where different in brackets)

Engine	Air-cooled parallel twin with piston-port induction, alloy heads, alloy barrels, the latter with iron liners, needle roller bearing for small- and big-ends, horizontally split crankcases
Bore	50mm
Stroke	50mm
Displacement	196cc
Compression ratio	7:1 (6.5:1)
Lubrication	Pump
Ignition	CDI flywheel magneto, 12 volt
Carburettor	2 × Mikuni 22mm (18mm)
Primary drive	Gears
Final drive	Chain
Gearbox	Five-speed (four-speed), foot-change
Frame	Full cradle, single front downtube
Front suspension	Telescopic forks: GT200X5 exposed stanchions, SB200 fully enclosed
Rear suspension	Swinging-arm, twin shock absorbers
Front brake	260mm disc (180mm full-width drum, SLS)
Rear brake	150mm full-width drum, SLS
Tyres	Front 2.75 × 18; rear 3.00 × 18

General specifications

Wheelbase	GT200X5 52in (1,320mm), SB200 51.5in (1,308mm)
Ground clearance	6.5in (165mm)
Seat height	30.5in (774mm)
Fuel tank capacity	2.2gal (10ltr)
Dry weight	GT250X5 290lb (131kg); SB200 276lb (125kg)
Maximum power	20bhp @ 8,000rpm (18.3bhp @ 7,500rpm)
Top speed	GT200X5 85mph (136km/h), SB200 75mph (120km/h) GT200X5 sports model with cast-alloy wheels; SB200 touring model with wire wheels

11 RE5

The RE5 (Rotary Engine 500cc) project was a brave but ultimately unsuccessful and extremely costly mistake for Suzuki.

The Wankel Engine

In 1974, much of the world's motorcycling press, including the American *Motorcyclist* magazine, were excited by what they perceived to be Suzuki's victory over rivals Yamaha to be the first to produce what was expected to be a mass-produced Wankel Rotary-engined bike. (In fact, the German Sachs empire, with its Hercules marque, could claim this 'first', with its W2000 machine, but with a much smaller expected production.)

On 1 October 1974, a six-day 'banzai charge' by assorted members of the press corp began. The plan was for twenty-four scribes from all areas of motorcycle journalism to ride in 250-mile (402km) relays from Los Angeles to Phoenix and back, assisted by a Cessna Citation aircraft shuttle service.

Suzuki made clear in its initial American advertising campaign for its new wonderbike that the engine was an 'NSU–Wankel Rotary'. Even though the rotary-valve principle had been known since the late nineteenth century, it was the German engineer Dipl. Ing. Felix Wankel who had first come up with the precise engineering design as employed in the RE5.

NSU's first contact with Felix Wankel had come in 1951 when its design chief, Dr Walter Froede, had first begun research into his own rotary-valve project, and needed information on

US advertisement for the new RE5, January 1975. Much was expected from this revolutionary design, but, although it was in many ways an excellent motorcycle, sales were never enough to meet the huge development costs.

RE5 Rotary side-panel badge.

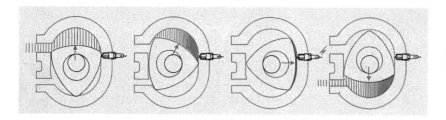

The operating cycle of the Wankel rotary engine.

sealing technology. As Wankel had been engaged in this area during the war, specifically on rotary disc valves for German naval torpedo engines, it was not unnatural for the two men to exchange ideas. Wankel soon entered into an agreement originally confined to rotary valves – with the NSU company. In late 1953, he discovered that the four-stroke cycle could be contained by an epitrochoidal bore containing an equilateral rotor. A year on, with Wankel's help, Froede succeeded in turning the inner and outer sections of this machine inside out, and thus created what was to emerge as the Wankel engine. As development continued throughout the late 1950s, unknown to the world, NSU and Wankel's project became imperceptibly interwoven.

Following an official announcement about the existence of the Wankel engine, the concept created by Wankel and Froede was to dictate NSU's commercial future to a degree that neither engineer could have imagined. By the end of the 1960s, no self-respecting producer of motor vehicles had ignored the possibility of applying rotary-engine technology – the Wankel engine was by now considered widely to be the engine of the future. This never quite happened, but the NSU factory and particularly Dr Wankel became much richer through a succession of licence agreements. A long list of well-known companies took up the option to use the new technology, including auto giants Ford, General Motors, Mercedes Benz and Mazda, two-wheel manufacturers BSA, MZ, Sachs and Van Veen, as well as all the Japanese marques. Suzuki took out a licence in early 1970.

Of the Japanese bike builders, the contest was between Suzuki and Yamaha, both producing working pre-production models: the Suzuki RX5 using a single rotor and Yamaha RZ201 with its twin rotor set up. Both were hi-tech, liquid-cooled, disc-braked superbikes. The Yamaha was conventionally styled along the lines of the XS750, while the RX5 hardly differed from the production RE5. Meanwhile, European manufacturers were to take a more low-tech approach, with their Wankel engines generally featuring air-cooling. Eventually, Suzuki was the only company in the Japanese motorcycle industry to take the Wankel rotary production plunge, while Mazda headed the country's four-wheel challenge.

Launching the Wankels

By the summer of 1974 the various Suzuki importers around the world were sending employees to Japan, to learn about what it was hoped would be a Rotary Revolution. They were soon reporting a super-smooth and torquey power delivery, combined with a higher than expected weight – and, most worryingly, a thirst for fuel, just as a fuel crisis was unfolding.

At the international Cologne Show in September 1974, three Wankels made their public debut. From Germany came the Hercules W2000 (sold under the 'DKW' brand name in the UK), powered by the fan-cooled Fitchel Sachs 294cc chamber engine (described by one journalist as 'looking somewhat like one of the Starship Enterprise's engine pods'). From

Holland, Van Veen managed to steal the show from Honda's Gold Wing by unveiling its OCR1000, a twin-rotor water-cooled monster that made the RE5 look small. Yamaha did not appear, while the BSA (now a Norton) was in working prototype guise, but several years from actual production. This left Suzuki and the RE5 as the final Cologne rotary exhibitor.

Both the Hercules and Van Veen powerplants could boast a measure of pedigree. The Van Veen engine had been developed via the car world, while the Hercules engine had been in use in snowmobiles for some time and had powered 'specials' such as the French Advancer and British Roto Gannet. The RE5 had no such heritage to fall back upon, so a 'major event' was laid on to launch the machine to the press. In keeping with the bike's intended role of long-distance tourer, half a dozen examples were ridden from Los Angeles to Phoenix and back. None of the journalists was able to break the bikes and, at that early stage in the RE5's career, things looked bright. One American journalist was optimistic about the new technology:

> Dawn … The Rotary … Wake Up! As of February 1 [1975] we'll all be members of the Antique Club of America when Suzuki unleashes the fabulous RE5!… The first practical new power concept in ninety years is about to whip the security blanket off the reciprocating engine – that which has kept it warm and alive since that memorable day in the evolution of personal transportation when man climbed down from behind a horse's rump and put something between his boots.

Bob Greene writing for *Motorcyclist* described the American press launch:

> Although a few still asked 'Why?' most were flatly impressed with what they saw, felt and heard. I was dazzled. Fearful that it might, as Mazda puts it, be electric-smooth and go h-u-m-m-m, the RE got off to a good start when its power impulses, though butter-soft, were still enough in evidence

to satisfy an old cycle hound, and the exhaust note registered more like a motorboat than a two-stroke.

Engine Details

The RE5 project was under the direction of Shigeyusa Kamiya, officially 'Head of Suzuki's Rotary Division'. His responsibilities included not just the engine development, but also the selection and employment of the basic cycle components. In the case of the chassis, the Japanese team certainly came up with a frame

A Heron Suzuki RE5 launch publicity shot, with period glamour assist.

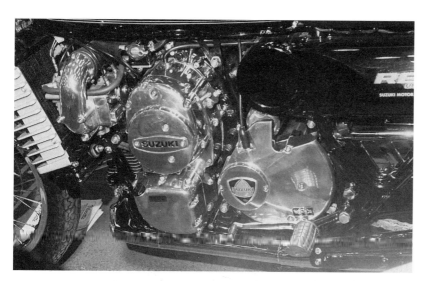

LEFT: Massive-looking structure of the RE5 engine, with its liquid-cooled housing and oil-cooled rotor. It displaced 497cc and maximum power was 62bhp at 6,500rpm.

BELOW: Exhaust header pipe with its cooling passage entry.

with which they could be satisfied, banishing as it did the 'hinge-in-the-middle' feeling that had afflicted most early large-capacity Japanese machines – particularly the original Mach III Kawasaki triple.

The late Don Leeson was a great Suzuki enthusiast. Writing for *Motorcycle Enthusiast* in 1987, he wondered whether 'it was the almost vertical mounting of the rear dampers which made the difference'. Whatever the answer to this question, the front forks, dual disc brakes and front hub were effectively GT750 (*see* Chapter 9) items, with the benefit of an aluminium rim to save a little weight. The rear rim was of the same material, whilst the drum rear brake was again taken straight from the GT750, with the brake plate retaining the cable stop of the GT despite rod operation on the rotary. Mounted on the front downtubes were the radiator for the water-cooling – the latter similar, but not identical to the GT750 component – with an oil cooler directly below.

The fuel tank carried 3.7gal (17ltr), scarcely enough for a comfortable 100-mile (160-km) range, and therefore a major drawback considering the model's 'long-distance touring' credentials.

Despite the RE5 being a single-rotor design, twin exhaust header pipes were fitted. A twin-shell construction was employed – this was necessary to cope with the high temperatures being generated. Grilles at the front of each exhaust allowed fresh air to enter and cool the inner shell along the length of the pipe before mixing with the exhaust gas just before the silencer (muffler) tip.

Carburation

Like the conventional reciprocating engine, the Wankel rotary engine converted a series of separate combustion chamber explosions into rotary motion. However, instead of a piston, a three-vaned rotor inside a combustion chamber shaped vaguely like a squashed figure-of-eight took the explosive force. By gearing a drive shaft inside the rotor the resultant eccentric movement of the rotor inside the epitrochoidal chamber allowed the production of particularly smooth power.

The simplicity of the Wankel rotary engine was a major attraction of the design, and it was in the over-complication of these components that the Suzuki development team, headed by Shigeyusa Kamiya, came unstuck.

One of the key reasons why a Wankel is so smooth on the highway is that the rotor only makes one revolution for every three of the output shaft. It therefore follows that the slow speed power impulses are relatively infrequent, leading to rough running. Because of this, carburation at slow speed becomes a major problem on a rotary, since gas velocity drops too low to atomize the fuel efficiently. Kamiya's solution was to fit the RE5 with a twin-barrel carburettor; although manufactured by Mikuni, it was basically of the Solex type. The primary bore was 18mm in diameter, and fed two small ports

in the chamber wall for slow running. The secondary bore was 32mm in diameter, feeding a single large port for high-speed use. Opening the throttle initially moved a butterfly valve in the primary bore, and thus the engine was running nicely on the two small ports of the 18mm section of the carburettor. Since the 32mm port back to the jets comprised quite a large proportion of the suction-chamber volume at this stage, a further butterfly valve – the port angle – was positioned in this port, close to the rotor tip. A secondary throttle cable linked the port valve to the twist grip, opening it once the primary valve was opened past 36 degrees.

The linkage was then arranged so that both reached the fully open position together, although the port valve did not actually open the big-bore part of the carburettor. Instead, this task was achieved by a vacuum switch controlling the secondary throttle valve, upstream from the port valve. Then of course there was the fourth butterfly valve for the choke, the fast idle linkage, the choke unloader mechanism … suffice it to say that the factory RE5 service manual runs to no less than fifteen pages on the carburettor alone, with special tools required to set up the various valve angles.

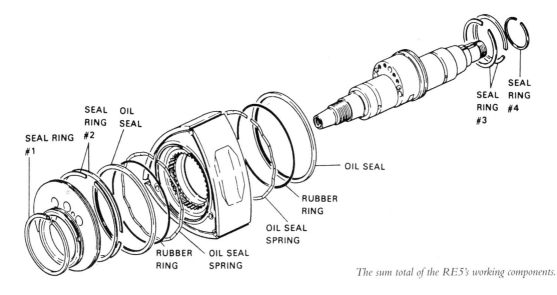

The sum total of the RE5's working components.

Ignition System

Just as important as the carburettor in achieving smooth low-speed running was the 12-volt ignition system. This featured a CDI (Capacitor Discharge Ignition) unit and special 18mm 'taper seat surface discharge plug' (Suzuki's description), which were the simple components along with the conventional bob-weight advance and retard mechanism. The points camshaft for the RE5's single-rotor engine carried two cams – one with one lobe, one with two lobes – and there were two sets of contact breakers! A speed relay driven from the rev counter and a vacuum switch connected to the carburettor were included in the control circuitry. Under engine braking the various sensors would combine to skip firing the plug every other chamber, thereby easing the snatching (jerking) effect from which the rotary would otherwise have suffered.

Sealing

Sealing the many faces of the rotor and at the same time achieving satisfactory wear of the tip seals in particular, had been a problem for all Wankel development teams. Suzuki addressed this problem by coming up with a self-compensating three-part seal for each apex of the rotor. The larger centre seal abutted its two smaller outers at a 45-degree angle. A spring strip bearing upon the two outer seals forced them upwards and outwards along the ramp formed by the ends of the centre seal towards the rotor housing.

Lubrication

The lubrication system of the RE5 was interesting if for no other reason than it employed more than one individual type. The seals for the rotor tips were lubricated by oil supplied by a two-stroke-type Mikuni injector pump. Oil for this was carried in a plastic tank under the dual seat, the same pump also providing a bleed to automatically lubricate the final-drive chain. Main engine lubrication was supplied by a rotary pump axial with the contact breaker points shaft. High pressure – of around 100psi – was employed to achieve an adequate flow to cool the rotor internals. Oil supply for this was carried in a finned aluminium sump mounted on the nearside (left) of the power unit, with a spin-off cartridge filter element mounted on the offside (right), its painted steel body standing out against the otherwise highly polished alloy on the remainder of the engine. A third oil supply was required for the five-speed GT750-derived gearbox. (The gearbox was a bolted unit construction style to the rear of the engine with ratios of 2.846; 1.736; 1.363; 1.125; 0.923.)

RE5's oil filter element on the offside (right) of the engine unit. Its painted silver finish contrasted with the polished aluminium or bright chromework.

With the engine output shaft sitting high in the motorcycle, primary drive was by way of a duplex chain. By comparison, the water-cooling arrangements for the rotor housing were simple, using many GT750 components. Unlike the GT750, the fan motor was to prove a necessary fitting! This electric fan cut in above 106°C and out at below 100°C.

Pre-Production Problems

In the five years between the signing of the licence agreement and the beginning of production, there were a number of problems, which had to be resolved by Shigeyusa Kamiya and his team back in Hamamatsu. Essentially, these involved the following areas: sealing, heat differential, carburation and porting, ignition, and manufacturing machinery unique to rotary production.

Probably the most important was the sealing process, which had cost German marque NSU dearly, with the quality control problems experienced by its R080 car. Sealing was complicated because of the length and shape of the area to be sealed and apex seal speed. Apex seal wear was eventually solved thanks to a new CEM (Composite Electro-chemical Material) plating process consisting of nickel-silicon carbide, the latter approaching the hardness of diamonds and being corrosion-resistant.

For the apex seals, Suzuki used a special material called Ferro-Tic, a combination of sintered ferrous alloy and titanium carbide, having only ½th the wear of cast-iron.

Since the cool induction ports and hot combustion areas were separate in a rotary and thus unable to share, as in a conventional four-stroke, heat transfer and control was an initial problem. Because of this, a cooling system was devised, which would transfer combustion heat over to warm the induction area. Exhaust heat was further reduced by a double shell header (exhaust pipe) and silencer (muffler) with an open air jacket between the two walls and a Ram Air intake at the front of the system to waft away heat *and* reduce noise level. Even the silencer (muffler) was a clever piece of design work, featuring as it did, a restricted low-speed passage, which opened via trap doors to permit high-flow passage at speed.

Riding the RE5

At first glance, the RE5 looked a big bike. Indeed, tipping the scales at around 540lb (245kg) 'ready to go', and with a wheelbase stretched to near 60in (1524mm), it was a daunting task for any rider of a shorter statue. There is also no doubt that the RE5 was designed around its engine – the 497cc unit put out 62bhp at 6,500rpm – but the real bonus for RE5 riders was torque band. Maximum torque was low at 3,500rpm (compared with other Japanese motorcycles of the era), and from 2,500 to 6,500rpm the torque curve was almost flat, giving a linear power flow. As one American magazine reported, 'This makes downshifting a thing of the past and the throttle response from anywhere in the torque band is excellent.'

At least one RE5 was successfully mated to a sidecar and, with a few changes (to gearing and the front forks, for example), made an ideal outfit.

Instrument Cluster

Above the headlamp sat an instrument cluster that was as radical as the engine design. According to *Motor Cycle World*, 'This does everything except tell time and weather, but the 160mph speedo is more for status than for function.' When you turned the ignition key, a green plastic cover popped open to reveal not only the speedo, but also the 0–9,000rpm rev counter, electronic gear indicator (which told the rider what gear he was in via a digital readout), coolant temperature gauge, fuel level idiot light, oil tank level light and turn signal indicator. The tail-light assembly was like the instrument cluster – of circular form in a space-age style.

ABOVE: RE5 with Squire sidecar, 1976. The Suzuki was more than capable of coping with a third wheel.

LEFT: The strange-shaped, circular instrument console.

There was also a lockable access panel covering both the fuel and water filler caps, at the front top of the tank.

Electric and Kickstarters

Although the RE5 was equipped with push-button electric starter, it also boasted a kickstarter. However, the latter was virtually impossible to operate. One road tester 'tried to start this monster with the foot lever and found it harder than a Harley to kick over. You really have to get it spinning to get it started, so the gearing is rather high.' This was with the engine hot. When the engine was cold, operating the kickstarter was, as described by another tester, 'a traumatic experience'. Another problem was that the kickstarter lever was mounted very high.

1975 RE5 Specification

Engine	Wankel rotary, with single rotor, liquid-cooled housing, oil-cooled rotor
Bore	Not applicable
Stroke	Not applicable
Displacement	497cc per chamber
Compression ratio	8.6:1 (corrected)
Lubrication	Wet sump, pressure feed to rotor shaft bearings via oil cooler, throttle-controlled pump for rotor tips and seals
Ignition	CDI, twin-lobe contact breaker with vacuum and speed sensors, single-lobe contact breaker back-up circuit
Carburettor	Mikuni 18–32mm HHD type, twin choke
Primary drive	Duplex chain, 1652 reduction, 23/38
Final drive	Chain, 14/43
Gearbox	Five-speed
Frame	Cradle type, all-steel welded construction
Front suspension	Hydraulically damped telescopic fork
Rear suspension	Swinging-arm, twin hydraulically damped shock absorbers
Front brake	Twin hydraulically operated 295mm (11.6in) discs
Rear brake	180mm full-width drum, SLS
Tyres	Front 3.25 × 19; rear 4.00 × 18

General specifications

Wheelbase	59.1in (1,501mm)
Ground clearance	6.7in (170mm)
Seat height	32in (812mm)
Fuel tank capacity	3.7gal (17ltr)
Dry weight	507lb (230kg)
Maximum power	62bhp @ 6,500rpm
Top speed	110mph (177km/h)

Testers' Reports

The 1976 edition of *Motorcyclist Illustrated Road Test Annual* published a particularly well-informed report of its experiences with the Suzuki rotary. The tester was generally complimentary in his summary:

I like the RE5. It is a long-legged tourer that will offer its owner a lifetime of easy-going cruising with – and this is a guess – the minimum of service and maintenance cost. Of particular merit are the paint finish (ours had a thick coat of metallic blue paint finished off with a clear varnish); the quality of castings used throughout the engine unit (Allen bolts all over as a bonus); the smoothness of the 497cc motor (which performs like a strong 750); fast cruising comfort (throw that handlebar away and fit a Trident flat bar), its handling (after switching to German Continental tyres). Small bitches on its weight (try and heave one on its centre stand and you're asking for a hernia), its thrust (cruising 35/37 mpg [8/7.6ltr/100km] – fast runs 30/32 mpg [9.5/8.8ltr/100km]); that low first gear and a wiring system that shrieks out for a Bolognese sauce.

The majority of other journals, certainly those in Europe (including Britain) had a more negative view of the RE5. According to *Motorcycle Mechanics*, 'The RE5 probably is a tribute to their [Suzuki's] technology, it's just a pity that the same expertise couldn't have been used to produce a complete machine instead of being concentrated into one or two comparatively small areas.' *Bike* carried out a comparison test between the RE5 and the Hercules W2000 (badged as a DKW), and came out in favour of the latter over the former: 'The Suzuki gives you a lot of very complex machinery for your money, which is OK if you want complexity, and technical sophistication for its own sake... but for my money the DKW is by far the most exciting bike of the two. It has the sort of handling that gives you confidence in any conditions.' *Bike* achieved 110.56mph (177.90km/h) and *Motorcycle Mechanics* 105mph (169km/h).

With a dry weight of 507lb (230kg), the RE5 was almost a third heavier than the German machine and the same as a Kawasaki Z1000!

A Suzuki GB service seminar for the RE5, with K. Machida, European Technical Manager, Suzuki Motor Co; Japan, spring 1975.

Public Response

Suzuki had a number of problems in marketing the RE5 to the public. First, it was some 25 per cent more expensive than the GT750 (*see* Chapter 9) at its UK launch in February 1975 – and the 750 triple was also 15mph (24km/h) faster. Second, even in the USA the RE5 failed to achieve the success for which Suzuki had hoped, finding itself in competition with the Honda Gold Wing, which came along at around the same time.

Faced with what could only be described as poor sales, Suzuki released an A version in mid-1976. For this updated model, some of the outlandish styling touches – notably the space-age instrument console and rear-light assemblies – were removed and replaced by components in the GT750 mould. The sophisticated engine

sensors were also deleted. However, none of these changes helped sales and by 1978 the RE5 was no more.

Surprisingly, RE5 owners are generally hyper-enthusiastic about their bikes, perhaps because of the kudos of an exclusive product, a generally good reliability record, and of course that uniquely smooth and torquey engine.

Company president Jitsujiro Suzuki, speaking at the Tokyo Show in 1974, had said, 'We see the rotary as the beginning of a new age in the history of two-wheel touring... it sets new performance standards in touring smoothness and comfort.' Sadly, Joe Public did not agree with him in sufficiently large numbers. Sales failed to fund the huge development costs swallowed up by the project, and Suzuki was left to rue the financial folly of its foray into rotary.

12 GS Series

With emission controls in the USA threatening to kill Suzuki's major export market for its all-two-stroke range, the company was effectively forced to enter the four-stroke field. Its first steps were taken with the twin-cylinder GS400 and four-cylinder GS750, both with double overhead camshafts, at the end of 1976.

A Class-Leading Motorcycle

Both GS models, the 750 in particular, showed considerable forward thinking. The 750 not only proved the fastest machine in its class, but also the most compact and best-mannered big

Originally Pip Higham was going to use a RE5, but, after reading Cook Neilson's test in Cycle World, *he switched his order to a GS750. He never regretted his decision.*

bike to appear from Japan up to that date. It was also instrumental in convincing market leaders Honda that its CB750 was in need of an immediate redesign.

Bob Goddard of *Motorcycle Mechanics* felt that, with the GS750, Suzuki had got it 'right first time'. With no previous four-stroke experience, Suzuki had shown the opposition – including the massive Honda organization, which had led four-stroke development both on track and road for many years – just how it should be done.

Officially, Suzuki engineers gave three reasons for going four-stroke: improved fuel economy, high performance potential in larger engines, and easier maintenance (read 'less maintenance for the owners over longer periods'). They declined ever to mention future air-pollution regulations in the USA!

A Proven Formula

In many ways, the Suzuki GS750 was a clever engineering-design mix between the Honda CB750 and the Kawasaki Z1. Suzuki's idea was to feature the cubic capacity of the Honda, in conjunction with the improved performance – via double overhead camshafts – of the Kawasaki. Following the problems with the RE5 rotary (*see* Chapter 11), Suzuki was wary of ploughing its own furrow, so the design team went for the proven formula, rather than innovation. As a result, the GS750 followed the classic layout pioneered by the likes of Benelli, Gilera, MV Agusta, Honda and Kawasaki: an air-cooled, inline (across-the-frame) four-cylinder, and, as with other production Japanese fours of the era, chain-driven camshafts and horizontally split crankcases. Apart for having two fewer cylinders, the GS400 followed the same route.

Design Details

Bore and Stroke Dimensions

However, the Suzuki design team was not content simply to create a Honda CB750 clone. So, they adopted not only dohc, but also short-stroke bore and stroke dimensions of 65 × 56.4mm respectively, giving 748cc. The smaller GS400 twin retained the same bore of 65mm, but with the stroke increased to 60mm, giving 398cc.

It is worth pointing out that, although today almost every four-cylinder engine is vastly over-square (short-stroke), this was not the case back in 1976 when the GS750 was launched. At that time, most Japanese manufacturers were still using square dimensions, such as the 66 × 66mm of the Kawasaki Z1, while Honda were using slightly long-stroke figures of 61 × 63mm for their CB750.

The GS750 produced a claimed 68bhp at 8,500rpm, whilst the GS400 twin put out 36bhp at the same engine revolutions.

Standard Japanese Practice

Where Suzuki did follow their Japanese rivals was in the design of the bottom end of the

motor, with the chain drive to the camshafts taken off the middle of the crankshaft, the starter drive (a two-stage gear drive) and alternator at the nearside (left) end, whilst the contact breakers were at the offside (right) end of the crankshaft.

There was a gear (straight-cut profile) primary drive, with the drive gear being mounted inboard of the offside cylinder. Since the driven gear was inboard of the clutch, this arrangement prevented the clutch being out too far.

There was a five-speed gearbox in unit with the engine, the crankcases of which split horizontally, in typical Japanese industry fashion, whilst the kickstart gear was mounted directly to the rear of the output shaft.

Simple though this layout was, the positioning of the kickstart to the rear of the gears had two distinct disadvantages: it made the engine longer than it would otherwise have been, and

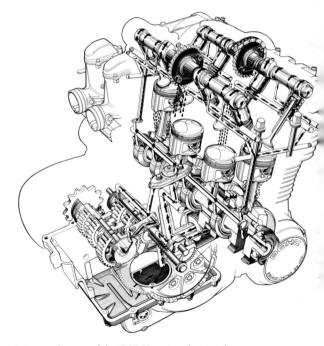

Cut-away diagram of the GS750 engine, showing the lubrication system.

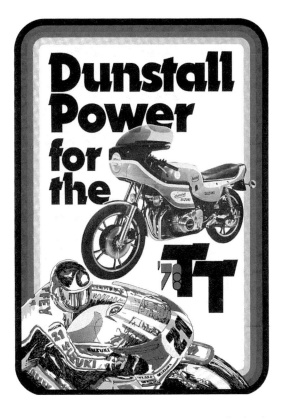

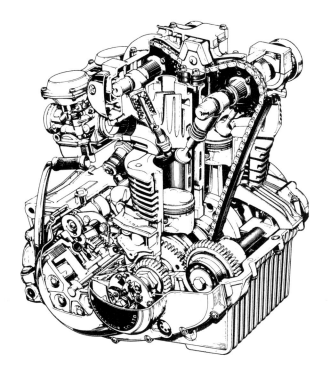

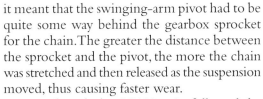

Like the GT750 before it, the new GS750 was offered with the Dunstall treatment.

The GS750's smaller brother, the GS400 twin. A major difference between the two engines was a balancer shaft in the four-hundred unit.

it meant that the swinging-arm pivot had to be quite some way behind the gearbox sprocket for the chain. The greater the distance between the sprocket and the pivot, the more the chain was stretched and then released as the suspension moved, thus causing faster wear.

Even though the GS400 twin followed the same basic layout as the GS750, helical gears were employed on the smaller engine for the primary drive (mainly, it is presumed, to cut the noise level), these being outboard of the engine and another change, the six-speed gearbox, but inboard of the clutch.

A 180-Degree Crank

The major difference between the two machines was the use in the four-hundred

twin of a balancer shaft. To achieve a better (lower) level of vibration, the Suzuki engineering team had not only fitted a balancer shaft, but also opted for a 180-degree instead of a 360-degree crank throw. In the latter, both pistons rise and fall together. With a 180-degree twin, there is one piston at TDC (top dead centre) and the other at BDC (bottom dead centre), so there is an out-of-balance force, equal to a half unit pulling upwards in one cylinder and another pulling downwards in the other cylinder. Although the forces are balanced vertically, they do not oppose each other, instead being offset. As a result, there is a rocking motion, tending to lift first one end of the engine and then the other alternately once a revolution. It is this 'couple', as it is known, which produces the distinctive, but by no means excessive, shaking vibration of the 180-degree twin. Another example of this format was the Honda CB72/77, while most British vertical twins featured 360 degrees. The latter configuration has the disadvantage of having increased vibes the higher the engine speed.

Even though the 180-degree crank is superior to the 360 one at high revs, both layouts suffer from vibration much more than a four (or a six). Suzuki employed the balance shaft gear driven at a 1:1 ratio from the crankshaft. There were two counterweights on this shaft, one opposite the big-end of each cylinder, and spaced at 180 degrees relative to one another. Ideally, these needed to exert the same effective centrifugal force as the counterweights on the crankshaft – and Suzuki could be said to have achieved this with the new twin.

How did the system work? The counterweights of the balancer shaft were set up so they were always facing in the opposite direction to the counterweights on the crankshaft. As a result, they exerted a 'couple' opposite the out-of-balance couple of the engine. In other words, the two couples balanced each other at all times. So Suzuki's twin-cylinder engine was in primary balance, and thus, in theory at least, had no more vibes than an across-the-frame four.

John Hartley commented on the layout in an excellent feature in *Motorcycle Mechanics* Engine Analysis series: 'In both engines [the GS400 and GS750] there is a secondary vibration, but this is much less than the primary vibration, and is less noticeable.' It is also worth pointing out that, because of its shorter firing intervals, the four will always give the impression of being smoother than a balanced twin.

A Modular Approach

Another feature of the GS400/750 series was the commonality to both powerplants of a relatively large number of components. The list included pistons, connecting-rods, bearings, valve gear (except the camshafts themselves),

the chain timing device, sprockets and tensioner arrangement, the oil pump, clutch pressure plate and discs (with more of the latter on the bigger engine), starter motor and alternator.

Diecast Aluminium Crankcases

Both engines featured diecast aluminium crankcases, split on the axis of the crankshaft and gears, the GS750 featuring a detachable sump plate at its base. On the GS400 there was an additional tunnel in the crankcase to house the balance shaft, this being forward of the crank shaft, but at the same level on the crankcase split.

According to John Hartley, 'Perhaps the most surprising thing about the bottom end of both bikes is that ball and roller bearings are used for the crankshafts, and the balance shaft... This presumably reflects Suzuki's experience with two-strokes and their lack of experience with shell bearings.'

Because of this, the crankshaft of the GS750 in particular was a super-strong and equally heavy piece of metal – and probably costly to manufacture. However, as John Hartley pointed out, 'it should last for ever'. This assembly was supported by no fewer than six main bearings.

Another example of Suzuki applying lessons learned in the two-stroke field was the use of rubber blocks between the fins of the cylinder head, to prevent fin 'ringing'. Each head was basically a single casting, split on the axis of the camshafts so that there were separate bearing caps and cam covers.

Each domed piston was equipped with three rings, the piston skirt to bore clearance being 0.002–0.0024in (0.05–0.06mm). Unusually, the gudgeon pin operated directly in the connecting-rod eye without a bearing or bush. Although at the time some car firms used this combination, they employed a force fit between the pin and rod, so that there was no relative movement. However, on the two Suzuki engines, a small clearance of 0.0003–0.0008in (0.008–0.02mm) was to be found, resulting in a steel-on-steel bearing. Not only was this unusual, it was also a low-cost option.

The GS750 had a compression ratio of 8.7:1, the GS400 slightly higher at 9.0:1.

On the GS750 there were four Mikuni VM26 SS carburettors, whilst the GS400 breathed via a pair of Mikuni BS34 constant depression type instruments – the latter being similar to the SU design. As one commentator of the day said, 'The main reason for using the BSs, no doubt, was to improve fuel consumption on the twin, since this is generally more important to the owner of a smaller bike.'

An Automatic Tensioner

Maintenance, or lack of it, was obviously a priority for the Suzuki design team when laying out the GS models. The engineers made key design improvements in this respect over their rivals – no one can have forgotten Honda's problems with cam chains in the late 1970s and early 1980s! Suzuki spent a significant amount of time getting it right first time when it came to cam drive and valve gear on the new four-strokes.

For a start, both runs of the cam chain were supported over virtually their entire length by steel blades featuring synthetic rubber facings, and there was a jockey sprocket on the horizontal run between the camshaft sprockets. The real bonus was the automatic tensioner, which required no attention unless the engine was stripped.

The tensioner consisted of a spring-loaded pushrod, this bearing on the tensioning blade of the rear chain run. The rear edge of the pushrod was tapered to form a wedge.

A lock shaft had a steel ball at its nose, and this ball bore on the wedge. As chain stretch occurred, so the pushrod moved outwards to take up the slack. As the lock shaft was also spring-loaded, this also extended, and the ball thus prevented the pushrod from moving backwards. This was a simple solution, but an effective one.

Camshaft Identification

To ease assembly, camshafts were marked 'IN' and 'EX', and 'R' and 'L', to identify which was which and where each end went. They were also given notched ends to ensure that the sprockets fitted correctly.

The camshafts ran directly in aluminium housings, and an interesting feature on the GS750 was that there were four camshaft bearings in two pairs, one cap being utilized for a pair of bearings. There were two caps per camshaft on the GS400.

The tappets were of the inverted bucket variety, inserted between the camshaft and the valves, and again running directly in the head. Adjustment shims were inserted into recesses on the top of the tappet and could be changed extremely quickly thanks to a simple small tool, which looked like a C-spanner. This was used to push down the tappet, thus leaving the shim free to be removed.

On the GS750, to absorb vibrations, there was a coil spring cush drive located in the driven primary-drive gear. A similar device was incorporated in the driven gear for the balancer shaft on the GS400 twin. These added to the smoothness of both engine assemblies.

At the rear of the primary-drive gear was a small gear that drove the oil pump. The clutch was a conventional wet multi-plate design, with the lubrication system designed to enable oil pressure to assist disengagement of the clutch plates on the seven-fifty four.

Another notable feature was the relatively narrow nature of both the 400 and 750, each shaft being supported by a single ball-race bearing and a single caged-needle roller assembly.

With its six speeds, the GS400 had a marginally narrower gap between first and second, but notably the actual ratios between second and fifth were identical. The faces of the GS750 gears were wider to cope with than the increased torque figures.

O-Ring Final-Drive Chain

To combat the potential problems associated with high chain wear, Suzuki commissioned chain specialists Takasago to create a special final-drive chain for the GS750. In this assembly, grease was forced into the gap between each pin and bush during manufacture; O-rings between the links prevented the grease leaking out. John Hartley was quite right to point out that 'sheer engineering common sense would lead to the chain being enclosed, but here the manufacturers seem afraid of losing the sporting image an exposed chain gives'.

The Chassis

The November 1977 issue of *Motorcycle Sport* reported favourably on the chassis of the new Suzukis:

> Once upon a time we used almost to accept that Japanese bikes were bound to lag behind European ones when it came to handling, and usually with good reason, for ten years ago they still had not learnt to harness the considerable power they developed... however, frame and suspension design have improved immeasurably... and the frame on the GS750 is a good example.

Motorcycle Sport was absolutely spot on. The new Suzuki's frame was of the duplex double-cradle type with massive gusseting around the steering head, with a single top tube running from the steering head to the point where the lower double top tubes began to curve downwards to complete the loop. The sub-frame ran straight out from the rear of the main frame and the continuation of the twin tubes forming the engine cradle carried on after meeting the top tubes and connected with the top rear sub-frame about half-way along the dual seat line. A smaller sub-frame served to accommodate the pillion footrests and the silencer. Needle bearings were employed for the swinging-arm pivots.

Complementing the excellent frame was an equally improved suspension, both front and

1976 GS400 Specification	
Engine	Air-cooled dohc parallel twin, two-valves per cylinder, alloy head and barrel, 180-degree crankshaft, gear-driven balancer shaft, automatic cam chain tensioner, four main bearings, three-ring pistons, bucket shim tappet adjustment, horizontally split aluminium crankcase
Bore	65mm
Stroke	60mm
Displacement	398cc
Compression ratio	9:1
Lubrication	Wet sump
Ignition	Battery/coil ignition with twin contact breakers; electric start, 12-volt
Carburettor	2 × Mikuni BS34 CV
Primary drive	Gears, 28/76
Final drive	Chain, 16/45
Gearbox	Six-speed, foot-change
Frame	Duplex, full cradle, all-steel tube construction
Front suspension	Telescopic forks, with exposed stanchions
Rear suspension	Swinging-arm, with five-way adjustable twin shock absorbers
Front brake	Single 280mm hydraulically operated disc
Rear brake	180mm full-width drum, SLS
Tyres	Front 3.00S-18; rear 3.50 S-18

General specifications

Wheelbase	54.5in (1,384mm)
Ground clearance	6.1in (155mm)
Seat height	31in (787mm)
Fuel tank capacity	3.1gal (14ltr)
Dry weight	379lb (172kg)
Maximum power	36bhp @ 8,500rpm
Top speed	96mph (154km/h)

1976 GS750 Specification

Engine	Air-cooled dohc across-the-frame four, eight valves, alloy head and barrel assemblies, six main bearings, automatic cam chain tensioner, three-ring pistons, bucket shim tappet adjustment, horizontally split aluminium crankcases
Bore	65mm
Stroke	56.4mm
Displacement	748cc
Compression ratio	8.7:1
Lubrication	Wet sump, trochoidal pump
Ignition	Battery/coil, twin contact breaker, electric start, 12-volt
Carburettor	4 × Mikuni VM26 SS, 26mm, piston-valve type
Primary drive	Gears, 44/99
Final drive	Chain, 15/41
Gearbox	Five-speed, foot-change
Frame	Duplex cradle, all-steel tube construction
Front suspension	Telescopic forks with exposed stanchions
Rear suspension	Swinging-arm, with five-way adjustable twin shock absorbers
Front brake	2 × 280mm hydraulically operated discs
Rear brake	Single 280mm hydraulically operated disc
Tyres	Front 3.25H-19; rear 4.00H-18

General specifications

Wheelbase	58.7in (1,490mm)
Ground clearance	6in (152mm)
Seat height	31in (787mm)
Fuel tank capacity	3.97gal (18ltr)
Dry weight	492lb (223kg)
Maximum power	68bhp @ 8,500rpm
Top speed	123mph (198km/h)

RIGHT: *Pop Star David Essex with a GS750L, the custom version of the GS750; Earls Court Show, London, November 1979.*

rear. Because of this, the handling and roadholding of the GS750 (and its smaller brother, the GS400, which used essentially the same layout) was exceptionally good for a Japanese motorcycle during the 1970s. The improvements were to benefit not only the road rider but also the production racer, with first the seven-fifty and, later, the larger-engined versions of Suzuki's four.

Press Reaction

Both press and the buying public were really impressed with the GS750. *Motorcycle Mechanics* had this to say:

> It has a combination of speed, acceleration, tractability and fuel economy superior to any 750 that has gone before, and fulfils both sportster and tourer markets quite adequately. It trickles through traffic like a lightweight, takes bends like it was

designed by a TT rider and is so comfortable to ride that a 150-mile [241km] non-stop run on a cold December night was a pleasure.

There was one area where Suzuki did not get it right first time – testers were less impressed with the brakes. The original (1977 model year) machines had a single disc front and rear and, in the opinion of *Motorcycle Mechanics*, 'the illusion of greatness was quickly shattered when putting the brakes on, especially in the wet when the Suzuki's single-disc stoppers front and rear showed themselves to be barely

1977 GS550 converted to 610cc (bigger bore), with GT750 forks, 4-into-1 exhaust, Works shocks, steering damper, Lockhart oil cooler and DID alloy rims; with James Trampe, rider (right) and friend Duncan Farash, Daytona March 2002.

adequate for the bike's size and performance'. Considering that the firm's GT750 triple of the same era *did* have dual discs up front, Suzuki had no excuse for making such a serious error. The GS400 had single-disc front and full-width SLS drum rear stoppers.

Motorcycle Mechanics recorded an electronically timed 123mph (198km/h) with the standing start quarter-mile (0.40km) being achieved in 12.9 seconds, a terminal speed of 101mph (162.5km/h). The same journal got 96mph (154km/h) from the GS400 with a standing start figure of 15.8 seconds and 85mph (137km/h)

As for updates, 1978 saw another 11in (280mm) disc tacked on the front, while 1979 brought cast-alloy wheels. Otherwise, there was little change for the GS750, which by then had been ousted from its number-one spot in the Suzuki range to number two, thanks to the new GS1000.

The GS550

Before the arrival of the GS1000, Suzuki developed the GS550, which, according to American magazine *Motorcyclist*, was 'the clear successor to the very capable GT550 two-stroke [*see* Chapter 7] triple'. At the time of its launch, in late 1977, many wondered how it would compete in a world dominated by Honda and Kawasaki in this sector. In fact, like the GS750, the GS550 could more than hold its own.

The 549cc (56 × 55.8mm) dohc engine was in essence a scaled-down GS750 with a compression ratio of 8.6:1, a quartet of 22mm Mikuni carbs, a six-speed gearbox and a maximum speed of 108mph (174km/h) from its 46bhp. Weighing in at some 100lb (45kg) lighter than the GS750, the GS550 had single-disc brakes front and rear, which, given the lighter weight, were more than adequate for the performance.

By 1979 a custom cruiser version of the GS550 was being offered and later still cast-alloy wheels were introduced.

In its September 1979 issue, *Motorcyclist* published a giant 'Middleweight' test, looking closely at the BMW R65, Honda CB650, Honda CX500, Kawasaki KZ650, Yamaha XS650, Yamaha SR500 and Suzuki's GS550.

Motorcyclist had some complimentary words for the Suzuki:

> With the best seat, the best brakes, the second-best handling and shared honors for most comfortable, the GS550 is a winner in anybody's comparison. Its shortcomings – some high-rpm vibration, a need for extra shifting and point-type ignition – aren't major and are made completely forgivable by the bargain price tag. In April we chose the GS550 as The Best Buy of 1979, and this test hasn't changed our minds one bit.

The GS850G

The dohc across-the-frame Suzuki four-cylinder family was enlarged still further by the addition of the GS850G, which featured shaft final

ABOVE: GS550 (1981 E variant). The five-fifty four provided a budget-priced entry to Suzuki's 4-cylinder dohc range.

RIGHT: GS550 engine unit: 549cc (56 × 55.8mm).

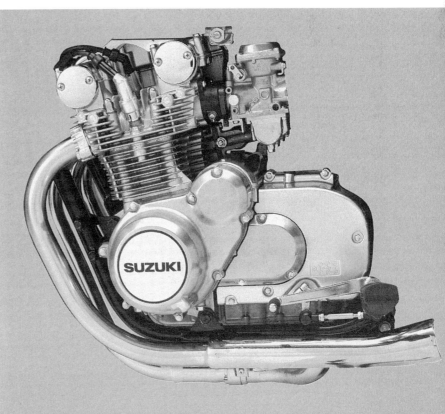

drive. This was a first for the Japanese marque and it was a particularly neatly executed system. Although the gear change was, according to *Motorcycle Mechanics*, 'not quite as slick as, say, those on the two-stroke triples', its selector mechanism was described as 'top class… The whole power train is fuss free. It's so good you hardly realize that the final drive is by shaft and not chain.'

Power from the crankshaft to the input shaft in the gearbox was damped via clutch springs. Transmission shocks between the input and output gearbox shafts were absorbed by a spring-loaded ramp and cam arrangement. The final shock absorption was by rubber bushes, which surrounded the six studs connecting the rear wheel to the drive system.

This system, which avoided the complication of a jackshaft, combined with the mild torque levels to eliminate the harshness often associated with shaft final drive.

Certainly, when compared with a BMW or Moto Guzzi of the era, the GS850 was more like a chain-driven bike – but much quieter in this respect. As *MCM* commented, 'The noise from chain thrash sounds positively raucous in comparison.'

Another first for Suzuki was the inclusion of self-cancelling indicators – an idea borrowed from rivals Yamaha.

Generally, the big Suzuki 'shaftie' was a great bike, although *MCM* criticized the headlamp as 'poor… the unit is a 45-watt item which lets the rest of the machine down badly'.

GS850G shaft-drive touring model: specially designed shaft final drive, with gear shock damper; gear shock absorber; rear hub damper rubber; tapered needle bearings in 850G swinging arm.

The GS850 engine was a bored-out GS750 (but with shaft instead of chain final drive). The bore size was up to 69mm, while the stroke remained unchanged at 56.4mm. The 850 also shared the 750's Mikuni VM26SS carburettors. Other details of the model specification included five-speed gearbox, cast-alloy wheels, and a 4.50 H × 17 rear tyre (compared to the GS750's 18in rubber).

The rear shock absorbers featured four damping adjustments – easily carried out with a thumb nail. A rubber protection sleeve had to be pulled up to expose the adjuster ring (at top of shock).

In most areas, the GS750 and 850 were very similar; UK GS850s differed from US models in that they did not have air forks or a stepped seat.

Although the shaft-drive four was intended very much as a de luxe touring bike, a power

Introduced for the 1979 model year, the GS850G was an excellent touring model, with the bonus of a shaft final drive that did not suffer from the usual torque reaction associated with this type of system.

output of 66.2bhp at 8,800rpm endowed it with a top speed of 115mph (185km/h) with fuel consumption averaging around 50mpg (5.66ltr/100km). Although it weighed in at 558lb (253kg), the GS850 was surprisingly easy to handle – except for getting it on the centre stand. Roadholding was also good, certainly for a tourer, both solo and with a passenger, making the GS850G an excellent choice.

As for prices, the GS850G cost £1,795 (September 1979), compared with £1,595 for the GS750 (March 1977) and £1,995 for the GS1000 (October 1978).

1979 GS850G Specification

Engine	Air-cooled dohc across-the-frame four, eight valves, alloy head and barrel assemblies, six main bearings, automatic cam chain tensioner, three-ring pistons, bucket shim tappet adjustment, horizontally split aluminium crankcases	Front suspension	Telescopic forks with three spring pre-load adjustment points
		Rear suspension	Swinging-arm, with twin shock absorbers featuring five spring pre-load and four damping positions
Bore	69mm	Front brake	2 × 280mm hydraulically operated discs
Stroke	56.4mm	Rear brake	Single 280mm hydraulically operated disc
Displacement	843cc		
Compression ratio	8.8:1	Tyres	Front 3.50 × 19; rear 4.50 × 17
Lubrication	Wet sump, trochoidal pump	*General specifications*	
Ignition	Battery/coil twin contact breaker, electric start, 12-volt	Wheelbase	58.7in (1,490mm)
Carburettor	4 × Mikuni VM26SS 26mm	Ground clearance	5.5in (139mm)
		Seat height	32in (812mm)
Primary drive	Gears, 49/87	Fuel tank capacity	4.8gal (22ltr)
Final drive	Shaft, 11/34	Dry weight	558lb (253kg)
Gearbox	Five-speed, foot-change	Maximum power	66.2bhp @ 8,800rpm
Frame	Duplex, full cradle, all-steel construction	Top speed	115mph (185km/h)

A pair of the new GS1000 models in the 1978 Australian Castrol 6-Hours race for standard production machines.

The GS1000

In terms of launch dates, the GS1000 was actually earlier than the GS850G. First displayed in public during late 1977, and made available in 1978, the newcomer was described by Suzuki's PR department as 'a regal combination of smoothness, stability and speed'.

Compared with the GS750, not only had the dohc five-speed engine been increased to 997cc (70 × 64.8mm), but also the balance of the machine had been beefed up to cope with the additional power and speed. This included larger 34mm carburettors, a strengthened frame and swinging arm, a double disc brake (also applied thereafter to the 750), cast-alloy wheels, wider-section tyres (3.50 front and 4.50 rear), larger-capacity 4.2gal (19ltr) fuel tank (compared with 3.97gal/18ltr on the 750) electronic ignition (points on the 750), and stronger clutch.

The result was an electrifying motorcycle capable of well in excess of 130mph (209km/h) with handling, roadholding and braking to match. The GS1000 became the bike to beat in production racing during the 1978 and 1979 seasons.

Besides the standard E model, Suzuki also offered the G model (shaft-drive tourer) and the S sportster. The S was basically the standard chain-driven bike, but with a new red or blue and white colour scheme and, more significantly, an abbreviated fairing. In truth, this was little more than a large cowling around the headlamp, with an 'aerofoil' lip at the base and a small screen on the top. It was really too small

ABOVE: Essentially the GS1000 was simply a bigger version of the existing GS750 motor. This is the S version, introduced for the 1979 season.

RIGHT: A 1979 GS1000; Brands Hatch, summer 1979.

ABOVE: *Pip Higham with his Kosman-framed GS1000 dragster; Melbourne, 19 August 1979. In 1980 it ran an amazing 8.5 seconds and 166mph (267km/h) at Santa Pod Raceway.*

RIGHT: *GS1000E, chain final drive. Like all GS fours, the exhaust system was 4-into-2.*

to have any real practical use, except to keep some wind off the rider's chest.

Other technical changes included air-adjustable front forks and rear shocks with a wide range of damping in addition to conventional multi-position spring loadings. The variations possible – although adjustment being made more difficult by the lack of an equalizer pipe between the fork legs – meant that any sort of ride could be achieved, from plushy armchair comfort to racer-like tautness.

A new instrument console, made possible by the fairing, incorporated a clock and an oil-temperature gauge in addition to the fuel gauge featured on the E and G models.

As for the twin, this became the GS425 (423cc, 67 × 60mm) for the 1979 model year, before being replaced by the GS450 (448cc, 71 × 56.6mm) for 1980. Running on a compression ratio, the 450 engine produced 41.5bhp at 9,000rpm. Weighing in dry at 386lb (175.5kg), the GS450 was generally agreed to have been a significant improvement over the GS400/425. Unfortunately, its production life was to be extremely short, measured in months rather than years, and it was superseded by the new GSX400 towards the end of 1980.

ABOVE: Vivid, full-action shot of a GS1000S, circa 1980.

RIGHT: The GS425 (shown) replaced the GS400 twin for 1979. This in turn was axed for 1980, and replaced by the GS450, but this too only lasted a few months before the new GSX400 arrived, towards the end of 1980.

The larger-displacement GS1000G weighed in at 562lb (255kg), but could still top 130mph (208km/h).

1979 Suzuki GS1000S Specification

Engine	Air-cooled dohc across-the-frame four, eight valves, alloy head and barrel assemblies, six main bearings, automatic cam chain tensioner, three-ring pistons, bucket shim tappet adjustment, horizontally split aluminium crankcases	Front suspension	Telescopic forks with adjustable air pressure. Exposed 37mm-diameter stanchions
		Rear suspension	Swinging-arm, four-way adjustable twin shock absorbers
		Front brake	2 × 280mm hydraulically operated discs
Bore	70mm	Rear brake	Single 280mm hydraulically operated disc
Stroke	64.8mm	Tyres	3.25 × 19 front; 4.00 × 18 rear
Displacement	997cc		
Compression ratio	9.2:1	*General specifications*	
Lubrication	Wet sump, trochoidal pump	Wheelbase	60in (1,524mm)
Ignition	Suzuki PEI electronic 12-volt 14-amp hour battery; electric start	Ground clearance	6.5in (165mm)
		Seat height	32.5in (825mm)
Carburettor	4 × Mikuni 34mm	Fuel tank capacity	4.2gal (19ltr)
Primary drive	Gears	Dry weight	530lb (240kg)
Final drive	Chain	Maximum power	87bhp @ 8,000rpm
Gearbox	Five-speed, foot-change	Top speed	132mph (212km/h)
Frame	Duplex cradle, with five cross tubes between the top frame tubes	E version:	Same specification but without fairing and different paintwork

As far as the fours were concerned, although the GS550 continued, the GS750 and GS1000 models were replaced at the beginning of 1980 by the new sixteen-valve GSX750 and GSX1100 models. The GS850G shaft, however, continued well into the 1980s, together with a 1000 version. For the full story of the hi-tech four-valves-per-cylinder GSX range, which was also to encompass the GSX250, *see* Chapter 14.

The GS series' place in history was assured, as Suzuki's first foray into the world of modern four-stroke motorcycles.

13   SP370/DR400

The Suzuki SP370 was the first of a new breed – a modern overhead camshaft single-cylinder family – and made its debut in 1978. Of course this tied in neatly with the new policy of moving into four-stroke technology, pioneered by the arrival in the previous year of the GS400/750 models (*see* Chapter 12). Later, Suzuki was to build a whole series that could be directly linked to the SP370, including the DR400, GN400, and ultimately, a decade on, the massive single lunger DR800!

Entering the Fray

The SP370 was inspired by the success that rival Yamaha had garnered with its XT500. The Suzuki design closely followed the larger machine's basic engineering principles, featuring a tall, sohc, two-valve engine, finished in black, and canted forward in a high-clearance frame. With a displacement of 369cc (85 × 65.2mm), the SP's engine ran on a compression ratio of 8.9:1 producing 25bhp at 7,500rpm.

With the company's history of participation in off-road sport (*see* Chapter 8), Suzuki's development engineers at Hamamatsu were also able to draw upon a wealth of experience gained from the exhaustive track testing in the world's motocross and enduro championships.

Handling On- and Off-Road

Even though at first sight the SP370 appeared to be quite bulky, and weighed in at 287lb (130kg) with a gallon of fuel, it was actually remarkably light, even nimble when ridden.

The frame was a single-downtube tubular steel job splayed out into a smaller-diameter twin cradle under the engine unit, and protected by a small, perforated metal sump guard. Although small, this was still extremely effective in making sure that rocks and the like did not damage the crankcase or other components.

The 1978 factory brochure said it all: 'Suzuki SP370. Suzuki's first 4-stroke, single cylinder dual purpose bike.'

The leading-axle front forks had exposed stanchions (fashion rather than function!), while the twin Kayaba rear shocks were reversed; the rear shocks were damped by gas, and adjustable. The rear brake (a drum, as on the front) was fully floating – to eliminate rear-end 'hop', according to Suzuki. Basically this involved the swinging arm and brake stay being parallel to each other and pivoted at each end. When the swinging arm descended its arc, the plate mirrored this precisely, due to the parallelogram formed by the swinging arm and brake stay. A brake cable, rather than rod, also helped.

The front suspension proved to have more than enough travel to cope with even the most unexpected changes in terrain when riding on the rough. There is no doubt that the leading-axle front-wheel spindle helped to keep the bike on line when bouncing down deeply rutted tracks. This system had a couple of advantages: longer travel suspension systems were possible, and the inertia of the front wheel mass was moved backwards towards the centre of the bike, which is where it should be. Also improved was the tracking of the front wheel while cornering and braking, by not altering the steering geometry as radically as conventional central-axle forks. The gas rear shocks complemented the good front-suspension set-up.

These benefits relate to the SP370's task as a trail bike, rather than as a pukka off-road competition mount. London-based Vic Camp Motorcycles converted several SP370s into road racers (as the same firm had with the TS250 model), so the handling must have been pretty decent, both for on- or off-road. It was a point underlined by off-road rider Charlie Harris, writing in *Which Bike?* in September 1978:

The Suzuki proved itself to be a real dual-purpose mount, capable of both effortless cruising on the road and with the ability to force its way across the roughest of country with incredible ease… In this respect it slots nicely into place in the off-road scene, sandwiched between the Honda XL250S and the Yamaha XT500… It had all the power of the Yamaha coupled with the lightness of the Honda, which must make it a serious candidate for the enduro rider. Also the 370 provides just the bike that the average trail customer is looking for. A bike that's not too heavy, has plenty of power and torque and has enough left to make touring on the road a reality.

Both tyres – a 3.00 × 21 front and a 4.00 × 18 rear – were of the knobbly variety, which was needed of course to provide enough grip on the dirt. Even so, Charlie Harris was to be 'pleasantly surprised' when he visited Brands Hatch race circuit for a speed test session:

When banked to the limit at high speed the rear-end drift is considerable (due to the tyre type) but controllable, good frame design is evident here because all that's needed to correct the situation is an easing off on the throttle.

The Engine

Besides its short-stroke bore and stroke dimensions and relatively mild compression ratio, the engine was provided with exceptional smoothness and a good spread of power across the range. According to *Bike*, it was 'beautifully simple, very tall as befits a single, and mounted high in the frame to ensure good ground clearance [actually 9½in/24mm]'.

The crankcases split vertically and the entire unit was finished in matt black paintwork with buffed (polished alloy) fin edges. The camshaft was chain-driven in typical Japanese fashion.

Besides having an oil-level window – in the offside (right) outer engine casing – it also had an 'easy-start' window in the cylinder head, which indicated the beginning of the firing stroke. Even though a lack of flywheel weight meant that in feel it was akin to a gutsy two-stroke rather than a big four-stroke single, power came in right from the beginning and just kept coming, with no sudden increases to

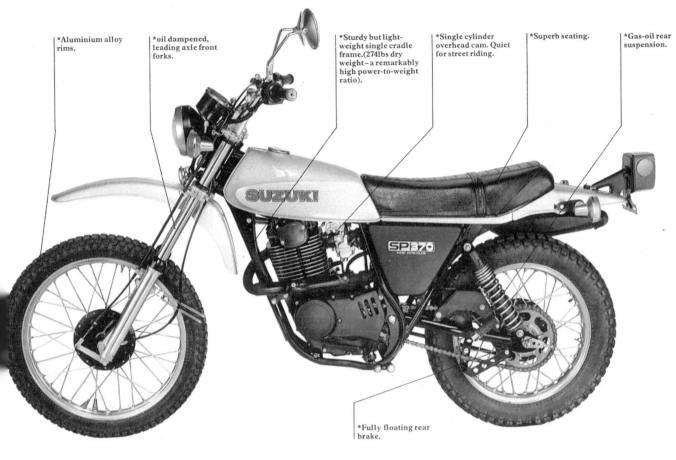

*Aluminium alloy rims.

*oil dampened, leading axle front forks.

*Sturdy but light-weight single cradle frame.(274lbs dry weight – a remarkably high power-to-weight ratio).

*Single cylinder overhead cam. Quiet for street riding.

*Superb seating.

*Gas-oil rear suspension.

*Fully floating rear brake.

ABOVE: *Features of the 1978 SP370 model, including engine and chassis.*

RIGHT: *The 369cc (85 × 65.2mm) sohc single-cylinder engine.*

watch out for. As *Bike* found out, 'although a handful of throttle will lift the front wheel without any effort, the motor is very docile'.

Lubrication was by wet sump with a 2.8 pint (1.6ltr) capacity, whilst carburation was by a 32mm Mikuni instrument. The engine was equipped with a conventional crankshaft-mounted flywheel magneto system, with the contact breaker points housed at the end of the camshaft well out of the way of water. John Bulley of *Bike* said he preferred this system to the Pointless Electronic Ignition system, because 'if anything goes wrong a zillion miles from the nearest cavalry outpost at least you stand a chance of fixing!' All the wiring was

1978 SP370 Specification

Engine	Air-cooled sohc single with two valves, chain-driven camshaft with automatic tensioner, alloy head and barrel, the latter with iron liner, vertically split aluminium crankcases
Bore	85mm
Stroke	65.2mm
Displacement	369cc
Compression ratio	8.9:1
Lubrication	Wet sump, gear pump
Ignition	Battery/coil; 6-volt
Carburettor	Mikuni 32mm
Primary drive	Gears
Final drive	Chain
Gearbox	Five-speed, foot-change
Frame	Full cradle frame; single front downtube, with perforated sump guard
Front suspension	Telescopic forks, exposed stanchions
Rear suspension	Swinging-arm, with twin shock absorbers
Front brake	150mm drum, SLS
Rear brake	150mm drum, SLS
Tyres	Front 3.00 × 21; rear 4.00 × 18

General specifications

Wheelbase	56.5in (1,435mm)
Ground clearance	9.5in (241mm)
Seat height	32.5in (825mm)
Fuel tank capacity	1.9gal (9ltr)
Dry weight	280lb (127kg)
Maximum power	25bhp @ 7,500rpm
Top speed	85mph (136km/h)

A Tester's Tale

During his 1978 appraisal of the SP370, Charlie Harris paid a visit to Brands Hatch, coming back with an interesting story:

After the track session we had some lunch and went over to the old motocross circuit which is at the back of Brands. It was used last about 10 years ago when the Trophie des Nations was held there. Part of the old course is still there with a couple of nasty deep bomb holes and a very fast straight. At the end of the straight is a sharp left-hander which has an adverse camber and is very stony, followed by a 1 in 3 hill. Tyre pressures were dropped to about 15 psi in each case and suddenly the bike was now a motocrosser. Leathers were donned and away we went. Diving into the bomb hole, the Suzy had a tendency to go in nose first and in fact I did find that subsequent jumping confirms that the bike was slightly heavy on the front end but this was overcome by putting the bars back and shifting my weight 2 to 3 inches rearward. The fast bumpy straight could be taken as fast as the bike would go. Thinking back 10 years I remember my 360 CZ MX bucking, and me doing a handstand all the way along this part of the course, how suspension has changed in a relatively small amount of time!

well designed, with snap connectors, which made the direction indicators easier to remove if wanting to do serious off-road work. The downside was that not only were there only 6 instead of 12 volts, whilst *Bike* questioned why Suzuki had not fitted a lightweight enduro-type lighting system instead of 'the oversize/ overweight headlight and rear lights'. The tester also felt that, while a rev counter 'may be needed on a screaming multi capable of reaching 12,000rpm,... it surely isn't necessary on a big, easy-going single'.

Maximum speed (on the tarmac) was 85mph (137km/h), but perhaps most significant were the SP370's consumption figures. *Bike* achieved 75/85 miles (120/137km) to the gallon, which was, in their opinion, 'remarkable considering the hammering the machine had to put up with'. In addition, 'the oil level remained the same throughout the test'.

Other notable features of the 1978 SP370 were its primary kickstart operation, alloy

At first Suzuki produced a larger 400-engined SP model, but then brought out the much more specialized DR400 (shown here).

wheel rims and its high-level black exhaust system. The September 1978 UK price was £825.

Future Developments

In 1979, Suzuki came up with a four-hundred version. On the original, the styling was akin to that of the 370, and the bike was still coded 'SP', but this was soon changed in favour of a much more purposeful-looking machine. Known as the DR400, like the SP400, the newcomer's 396cc engine size was achieved by increasing the bore of the cylinder to 88mm; the stroke remained unaltered at 65.2mm.

Technically, the SP400 and DR400 were also different, the latter having a higher 9.27:1 compression ratio and a 36 instead of 33mm

carb. The SP400 produced the same output (25bhp) as the 370 version, whereas the DR400 put out 27.6bhp (at 7,000rpm). The SP400 cost £885 and the DR400 was £945 (both in September 1980). The DR400 also had a wider-section (4.60) rear tyre.

At the end of 1980 a purely road-going touring version was introduced, with new styling and notably a disc front brake; this was coded GN400. The wheel sizes were now 18in front and rear, while power output was quoted at 27.6bhp. However, I can confirm from personal experience, having owned and ridden a GN400 during the early 1980s, it was an excellent bike spoilt by its weak 6-volt flywheel mag electrics. They might have been acceptable for a trail bike, but for a serious touring machine they were not good enough. It also had a bad habit of refusing to start when hot.

GN400 touring model.

The 1982 model year saw the arrival of Suzuki's smallest four-stroke, the 124cc (57 × 48.4mm) DR125, with a six-speed gearbox and sharing many of the engine components with the GN125 road model.

By mid-1984 Suzuki had increased the range still further with the new DR600; its 598cc sohc engine featured twin plug ignition, four valves, dual exhaust system (twin exhaust port head) and an oil cooler, to allow extended, high-speed cruising under the most arduous conditions. Maximum power output was 44bhp at 6,500rpm and it weighed in at 299lb (136kg). It was offered in 'S' and 'R' versions,

the latter a Paris-Dakar styled bike at extra cost.

'Mr Big', shouted the headlines of the motorcycle press in December 1987. They were referring to Suzuki's DR750, a bike that had been designed in Japan by Toshiyuki Endo, with input from Europe, most notably via the former 125cc World Motocross Champion and multi-time Paris-Dakar Rally winner, Gaston Rahier. Ultimately, the seven-fifty proved something of a failure, certainly in terms of sales.

It is fair to say that the sohc single-cylinder Suzuki line owed its origins to the company's first four-stroke trail bike, the 1978 SP370.

14   GSX Series

The GSX1100, which was new for 1980. It moved on the Suzuki dohc range by a considerable margin, with four-valves-per-cylinder, TSCC (Twin Swirl Combustion Chamber), new valve gear and a total redesign of bearings and crankshaft.

Whilst Honda debuted its CBX and Kawasaki its Z1300, Suzuki bided its time. Both Honda and Kawasaki got a considerable amount of flak: typically, the massive across-the-frame six cylinder models were criticized as being 'too heavy', 'too complicated', and too much of almost everything else.

By the time Suzuki launched its own megabike, the GSX1100, Yamaha already had its XS1100. The latter was, like the Honda and the Kawasaki, a big, heavy beastie – even though, like the new GSX, it had 'only' four cylinders.

The April 1980 issue of *Bike* magazine was complimentary about the arrival of the GSX1100:

> It was time for Suzuki to get their act together and the production has proved to be one of remarkable

subtlety. There is no plethora of cylinders or shafts, no gigantism and hardly any gadgetry. There has been some weight watching, there is certainly prodigious performance and there is a nicely refined ride.

Apart from the Z1300's chip-controlled fuel-injection system, the 1980 GSX1100 was bang up to date, with class-leading suspension, brakes, ignition and combustion chamber design.

The GSX Range

There was a whole family of GSX models: the star of the 1980 range was the 1100, but Suzuki also produced a 750 four and a couple of twins – a 250 and a 400 (the latter for the time being reserved for the Japanese home market only).

LEFT: *The second GSX1100 ever made (engine number 100004, frame number 500002) was turned into a drag racer by Pip Higham and went on to become one of the best and most successful Pro-Stock bikes ever seen in Europe. The bike and rider are shown here in action at Santa Pod, circa 1981.*

ABOVE: *Pip Higham's GSX1100 'The Deuce' Pro-Stock dragster; Bonhams Auction, Stafford, 16 October 2005.*

LEFT: *Eight-valve GSX250 engine with ultra-short-stroke bore and stroke dimensions of 60 × 44.2mm.*

BELOW: Valve covers removed showing the camshafts, valves and cam chain of the GSX250 engine.

When Suzuki introduced its first modern four-strokes in 1976, it adopted nominally over-square bore and stroke dimensions; the GS750 had 65 × 56.4mm. With the GSX series, this was taken a stage further, with the new 750 having dimensions of 67 × 53mm, and the 250, 60 × 44.2mm. However, since the 1100 was derived from the GS1000, it was less over-square, at 72 × 66mm.

Twin Swirl Combustion Chamber

The GSX series featured four-valves-per-cylinder technology. According to Chief of Suzuki engine design, Sadeo Shirasagi, this was in order to get 'good performance and good low-speed running as a priority'. However, as John Hartley commented in a technical feature on the GSX range in the April 1980 issue of *Motorcycle Mechanics*, four-valves were 'usually a bit short of low-speed torque'.

To achieve better performance both at the top and low end of the engine speed range, Shirasagi studied ways of achieving superior combustion at low speeds compared with traditional four-valve layouts. The result of his

investigations was TSCC (Twin Swirl Combustion Chamber). The whole concept was to provide as wide a spread of torque, much further down the scale than before, while allowing the benefits of four-valves per cylinder.

The Suzuki design featured smaller valves than were conventional in four-valve set-ups at the time, and the angle between inlet and exhaust valves was less than on the latest Honda 750. As an example, on the Honda engine, the angle was 63 degrees, while the inlet and exhaust valves were of 25mm and 22mm diameter respectively. The equivalent dimensions for the GSX750 were 40 degrees, 23 and 20mm. The

same valves were also to be found in the GSX400 twin, whilst those on the GSX1100 and GSX250 were 27/25mm and 21/18mm respectively.

John Hartley explained the difference in *Motorcycle Mechanics*: 'The advantage of those smaller valves and the different angle is that the gas going into the cylinder goes down more vertically, and is less obstructed by the valve

There was also a GSX400 using the same formula as the GSX250. This example was owned by the author during the early 1980s.

Like the sixteen-valve fours, the eight-valve GSX400 also boasted Twin Swirl Combustion Chambers (TSCC).

guide, and less shrouded by the sides of the combustion chamber.' The actual chamber itself was somewhat different too, having a peak running down the middle from inlet to exhaust side. This peak divided the chamber into two sections, each for one inlet and exhaust valve. The spark plug was located in this peak (centrally between the four valves) and was thus nearer the piston than usual.

Design chief Shirasagi explained that his idea 'was to keep the air swirling in each half of the chamber, so that there are two movements of air/fuel alongside the spark plug at ignition'.

Another important feature was the shape of the chamber, which left a squish area at the ends of the chambers, adjacent to the pair of inlets and to the exhausts.

The squish areas were sections of the cylinder head that were flat, which came close to the piston on the compression stroke. The result was to force gas out at high speed and centred in the middle of the chamber, and thus the plug, providing maximum flame propagation.

ABOVE: Twin front downtubes of the 1981 GSX400; note the finned circular cover at the bottom/middle of crankcase, under which lived the engine's oil filter element.

RIGHT: As with the GS series, Suzuki also offered custom versions of the GSX family, including this GSX400L model.

The mighty 1075cc (76 × 66mm) GSX1100 engine, which put out a class-leading 100bhp at 8,700rpm.

New Valve Gear

Another feature of Suzuki's switch from two to four valves was that, in place of the original GS-type inverted bucket tappets, the new GSX range sported short 'finger'-type rockers. These were forked, enabling one cam lobe to operate two valves, and there were now conventional screw adjusters at the ends of the rocker arm for valve clearance adjustment.

Proof of the efficiency of Suzuki TSCC system was that its engines needed less advance than comparable Honda ones (32 degrees against 37 degrees). Suzuki tests showed that, for a given valve area, the TSCC layout provided higher specific power output figures than other designs. As an added bonus, compared

with Honda, fuel consumption was some 10 per cent less.

Crankshaft Design

When Suzuki introduced its two-valve GS series of four-cylinder engines, it employed the built-up type of crankshaft it had employed on its two-stroke engines. This was heavy and expensive, with a combination of ball and roller bearings. On the new GSX power units, the design team opted to use plain bearings and one-piece crankshafts; the connecting rods featured split big-end eyes. According to Suzuki sources, this change meant not only less weight, but also the possibility of making the engines more compact.

In basic form, the GSX engines resembled the GS ones, with gear primary drives direct to the clutch, the starter motor mounted above the gearbox housing, and a single chain drive to the dohc. On the four-cylinder models, primary drive was taken right next to the web on the outside of the second cylinder. In reality, therefore, on the fours there was a two-piece crank, the end crankpin, journal and gear being formed in one piece, which was subsequently pressed on to the other piece.

As for the twins, the GSX250/400, these, like the GS models, used 180-degree cranks with a single balancer shaft (*see* Chapter 12 for a full technical description).

GSX750/1100

Special Features

For the GSX750/1100 models Suzuki had introduced a few special features. In common with all the models in the new range, these had CV (constant velocity) carburettors, automatic chain tensioner and self-lubricating final-drive cam-chain ('O'-ring type), while tapered roller bearings and needle roller bearings were specified for the steering head and swinging-arm pivot points respectively.

Besides the GSX1100, Suzuki also offered the GSX750. This smaller-engined bike had a steel instead of alloy swinging arm, and no air assistance for the front forks or multi-adjustable damping – plus a lower purchase price.

Considerable effort had been put into beating the problems associated with braking performance. Not only were there new slotted discs on both wheels (the slots claimed to reduce pad wear), but the pads themselves also had modified material, with additional metallic particles added to the compound to improve wet-weather stopping power.

On the GSX1100 there was a forged aluminium swinging arm, which contributed to reducing weight.

The Suspension

The GSX1100 employed a new air/coil spring front-fork assembly, with four-way adjustable damping. In these new forks, a steel spring (softer than normal) was fitted in the upper section of the fork. Also located in this portion was the air spring – compressed air being trapped in the fork – above a piston located in the lower fork leg. Air was pumped into the forks via a valve, one valve being employed for both legs. To adjust the damping force, a ring (at the base of the leg) was rotated.

John Hartley was unsure about this set-up:

Why use this type of spring? Well, the point about air springs is that as the suspension is deflected, so the spring rate increases. That means that you can have quite a soft rate for the first inch or so, to soak up normal bumps, and then the rate increases with travel to absorb the shocks from larger bumps or at higher speeds. That means more comfortable riding.

Essentially, Suzuki was aiming to give the rider softer springs, and more suspension travel, but with a progressive rate to absorb shocks. Although it had not yet introduced features such as monoshock rear suspension or inverted (upside-down) front forks, the Suzuki development team had realized that softer springs did not necessarily equal poor handling. As proof of this, it offered the example of the company's own RG500 racer, which did have quite soft suspension, but at the same time provided excellent roadholding.

In their respective classes, all the models in the 1980 GSX range featured more suspension

RIGHT: Nick Andrews with his GSX1100 production racer, Carnaby Raceway, East Yorkshire, 1982.

BELOW: A GSX1100 converted to an open class racer during the 1980s, but still largely stock, except for 4-into-1 exhaust and engine protection bars.

travel than the GS models. For example, on the 750, at the front, the increase was between 2in (50mm) to 6.3in (160mm), depending upon adjustment; at the rear, the figures were 2.75 to 3.3in (70 to 85mm).

Instrumentation and Other Features
On the GSX750/1100, instrumentation followed automobile rather than motorcycle fashion, with a printed circuit layout in the massive console, which also housed the speedometer, tachometer and fuel gauge. Besides the normal warning lights for functions such as oil, neutral, high beam and turn signals, there was also an outline of a motorcycle illuminated by warning signs at salient points. A failure of electrics or fluids would cause an appropriate 'idiot' light to glow in response.

Other notable features of the GSX1100 included a quartet of Mikuni BS34SS carbs, a five-speed gearbox, a 12-volt 14-amp hour battery, electric start, 60-/55-watt halogen headlamp, triple 11in (275mm) slotted disc brakes, cast-alloy wheel with Bridgestone V-rated tyres (3.50 × 19 front; 4.50 × 17 rear), and self-cancelling indicators.

Performance

The top-of-the-range GSX1100 (1075cc – 72 × 66mm) engine put out 100bhp at 8,700rpm. Although 100bhp may seem tame by modern standards, back in 1980 it was a class-leading figure. *Bike* magazine achieved an electronically timed 137.6mph (221km/h) and did the standing ¼-mile in 11.38 seconds, a terminal speed of 117.6mph (190km/h).

The UK price of the GSX1100 in April 1980 was £2,399 (including VAT).

GSX750

The GSX750 was essentially the same as the larger bike, but with a steel swinging arm and less powerful engine. The 67 × 53mm dimensions were notably shorter stroke than the GS version, giving a displacement of 747cc. The GSX750 lived very much in the shadow of its bigger brother and the British importers were eventually forced to off-load an entire shipment at a loss-making price (less than rival 550s!). It was not a poor motorcycle by any means, but anyone who wanted a GSX four would plump for the 1100.

New Ranges and Models

In the autumn of 1981 Suzuki introduced an entire family of revised air-cooled fours, with futuristic styling, known as the Katana, in a number of engine sizes. The Katana styling, provided for Suzuki by the Target Design Company, which had offices in West Germany and Britain, was headed by one-time BMW employee Jan Fellstrom.

1980 GSX1100/750 Specifications
(750 in brackets where different)

Engine	Air-cooled dohc across-the-frame four, sixteen valves, alloy head and barrel assemblies, TSCC (twin swirl combustion chambers)
Bore	72mm (67mm)
Stroke	66mm (53mm)
Displacement	1075cc (747cc)
Compression ratio	9.5:1 (9.4:1)
Lubrication	Wet sump
Ignition	Electronic, electric start; 12-volt
Carburettor	4 × Mikuni BS34SS 34mm (BS34SS-32mm)
Primary drive	Gears
Final drive	Chain
Gearbox	Five-speed, foot-change
Frame	Duplex cradle, all-steel welded construction
Front suspension	Telescopic fork with air-oil; balance tube connecting the two stanchions, coil spring preload
Rear suspension	Alloy swinging-arm, with multi-adjustable twin shock absorbers★
Front brake	2 × 227mm hydraulically operated disc
Rear brake	1 × 227mm hydraulically operated disc
Tyres	Front 3.50 V19 4PR Bridgestone; rear 4.50 V17 4PR Bridgestone (3.25 front; 4.00 rear)

General specifications

Wheelbase	60in (1,524mm)
Ground clearance	6in (152mm)
Seat height	32.5in (825mm)
Fuel tank capacity	5.3gal (24ltr)
Dry weight	GSX1100 540lb (245kg); GSX750 512lb (232kg)
Maximum power	100bhp @ 8,700rpm (80bhp @ 9,200rpm)
Top speed	GSX1100 138mph (222km/h); GSX750 120mph (193km/h)

★ 750 without air assistance, multi-adjustable damping, plus steel swinging arm

Suzuki also marketed the GSX four-cylinder models with Katana styling from 1981. This is a 1982 GSX1100 Katana model.

In 1983, Suzuki offered the more conventionally styled GSX ES range, comprising 550, 750 and 1100 models. The smaller model featured an all-new square-section frame, and 'Full Floater' monoshock rear suspension, the latter having been developed from the company's motocross bikes.

Finally, at the Cologne Show in September 1984 Suzuki launched the new GSX-R750 Super Sport model. Developed from the 1983 World Endurance Championship-winning model, the GSX-R was the work of Yasunobo Fujji. Featuring a new oil-cooled 100bhp sixteen-valve engine, six-speed gearbox, alloy frame and monoshock rear suspension, it set a new standard for production Super Sport motorcycles of light weight and high power. This new breed of motorcycle has been a priority with manufacturers ever since, but it is the Suzuki engineers who can claim to have invented it. Tracing its origins to the GS/GSX series of fours, it is still influencing engine design today.

Suzuki Codes/Names

Name	Code	Name	Code		
Adventurer	GT185	Invader	T200	*From the 1971 model year Suzuki*	
Apache	TS400	Le Mans	GT750	*began to use letter suffixes, as follows:*	
Bearcat	B105P	Patroller	GT750 Police		
Blazer	TC100	Prospector	TC125	1971	R
Cat	TC120	Raider	T305	1972	J
Challenger	TM125	Rover	RV90	1973	K
Champion	TM250	Savage	TS250	1974	L
Charger	A100	Sebring	GT380	1975	M
Charger	T500	Sierra	AS100/TS185	1976	A
Cobra	T500	Sovereign	M15	1977	B
Cutlass	F50	Stinger	T125 (horizontal	1978	C
Cyclone	TM400		cylinders)	1979	N
Duster	TS125	Student	B120	1980	T
El Camino	250TC	Super Six	T20	1981	X
Exacta	RL250	Titan	T500	1982	Z
Gaucho	TS50	Tracker	RV125	1983	D
Honcho	TS100	Trail Cat	TC120	1984	E
Hustler	T250/GT250	Trailhopper	MT50	1985	F
Indy	GT550	Wolf	AC100		

Index